Come back to Mona Vale

Come back to Mona Vale

Life and death in a Christchurch mansion

Alexander McKinnon

OTAGO UNIVERSITY PRESS
Te Whare Tā o Te Wānanga o Ōtākou

For my mother and father

But evil things, in robes of sorrow,
Assailed the monarch's high estate;
(Ah, let us mourn! – for never morrow
Shall dawn upon him, desolate!)
And round about his home the glory
That blushed and bloomed
Is but a dim-remembered story
Of the old time entombed.

Edgar Allan Poe

Author's Note

The names of almost all the living have been changed.

Family Tree

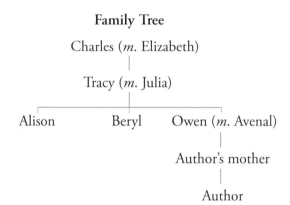

Charles (*m.* Elizabeth)
|
Tracy (*m.* Julia)
|
Alison   Beryl   Owen (*m.* Avenal)
|
Author's mother
|
Author

1

Christchurch sits at the far edge of a ruled page at the bottom of the world. To the east, nothing but the Pacific Ocean. To the west, the flat expanse of the Canterbury Plains crossed by rivers that tumble from the Southern Alps 100 kilometres away and run blue and clear and cold for the coast. It's a city of tall trees, small streams and changing seasons; public parks and private gardens under a wide sky.

And it's where my mother grew up, in a large white house surrounded by lawns. Her parents were called Owen and Avenal and they lived there still. We used to visit them several times a year. You could see their place from the top of the road, the stone wall jutting forward of all others, buttressed by a higher shield of green. Through wrought-iron gates, designed by Avenal, a drive curved to the house that stood as if in a clearing in the woods. It was symmetrical such as a child might draw: the roof pitching left and right, pierced by chimneys, the windows evenly placed.

We'd arrive and rush through the rooms, breaking the peace that otherwise prevailed. My sister, the youngest, was always awarded my mother's old bedroom with her white canopy bed (a twenty-first birthday present). My brother and I took two rooms opposite. One was small and dark. The second, small and too bright, was a former sunporch that had fallen victim to realism about the Canterbury winters and been filled in with walls of glass. It baked in summer and was frigid in winter. Its bed felt like a metal cot; the one in the other room had lumps. The bedspreads in both were the colour of brass and about as soft.

Each morning the sun would pour through a clerestory window high above the stairs and refract through a chandelier into a thousand rainbow shards that danced on the cream walls. While our parents slept, we'd creep from our dark rooms and step into a world of light and colour in search of breakfast.

Owen and Avenal's door would be ajar and we'd pause and listen. The hum of the radio meant they were awake: news, or hymns. We'd push through and they'd be sitting up in bed, Owen in pyjamas and a navy dressing gown, Avenal in a satin housecoat, drinking tea. We'd clamber up and try to sit still while Avenal dispensed toast: paved in butter, dipped in marmalade and handed to us on translucent china plates. We'd try not to spill too many crumbs. Owen would smile.

Owen was always the first to rise. He'd shower, dress into a dark three-piece suit and head downstairs, walking past portraits of himsef and Avenal. He'd stop at the bottom each day and wind the longcase clock that stood there, guarding the entrance to the drawing room.

The clock was dark and polished and twice the height of a child. Owen would draw a heavy brass key – inscribed 'Made in England' – from the clock's abdomen and use it to turn the three cogs built into the clock's face. The chime was the house's background music and I came to know its melody by heart: an ascending number of four-note chimes – tetrarchs they're called – to match the quarter-hours and deep gonging for each hour. This sequence is known as Cambridge Quarters and it was only decades later, listening to Big Ben and thinking how familiar it sounded, that I realised it's something of a global standard.

Owen would move from the clock to the library, where shields and spears and guns and arrows hung above dark shelves. He'd take the basket from beside the hearth out through the hall, the kitchen, the laundry and the back porch, to the woodpile stacked by the garden shed. Sometimes he'd have me or my brother as acolyte, trying to carry two or three logs in our arms to supplement his haul but conscious of getting bark and splinters all over the jerseys Avenal had knitted us. Once the fire was started we settled back, just in time for the first laden tray to arrive, with pikelets, cake, a silver pot of tea.

If we children grew bored by such static pleasures, there was much to explore besides. The house had grown in twists and kinks over the years. A bathroom sat halfway up the stairs; a hidden hatch in a bedroom wall led to an attic; the dining room had a stonework cave that had been a woodstore and now held toy cars. The drawing room even had an organ – though it would be reasonably obvious if a child trespassed and started to play.

The most enticing spot, though, was the Fun Room, a small windowless space beneath the stairs that sat between the hall and the furnace, which was known as Mephistopheles. The Fun Room's door was solid, the handle high enough to keep Edwardian children out. I can't remember how we used to open it – perhaps someone would jump, get a purchase and use their weight to turn it? The door would give inwards with a thick click and we would tumble in as a gust of warm diesel air escaped over our heads.

We might succeed with the door handle but we could never reach the black Bakelite light switch, and so we'd fumble in the darkness for the room's bounty – superannuated toys who remembered the fall of Paris and now eked out lives in wooden boxes. There was a faded-red steel fire engine with sharp edges, several toy tractors made of lead that thankfully no one told us not to lick, a balding teddy bear with hard limbs that could hurt and a doll with blue-rinsed hair who always wore a sundress.

The most fabled prizes were Owen's hats and coats, hanging on the wall. The hats were neat and grey, like his suits. He always wore one when leaving the house, resting on silver hair that he had cut once a week by a barber in a white coat. I suppose he was a member of the last generation for whom a hat was not affectation and we'd don them as tribute, emerging from under the stairs just as he might. Owen never seemed to mind. He would sit in the library and chuckle if he spotted us. He had great tolerance for a damaged crown and would just pat it back into shape and hang it back up. In fact he seemed tolerant of everything.

The garden around the house also held secrets and adventure for little explorers. At the front was a wide apron of lawn. It was a good lawn for dogs, for games or for parties. My parents had their wedding breakfast here, in a big white tent. My grandparents celebrated their golden wedding anniversary the same way, Owen in tails and Avenal in a cream ball gown, a cast on one arm – she tripped getting in the car to drop me back at school one Sunday – and a single long satin glove on the other.

The other side of the drive was – is – a dense, dark mass of laurels and several autumns' worth of leaves, known as the Secret Garden. It was always hung with darkness, but within the shrubbery there was a pond the size of a shallow bath, a gently arched stone footbridge and the occasional statue or urn. It was a child-sized Romantic landscape, hidden from view and available only to those who ventured in to retrieve a ball or play hide and seek.

At the rear was an orchard with a dozen trees planted by a prior owner at decorative intervals, their bases encircled by flowers. The planter chose cleverly: the trees fruited in sequence through the year. Owen used to eat the apples, core and all, and then sort of shrug his jowls in an unusual half-smile. Avenal would shake her head and say, 'Owen, really,' but smile herself.

The orchard was once turned into a racetrack. When my brother was eight or nine, Owen made him a car, a real car, about 1.5 metres long. It was low to the ground, with a petrol engine, a steering column and a steel chassis, and could accelerate as fast as a parent's nightmare. Despite the suits and the quiet demeanour, Owen was a mechanic really: from crisp cuffs emerged incredibly strong hands that could open anything.

First my brother and Owen zoomed it up and down the road, until my mother and Avenal quickly proscribed this lunacy. Owen complied and they moved out the back and slalomed among the fruit trees, my brother at the wheel and Owen, in a summer suit, chuckling with his back to the drawing room window. At the top of each lap there was a sharp turn around a laurel bush to avoid crashing into a chimney. The lawn was quickly turned to mud. When Avenal saw this, the car was wheeled in final disgrace into the back garage.

Along the south side of the orchard ran the old pool. It's still there now: a large concrete oblong set above ground with roses down each side. Owen built an Aga into one end to heat the hollow walls in a design that's essentially Roman. In black and white photos from the pool's heyday it's heavily and darkly hedged for privacy and the pale grey water looks refreshing and peaceful. I never knew it thus. To the lasting regret of all grandchildren, Owen and Avenal filled it in when my mother, the youngest, left home. It's ever since been a home for compost and wilding flowers and sycamores.

The author in the garden at his grandparents' house in Christchurch, 1980.

Avenal and Owen outside their home, 1993.

At the back of the pool the orchard has an outlier: a giant pear tree 20 metres tall that's sprung out of sequence and flourished. It spills its butter-nut-sized fruit in a skirt around its base, as if in despair at the burden. It must have produced several thousand pears weighing about half a kilo each. Avenal would fill wheelbarrow after wheelbarrow and, dressed in frock and sunhat, go up and down the road, offloading them onto neighbours. People remembered that.

Beyond the pear was a Wendy house known as Acorn Cottage. It had been built as a sort of Hameau de la Reine for the playtime of my mother and her three brothers. It looks like an alpine chalet, or a cuckoo clock, with white masonry walls and a steep, curved, brown shingle roof. There were two rooms, one below and another under the eaves, up steep ladder-like stairs. It looked out on its own lawn but even in those days was wrapped by cobwebs and I didn't often venture inside.

Rising above the whole landscape is a giant oak. Its height looked infinite to me, but I suppose it was around two or three times the height of the house. If you're a little weak with heights, as I am, and instead of climbing it you stood beneath and looked up, it was enough to make you dizzy. Its branches spread for ever. My mother and her brothers called it Robin Hood Oak. But it must have been planted long before they imagined the merry men hiding in its branches. Every autumn, its acorns dropped like gunshots on the roof below. Then they sat there in their hundreds, shorn of their little hat-like cupules.

The four children of Owen and Avenal on the drive, c. 1955.

Looking at it, you could see why every ancient culture in Europe worshipped oaks, and linked them to their senior gods: Zeus, Jupiter, Thor for the Teutons, Perun for Slavs. When early Christians cut down oaks, George Frazer says in *The Golden Bough*, 'the people loudly complained that their Sylvan deities were destroyed'. You can imagine a sort of paganism coming from these giant, strong trees, holding their arms in mid-air for century after century. In my grandparents' garden, though, it could not have been a threatening faith of demons and vengeance, but a soft social code of trees and grass, daisies and lavender: more Kenneth Grahame than Norse saga.

Owen and Avenal's home was more hermitage than pleasure dome. Our stays with them were regulated by teas and meals and church. The main visitors were relatives. Of my mother's three brothers, one was abroad (but with a container-load of his beloved French furniture stored somewhere in Christchurch) and the other two lived within a mile of their parents. Her eldest brother had built himself a house resembling a Greek temple by the banks of a stream. He collected cars and would roar up the drive in something new and shiny. My brother and I would idle close enough that the safest thing, for the car, was to take us for a drive.

Another uncle had an indoor pool and bred Great Danes in a large house overlooking Elmwood Park. At one stage he had over a dozen of them, making visits to his house an exercise in juvenile bravery. In wintertime he would take us all into the mountains for skiing, in cars that smelt strongly of hound.

The most regular visitor to Owen and Avenal's, though, was Great-Auntie Beryl. She lived on a hill, dabbled with a lavender rinse and rarely went to bed before three in the morning. When I think of her, I see her dressed for cold weather: worsted skirt, thick tights, flat shoes, cream blouse and wool cardigan. She wore her hair in a permanent curl and a cross around her neck. She always remembered birthdays.

Beryl was Owen's older sister. The story went that, when she was three, she asked for a baby brother for Christmas and, sure enough, on 25 December 1919, Owen arrived. Beryl had treated him as something between a miracle and a toy ever since, though she reserved for him the immemorial tone of the elder sister to the beloved brother: 'Owen, you mustn't'; 'Oh Owen, really.'

Beryl could turn up at Owen and Avenal's at any hour, but her nocturnality prejudiced her in favour of late afternoons. She would appear at the door with a blue leather handbag the size and weight of a small planet, knitting needles and Bibles and bits of paper sticking out in all directions. Her greetings were full of blessings as she dispensed kisses and face powder to all. By the time I knew Beryl, she was stooped by age and widened by fruitcake but she retained round, red cheeks, fair skin and a voice as soft as a brook. With her conversational focus on Christ and God's Plan, it felt like a visitation from a retired but still conscientious cherub.

Beryl and Avenal would sit near the fire in the library, heads together, sometimes with my mother. The only snippets I ever grasped were heavy with religion. Across from them on the sofa, Owen took what was on offer from the tea tray and napped without offending anyone, his hands clasped across his waistcoat.

Tea and baking sustained Beryl through the day but she still ate heartily at night, and each visit to Christchurch we'd dine with her at least once. We would pile into the back of Owen's grand old car, five of us across the lambswool back seat, he and Avenal in front, and drive across town and up into the Cashmere Hills.

Beryl shared her home with a companion we knew as Ella. She was a larger and whiter-haired version of Beryl and Beryl had only tried to kill her once. They had returned home, Beryl driving, and parked the car in the usual spot at the top of the steep drive that ran like a hairpin off Dyers Pass Road. Beryl got out first but she'd forgotten to set the brake. As she shut the driver's door, the vehicle began to slide backwards with Ella still belted inside.

The car gathered pace, failed to make the first of several sharp bends and sailed over the edge. Ella and car would have landed on the road 5 metres

Beryl (right) and
her companion Ella
having tea,
c. 1970s.

below if it hadn't been for a large rhododendron growing sideways out of
the bank. It held them aloft until the fire brigade arrived to save them. The
nearest fire station was some distance away so I like to think that after Beryl
had telephoned for help she would have returned to the precipice and, leaning
over, chatted with Ella until help came. Despite this event, or maybe because
of it, Ella once said to my mother that she thought of us all as family. We
called her auntie, and my brother named his daughter for her.

On our visits we'd arrive at the top of that same steep drive to find
everything in darkness. Once the car's lights were off, it would be pitch black
and we'd be nervous about stumbling down the bank. There were a few steps
up to the front door, which Beryl would have left unlocked. We'd fumble our
way in and reach for a light switch, hidden behind a clock.

The light would show us to be in a small hall. Beryl had built the house to
meet her idiosyncratic needs. She and Ella lived on the first floor – with views
over the city to the Southern Alps – while almost the entire ground level was
given over to a giant music room. This contained several pianos and much
else besides. Beryl's great passion had been opera. In August 1939 she was
one of four finalists in the Melba Bequest Scholarship and she had often been
a prize-winner in national and local singing competitions. She later taught,
and the music room was her classroom.

We'd head up the stairs. These were narrow and steep. We'd be in single
file, with Owen leading the way towards the gloaming emitted through the

net curtains of a pair of French doors at the top. He'd open these and we'd emerge like voles, blinking, into a blaze of light and Axminster that was hot like a sauna.

Beryl and Ella's drawing room was long with a fireplace at one end and views at the other. The walls were decorated in cream damask and all the furniture was Victorian – walnut and stretched silk. Ella would be sitting alone on one of those low-slung armchairs. She'd greet us but not, I recall, rise. The design of the furniture was a poor complement to her own and I think it was more graceful just to sit still.

There were shelves full of colourfully bound, embossed books either side of the fireplace and porcelain figurines were cast in an eternal promenade around the mantel. The tables were covered in lace and there were plenty of pictures hung. There was the odd bundle of music, encased in a plastic bag and sitting on a shelf or a speaker. You might go to sit down and find that one of Beryl's many Persian cats was there already. It would screech, jump off and speed for cover further into the house, legs swamped by fur so that it looked like a rapidly moving wool cushion.

But this room was orderly compared with the one that lay beyond, where every flat surface held piles of papers, records, sheaves of music, books. There were plastic bags by the door full of things to be given away, with tags written in Beryl's distinctive copperplate. There were stacks of cake tins, cassettes, letters. Every drawer was bursting, every seat was taken by velvet cushions.

Beryl would emerge from this direction to say hello. Her head would pop around the door into the drawing room, followed by the rest of her in an apron. 'Oh, hello dears,' she'd say, with kisses all round, and explain that she was overseeing dinner preparations. She didn't always cook by herself and often there would be completely different people there helping. As a child it was discombobulating to find a series of new faces at every visit.

'I'm just getting things ready,' Beryl would go on to say, 'We'll eat soon.'

This was a lie. Dinner would be hours away. It was invariably a roast, which we all loved, but the absence of aroma supported the general suspicion that preparations had only just begun. Owen's response to this reality was to sit quietly and wait, sometimes with eyes closed. I am not sure what I did. I suppose I just sat and listened, and I think my siblings might have slept. There was little in the way of toys and the house felt too full of hazards for exploration. Avenal and my mother would go and see how far along things really were. My father would read.

At some point, normally between nine and ten, we'd be called through to the dining table where the women who had helped Beryl prepare the meal would now serve it, moving in silent ellipses around a scene they no doubt found as improbable as I did. Owen would say grace. The roast would be followed by trifle, or a boiled pudding and custard. It would be very late by the time we were done and we'd all want to head home. The last conversation would be Avenal and my mother trying to commit Beryl to a bedtime. Beryl would reply, 'I just have one or two letters to write,' and we'd leave knowing she'd be up all night.

2

Christchurch was the dream of the Canterbury Association, a colonising force that developed in early Victorian London. It was founded on 27 March 1848 by a meeting at what was then 41 Charing Cross, a three-storey brick building with an attic above apparently lived in by a John Hill. Next door was the Salopian Coffee House. The Charing Cross address is now 22 Whitehall and became the offices of Glyn, Mills & Co., a private bank that had serviced the Hudson's Bay Company. There's a black plaque there now, at waist height, with the Canterbury coat of arms.

A royal charter followed for the association in 1849, no doubt helped by the distinction of their membership. The president of the management committee was the Archbishop of Canterbury himself, John Bird Sumner (though he was known at Eton as 'Crumpety'), who gave his title to both the organisation and the envisioned province. Other members included the dukes of Manchester, of Buccleuch and of Newcastle, the marquess of Cholmondeley, the earl of Harewood, the earl of Shaftesbury and the earl of Devon.

There were plenty of other peers and baronets and bishops and churchmen too, plus a nephew of Samuel Taylor Coleridge (who had a high-country lake named after him), two sons of William Wilberforce (who got a river) and a member of the Baring banking family. The association's driving forces were Edward Gibbon Wakefield, a convicted kidnapper and experienced colony-founder, James Edward FitzGerald, who went on to be Canterbury's first superintendent, and John Robert Godley, a politician from the Irish Ascendancy. Christchurch city, to become Canterbury's capital, was named in advance of its foundation for Godley's old Oxford college.

The first organised wave of settlers left almost directly for Plymouth from a special service of farewell at St Paul's Cathedral, where the Archbishop of Canterbury anointed them Pilgrims and bade them cross the earth and found an ideal Anglican society in the south seas, away from the soot, industry and corruption of mid-Victorian London. If you were wealthy enough to have bought land before leaving, then there was a banquet and a ball for you too.

At the service the Pilgrims sang their own, eponymous, hymn, and maybe it still rung in their ears as they were outward bound from Plymouth Sound a few days later:

Heaven speed you noble band,
Link'd together, heart and hand,
Sworn to seek that far off land,
Canterbury Pilgrims!

The Pilgrims sailed on what came to be known as the First Four Ships – the *Cressy*, the *Sir George Seymour*, the *Charlotte Jane* and the *Randolph*. The aim was to transport a whole cross-section of society, from sturdy labourers to landed gentry. The differentiation began at the ticket office. Those who booked passage south in cabins were called colonists and were served by a steward. Those in steerage made their own meals and were known as immigrants.

On board ship, they prayed every morning and held church services each Sunday. They brought cows and an organ and a bell too, to go in the first church, St Michael and All Angels. For a period it was the colony's only timepiece, rung on the hour, every hour, during daylight.

The journey took 100 days before they rounded the giant earth fortress now called Godley Head in December 1850, sailing into a harbour that used to be a volcano. There was a small port settlement, later named Lyttelton, but caldera walls formed a steep and rocky barrier against the plains beyond. After a few weeks the Pilgrims moved over the hills via a narrow bridle path. As local writer Dame Ngaio Marsh reflected over a century later, 'They climbed the Port Hills and reached the summit where, with a munificent gesture, their inheritance was suddenly laid out before them.' What they surveyed were those wide plains and, in the distance, the Southern Alps: tanned in summer; painted white to a waistline in winter. Many of the new arrivals had perhaps never seen a mountain or stretches of land so lightly populated.

Here was the site for their perfect Anglican city, to be raised from the flax and swamp. A couple of years earlier the New Zealand Company, another colonising organisation with business links to the Canterbury Association, had bought, according to their own standards, all that the Pilgrims could see. They claimed title to 20 million acres (8 million hectares) along the eastern side of the South Island, in fact, in return for a payment of £2000. For Canterbury wasn't uninhabited. Its Māori residents knew the area as Waitaha and had been there for 400 or 500 years. This is part of colonial New Zealand's original sin. Local Māori were pushed to the poor land at the margins and continue to fight for redress over a century and a half later.

The Pilgrims' first homes were tent-like huts with flaxen roofs. The whares, as the Pilgrims called them, borrowed both name and architecture from Māori. The spot where these first huts stood is now known as Settlers', sometimes Pilgrims', Corner. It's marked by a stone memorial, which most boys I was at school with knew to be a good, shady place for drinking beer bought from the off-licence at the far side of the park. The settlers gradually built houses with wide gardens, or cottages with none. They lined the banks of the Avon with weeping willows said to have been grown from cuttings taken at the grave of Napoleon on St Helena. There were long hot summers, and icy winters that capped the Alps with snow and blanketed the plains. A racecourse, polo grounds and cricket fields appeared. There were church bells and hymns. There were families who valued where they'd come from as much as where they stood now, and they used this nostalgia to form their new landscape.

The original plan for Christchurch was drawn by Canterbury Association surveyor Edward Jollie in 1850, and you could navigate with it today. The cathedral sat at the city's core, in the centre of a grid of squares and avenues designed to aid land sales. At the end of each day Jollie and his fellow surveyor Captain Joseph Thomas put their feet up on a table in their ramshackle study at the edge of the world and baptised the new landmarks by bouncing names off one another 'to hear if it sounded well'. The streets were named for Anglican bishoprics, the town squares for martyrs and, in time, the marketplace for the Queen.

When the serious building started it wasn't with the sticks of the Pilgrims' huts but with stone – local black volcanic stone rendered into the neo-Gothic that had been the fashion when they'd left home. The style's rise has been attributed to the French. Blood-soaked revolution and Napoleonic wars put an end to easy travel to the Continent to absorb classical models. Instead, Englishmen looked to home for inspiration. English Gothic was suddenly romantic, pastoral, democratic as opposed to the classical absolutism of the Continent. Think Camelot as opposed to Versailles. This so-called Gothic Revival came to be led by the church, was taken up by gentry and then

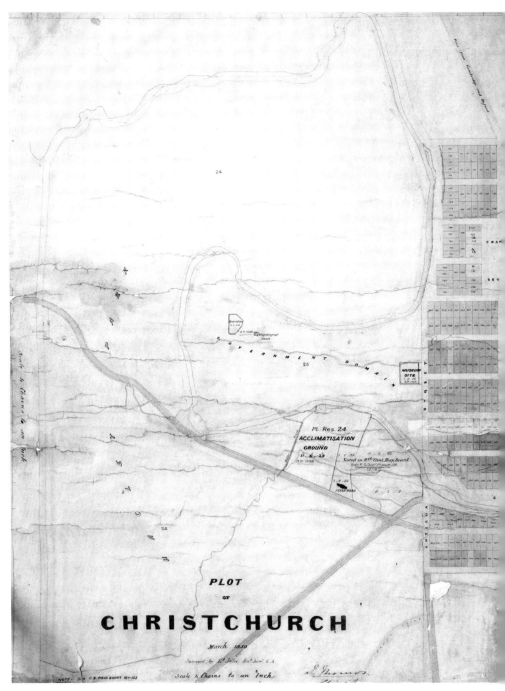

Edward Jollie's original plan for Christchurch. WIKIMEDIA COMMONS

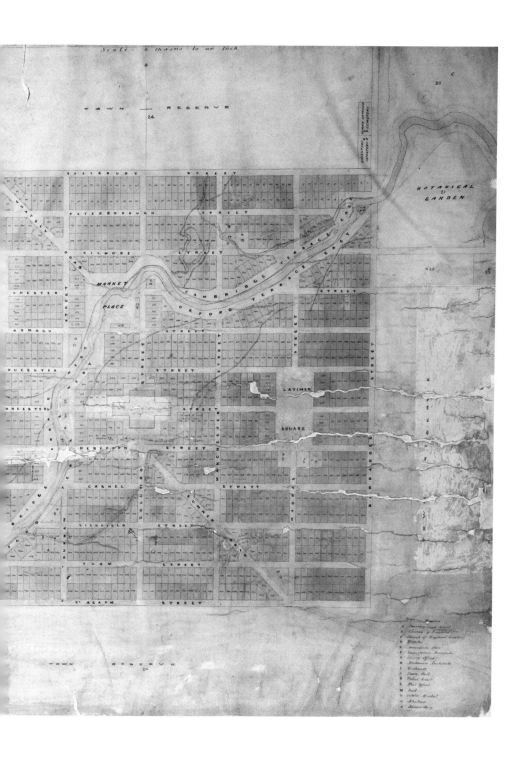

immortalised by Augustus Pugin (the son of a French refugee) and Charles Barry at the Palace of Westminster. The timing was perfect for Christchurch, and the style's morality suited the colony's self-professed progressive goals.

In a world of high-rises and cheap glass it's easy to forget now that the original medieval Gothic architecture was all about letting in light. Norman or Romanesque buildings needed thick walls to support the weight of a stone roof. Windows had to be narrow and deep and admitted little sunshine. The development of load-bearing buttresses allowed for shallower walls and wider windows. Wealthy churches filled these with coloured glass, the better to communicate God's majesty. You can imagine the red- and blue-washed awe of labourers, soldiers, villeins, as they came to give thanks for whatever horror they had just avoided.

Of course, we now see Gothic Revival as old-fashioned, as Edgar Allan Poe or the Addams family. Yet in its time it was anything but. Horace Walpole's mansion, Strawberry Hill, which started it all, was light, airy and picturesque. The style was approachable, romantic, flexible and practical. It let people see what a building did while echoing supposedly old values. In Christchurch, New Zealand, as in England, the Gothic could be both ancient and modern.

Aside from the cathedral, the plan for Christchurch ordained two other major public institutions: a public domain that became 1000-acre (404ha) oak-filled Hagley Park, and a collegiate school for boys to educate the scions of transplanted (or would-be) squires.

The English naming traditions continued too: among Christchurch's suburbs there are Addington, Bromley, Woolston, St Albans, New Brighton. Towns such as Oxford and Springfield had sprouted in the hinterland as many of the wealthiest settler families established themselves on large landholdings, made easily available in return for an application at the Land Office in Christchurch.

The land grants were often enormous. By 1859, according to the great historian of early Canterbury farming Leopold Acland, Canterbury had been parcelled out into about 200 giant farms. What developed was a land-owning culture that may have been a gentry, or at least thought of itself as such, but with a backdrop out of Switzerland or the Tyrol.

Some farms had Māori names, like Orari or Okuku, but the vast majority looked to the northern hemisphere: Broadlands and Buccleuch, Coldstream, Craigieburn, Fernside, Haldon, Rokeby, Lavington and so on. Still others made play of their runholders' classical educations: Mount Algidus for the hills south of Rome; Acheron for the river in Northern Greece. Samuel

Butler, a near contemporary of Bishop George Selwyn at Cambridge, came out to farm a place called Mesopotamia, named thus because it sat between two rivers like the original in the Middle East.

The new farmers included men such as Charles Clifford, the Rhodes brothers, Charles Tripp and John Acland, John Grigg, FitzGerald himself and other politicians: Sir John Hall, William Rolleston, William Moorhouse. Many took their profits and channelled them into manor houses. They'd never match Blenheim or Woburn or Houghton, of course, but they'd have been as good and as grand as much of what was being built by the kinfolk in the English countryside at the time. There'd often been a coat of arms or an escutcheon embedded above the doorway or in the side of a chimney. This hinterland made the farmers wealthy, and parts of Christchurch too.

By 1900 the city had risen in a mass of grey stone, dark towers, finials and battlements and steep roofs. It had a university, churches, a gaol, a hospital. There were provincial council chambers for the voices of the (European) citizens. Canterbury Museum had opened in 1870, only about a decade after the Oxford University Museum, which it in part resembles. The cathedral was finally finished in 1904, complete with a font from the dean of Westminster Abbey, brother of the naval captain who had beaten a French ship to raise the Union Flag over Akaroa.

Christchurch Cathedral, 1980s. WIKIMEDIA COMMONS

3

When I was coming up for 10 and Great-Auntie Beryl was 72, she decided to marry for the first time. Her groom was a widower of similar age called Peter. Peter had white hair swept back from his forehead, wore emblemed jerseys and striped ties and had been a fighter pilot for the Royal Air Force. After the war, he'd left England for Christchurch and a career of religious devotion. This is how he and Beryl had met.

Their wedding was to be in the cathedral. Beryl's commitment to the church over decades qualified her for this, but I can also remember my mother saying that a cathedral wedding was what Beryl had always wanted. It was the only intimation I'd ever had that spinsterhood might not have been her intention. Picking up on the muffled chuckles of my uncles and aunts, I too thought it amusing that someone like Beryl – soft, woolly, living with Ella – would be interested in marriage at all, especially at her age. Such family chatter wasn't unkind, or wasn't meant to be. It was driven instead by genuine surprise and curiosity. I think everyone would have been less intrigued if Beryl had joined a nunnery. As it was, marriage confirmed that Beryl was inimitable, not predictable.

A fairy-tale ceremony was planned, driven by a pre-Raphaelite aesthetic. Beryl wore a high-necked, long-sleeved wedding dress in cream with plenty of smocking. There were half a dozen matrons of honour, including my mother and my grandmother, in similar frocks with large sleeves and wide skirts. All Beryl's great-nieces and nephews had roles too. My two older female cousins were maids of honour, my three-year-old sister a flower girl, and Beryl's three other great-nephews and I were pages. We were to parade up the aisle in Beryl's train and sit up the front as her attendants.

The costumes for the young entourage were inspired by a collection of miniatures that hung in brass frames in Owen and Avenal's drawing room. These showed my mother and her three brothers as pre-schoolers, but apparently dressed for a Victorian picnic. My mother was in a cream dress, sashed with blue silk, and the boys in ecru shirts with Fauntleroy collars and blue silk ribbon bowties. From this Beryl extrapolated the addition of blue corduroy knickerbockers and white hose. We were taken into Ballantynes, the fancy local department store, to have it all tailored for us.

Owen was to give Beryl away. He and Peter wore comparatively modest morning coats. Hundreds were invited, and flowers were ordered and hung down the nave. A local Christchurch paper got involved, no doubt amused like many others by a grand septuagenarian wedding. They put the elderly couple on the front page.

I looked forward to my role and my uniform. I enjoyed the mounting fuss and excitement. On the wedding day itself my cousins and I gathered at my grandparents' house to dress. We pulled on stockings, buttoned knickerbockers, tied silk ribbons and had our hair brushed until it shone. Then we were shuffled into a line of cars and driven into town.

At the time of Beryl's wedding, Cathedral Square was less an expression of confident Anglicanism than a woebegone windscape of grey slate and pigeons. A pub catered to the newspapermen who got off work at midnight, there were a couple of banks and the sort of convenience stores that sold single cigarettes, and in one corner was an empty office block, riddled with asbestos. For all its roughness, the square still attracted visitors: tourists photographing the cathedral, passers-by with time and curiosity to spare, shoppers, wayfarers with nothing else to do and nowhere better to be, policemen keeping an eye on them. Sometimes even actual worshippers.

The journey to the cathedral wasn't long. As we drew up, I could see a crowd of onlookers gathered by the cathedral doors, attracted by the activity. Their presence confirmed to me, for the first time, the full horror of what was about to occur: I was a 10-year-old boy, about to step out into the town square wearing a shirt from Byron's childhood, and tights. If there had been room in the car's footwell I would have stayed there, but the doors opened and out we stepped. I was grateful that the adults provided camouflage. I stayed close to them and entered through the Great West Door with my head down and at a faster pace than is becoming for a page.

During the service I sat at the front on the cold tiles and tried to keep my younger brother still. Across the chancel from us, a beautifully dressed aunt governed my youngest cousin's mischief and my sister fell asleep on the altar steps.

I still have a copy of the service order, found years later among Beryl's possessions. It reminds me that the final hymn was one of my favourites, 'Love Divine, All Loves Excelling'. I had it at my own wedding:

Finish, then, Thy new creation;
Pure and spotless let us be.
Let us see Thy great salvation
Perfectly restored in Thee.
Changed from glory into glory,
Till in Heav'n we take our place,
Till we cast our crowns before Thee,
Lost in wonder, love, and praise.

As the final notes rose to the rafters, we prepared to follow in Beryl's wake down the aisle and back into the waiting cars. There were photographs first, a vast and elderly wedding party gathered on the cathedral steps. Just behind them, engraved into a limestone block inside the porch, if I'd known then to look, I would have seen a small blue arrow pointing to the ground and beneath it the inscription: 'This is the Christchurch benchmark. From this point all levels were taken.'

We drove down Gloucester Street towards Hagley Park and traced its boundary along Park Terrace and then Harper Avenue, before turning into Fendalton Road. After a journey of only a few minutes the cavalcade arrived at a gothic folly of a gatehouse, all steep roofs and fretwork, overseeing high grey gates. We turned and followed the gravel drive snaking between flowerbeds on one side, the Wairarapa Stream on the other.

The drive widened, and we slowed. The trees stood back and in front of us was a large house, the ground floor in brick with stucco above followed by a high roof. The cars pulled up, one by one, beneath a porte-cochère that enclosed the front door like a fortress.

The door was dark, massive. It opened and we were taken into a double-height hall. There was a stone fireplace, bigger than me, in one corner. Ahead, a carved staircase rose around two walls to an ornate gallery. The hall was dim, the day's dying light further muted by stained glass. This was Mona Vale, and it had once been Beryl and Owen's home.

I'm afraid that neither then nor now have I found the house beautiful. The brick rustic and white roughcast upper floor seem mismatched and too much the archetype of suburban-Elizabethan. The twin gables that face east towards the river are a shade too high and give the house a top-heavy look, a

Mona Vale from the driveway. WIKIMEDIA COMMONS

pair of thick eyebrows shrugged in surprise. And the roof ought to be slate, I feel, not the Marseille tile that clashes with the brick.

It is really a late-Victorian country house, with all that implies: the monumental triumphs over the delicate. It was built at the turn of the century by a businessman called Frederick Waymouth, who exported meat, and his wife Alice, a keen gardener. The couple turned to architect Joseph Maddison for the design. Maddison was known, among other things, for abattoirs, which may have been the link, and has been described as preferring functionality over ornament. I think it's fairer to say his usual scale was institutional. His neo-Georgian government buildings, sitting in the cathedral's shadow, are handsome and arguably his masterpiece.

And the monumental can be impressive: Mona Vale's total of 9000–10,000 square feet (830–930m^2), so the council records told me, and the garden setting make up for any lack of finesse. The house overlooks the confluence of two rivers, populated by ingratiating ducks. There are bridges, weirs, an octagonal rose garden, endless trees, manicured lawns, floral borders. There is a separate lodge at the rear gates too, and a sloping dell where these days they put on Shakespeare in the summer.

Waymouth sold the house, then known as Karewa, soon after completion to Annie Quayle Townend. She was famous as the country's wealthiest woman. In 1905 she had inherited £1,000,000 from her father, the miserly landowner of a huge sheep station. He was called George Moore but nick-named Scabby for his refusal to drench his stock. Annie rechristened the house Mona Vale in honour of her mother's family home in Tasmania, at the time the largest in Australia. She added nine acres (3.6ha) to Mona Vale's original four, a bathhouse, and a fernery that she purchased from the 1906–07 New Zealand International Exhibition held in nearby Hagley Park.

Annie Townend, by the by, was a woman of some purpose. She married a divorced doctor almost literally before her father's blind eyes, despite his express opposition. She owned a second large house by the seaside and when she got into dispute with the local borough council, she put it behind a traction engine and moved it to the next-door county. She died without issue and, among other things, her estate paid for the Begonia House at the Botanic Gardens.

In a city of grand homes Mona Vale became one of the city's great estates, if perhaps a little showy. That's how it was known, as the showpiece of Christchurch. It passed through several more hands before it was bought by Owen and Beryl's father, Tracy. When it was up for sale in 1920, the advertising copy said that 'every day its velvety lawns, beautiful shrubs and

The entrance to Mona Vale.

The staircase at Mona Vale, c. 1960.

trees, and the clear-flowing river, attract and hold the attention of passers-by'.

Beryl's wedding was my first visit. By then Mona Vale was owned by the city and run as a function venue, café and public gardens. On the ground floor, Devonshire teas were sold to bridge groups and tour bus parties. You could take punt tours with a landing at the edge of the lawn below the drawing room. Upstairs was for larger events and, arriving to a party not just for grown-ups but for the elderly, I followed everyone up. At the top was a single large space, all the walls of the lost rooms missing, all the decoration gone. It was painted white and bright like a bingo hall.

Guests sat at long tables on metal chairs covered in red velour. The family – the only people I knew in the room – were seated together, infants and children interspersed among the uncles and aunts who were younger than I am now and probably all wondering whether Beryl was going to serve wine. I'm pretty sure she didn't.

There were battalions of speeches. It felt long for me; it would have felt longer for the adults. An aunt, more given to confidences than most, leant over and, pointing to where Beryl was sitting at the top table, said, 'She's sitting exactly where her old bedroom used to be.' And it struck me as odd, on this odd day, for an elderly woman to get married in her old bedroom. I also didn't understand why you'd want to come back to something you'd sold and so presumably didn't want any more.

At a certain point in the wedding breakfast, maybe it was after the pudding, the children were granted leave. We sped down the bannisters, out through the drawing room doors and onto the terrace. There were – are – large trees on either side and beyond the terrace the lawn slopes to the river. The dew was making it slippery and hard to keep our knickerbockers clean. It was dark by now and we played close to the house, staying in the half-light that fell from tall windows.

My mother later told me about her first and only visit to the house, in 1954, when she was five. Her parents took her on her own, no siblings. They drove over from their home, not far away, the same home that I came to know, pulled up under the awning and knocked on the door. A nurse in a blue uniform opened it. It was dark inside. No one said anything as, the nurse leading, they went straight up the stairs, just as we'd done.

There's a verandah in the middle of the house on the first floor, set between the high gables that face the Avon. Behind the verandah was Tracy's bedroom – its walls gone now with all the others, but it was about where the bridesmaids sat. The nurse led my mother and her parents in. Tracy lay in bed, paralysed by a stroke. He faced ahead, his arms lying straight on top of the bedclothes.

Someone fetched a low stool. My mother was motioned to stand on it. Then someone indicated that she should take Tracy's hand. She picked it up and remembers it was stone cold. Tracy couldn't turn his head or his eyes to look at her. After a few moments, my mother replaced the hand on the bed and stepped down from the stool. Then they all went back down the stairs, followed by the nurse, and left. No one had said a thing. Tracy died a few days later – over there, by the verandah. This is the only story I remember being told as a child about Mona Vale.

4

Having a childhood image of any long-departed great-grandparent is unusual. I know it was for me. I knew the names of no others, let alone where they lived and died. Just Tracy.

Maybe it's fitting that I first encountered him in his death, given the long shadow that death was to cast. But, if anything, the way Tracy developed in my child's eye was the reverse. He was the vital life-giver, prominent even if not fully knowable. There was the family catechism: In the beginning the world was dark. Then there was Tracy. He built a company from nothing. He was successful. He created a beautiful world around himself. He filled it with treasure and his treasure brought light. And on the final day he rested, at his new firmament of Mona Vale. It was impressive, memorable and well understood.

Part of it was just his name: memorable also, unusual, possibly eccentric. Who'd ever heard of a man called Tracy? 'French,' relatives would say, and I'd repeat the same years later if ever some incredulous friend sought an explanation.

Tracy was indeed a named presence, a mythic overlord. And, as I was to learn, in many ways still alive: his will still being done. If I'd been able to interpret it at the time, I'd have noticed this occurring, since Tracy's name appeared regularly on our kitchen table. Large white envelopes would arrive for my mother, containing letters emblazoned with 'TRUSTEES OF THE ESTATE T.T. GOUGH'. These gathered in complicated geometric arrangements and sometimes lead to telephone calls long into the evening between my mother and her brothers. When the piles reached a certain height they would be moved and placed on top of earlier piles, or on chairs off to one side, so that we could eat.

Tracy's appearances as a human force distinct from his achievements, his name, his estate, were rare though. I remember only two examples, both of which cast Tracy benevolently. The first involved how Owen and Avenal met.

The rule of thumb in Canterbury is that the truly great rivers – braided ones of the sort you find in other landscapes of great drama such as northern Italy, the northwest of the Americas, the Himalaya – always kept their original Māori names: the Hurunui, the Waimakiriri, the Rakaia, the Rangitata. One likes to think it was a rare mark of deference by the settlers. The lesser waterways all used to sound entirely English; names borrowed from early churchmen and settlers and superimposed over the originals: the Ashley and the Clarence among those to the north, while heading south from Christchurch, there was the Selwyn then the Ashburton. The Selwyn was named for the country's first bishop. In the early twentieth century its lower reaches were a popular spot for holidaymakers from Christchurch, a sort of Henley-in-the-wild, where long grassed meadows merged into riverbanks that sprouted wooden jetties and little white boats.

Tracy used to take the family here each summer. One year a new family took the place next door. There was George Holcombe, who was English, the son of a lawyer and something of a gentleman. George had left London for Western Australia to try mining and when this didn't work he became an accountant in Perth. He was completely unqualified for either job, which I find unreasonably endearing.

The Selwyn River, 1920s. CREATIVE COMMONS

Avenal as a young girl, c. 1926.

Owen at home in Sumner, aged about six, c. 1925.

George was married to Edith, the prettiest girl in Australia, he used to say, and an heiress in her own right. With her inheritance they tried farming in Australia but again it didn't seem to suit and they eventually arrived in Christchurch. They had two children: a boy and a younger girl, 12 years apart.

With a brother so much older, the daughter, Avenal, was used to making her own fun. She entertained herself by skipping alone in the garden. One day she was running out of moves to execute when she realised that the large house next door had a flagpole. This doesn't entirely surprise me: of course Tracy's summer cottage would have a flagpole. Avenal thought that tying the skipping rope to the flagpole would add variety and so she went over and knocked on the door to ask permission. It was opened by a small boy with hair the colour of white lightning. Avenal had been expecting an adult.

For Owen, several months younger, Avenal was the loveliest girl he'd ever seen, and very grown-up. He not only said she could use the flagpole but also offered to hold the other end of the skipping rope. She accepted, and so he stood there all afternoon while she skipped, the quiet, compliant, little blond

A family group at the cottage by the Selwyn River. Beryl, in white, seated far right.

boy and the dark-haired girl. Avenal and Owen spent that whole summer, 1926 I think, playing together. Their parents became friends, the two mothers especially so. At summer's end both families returned to Christchurch. Later, the Holcombe family would move again – George, I feel, was often on the lookout for a job that might properly suit – and it wouldn't be till they were on the cusp of adulthood that Owen and Avenal renewed contact.

• • •

Tracy also appeared in the background of our family holidays, decades later, again by the water, again with Owen and Avenal.

I knew he had been a sailing enthusiast, I knew he owned yachts and I knew he raced them. My informants were small silver cups dotted on mantelpieces and bookshelves around Owen and Avenal's home. These – too shiny not to be touched by wandering children – told me that Tracy often won, often in his yacht *Marangi*: sleek, classic and famous. He made the papers when he bought it. He'd owned a motor launch called *Kereru* and then a 50-footer (15m) called *Friendship*, which lived in Queen Charlotte Sound at the top of the South Island. The navy commandeered *Friendship* during World War II and by the time they were done it was, in his eyes, ruined.

He sold it, and for decades it was the main passenger vessel around the Sounds, dropping people at isolated coves. For thousands and thousands of people, stepping onto *Friendship* was the start of a holiday. Commemorative teaspoons were made – Owen and Avenal had one.

But at the time Owen left school, *Friendship* was Tracy's pleasure launch and he offered her to Owen for the holidays. Owen and a friend spent the whole summer pottering in and out of the endless green, sunken valleys of the Marlborough Sounds. I remember overhearing Avenal describe that summer as an idyllic time for Owen and how it had made him vow to move there one day.

It took him more than 30 years. It was only as he faced retirement, long before I was born, that he and Avenal bought an isolated piece of ex-farmland, perched on an island at the head of a deep bay. We have the 1968 telegram still, strips of white stuck to a yellow sheet: 'Your offer accepted. Property Arapawa Island. Please wire deposit.'

They cleared the gorse and bracken with fire – a common shortcut then. It burned wildly out of control and blackened hundreds if not thousands of hectares, required monsoon buckets and resulted in some substantial invoices from emergency services. I can imagine Owen standing there, watching, knowing he could do nothing about it and therefore not getting flustered but hoping for the best. From the resulting dirt Owen and Avenal raised a long,

Tracy's yacht *Marangi*.

Tracy's one-time launch *Friendship* in the Marlborough Sounds.

low house with a verandah facing out over the water. Theirs was the only dwelling in the bay; you couldn't see any others whichever way you looked, just water, curves and hills. Owen and Avenal had planned to live here permanently. They'd shipped up furniture, desks, their sofas and bedroom suite. They'd even bought another organ, like the one in Christchurch, so that Owen would be able to fill the bay with worship on high days and holy days. The idea of moving permanently collapsed only when an estate agent told them that their Christchurch home was so unfashionable there was virtually no market for it. So this island bungalow became their escape, and we came too.

It's where we spent most summers and Easters. We'd all converge at Picton. We'd come from Wellington by ferry or sometimes by small plane, flying low and looking out over the pinched velvet handkerchiefs that make up the hills, drooping into indigo seas. Owen and Avenal would come from the south, by car. When I became a little older, I'd join them occasionally. It was a migration each time. They'd fill the boot and back seats of Owen's old Rolls-Royce with provisions for what might be months. Then I'd wedge myself into the middle of the back seat, stuck between the picnic basket and the linen.

We'd leave early and Owen always took it carefully. We'd stop for lunch just south of Kaikōura where the highway emerges from the hills of North Canterbury and comes down to the sea. This was about halfway to Picton and

Owen (left) and a friend at Picton, 1938.

Owen would pull into the same lay-by each time and park facing the surf. Avenal would reach back for the lunch and hand it out and we'd sit watching the breakers roll in from South America, eating curried egg sandwiches and drinking tea from a thermos.

Then it was following the coast, past Kēkerengū, then the little limestone church of St Oswald's at Wharanui, its graves hedged by rosemary; the hills of Ward and the Lion's Back, Seddon, the Awatere and its single-lane bridge; the turn-off for Molesworth Station and its landscape of dust and scree; then Blenheim and at last the final winding through the Koromiko Valley and down to Picton: beach, shops, cafés, pubs, a war memorial, ferries, fishing boats and *Aroha*.

Aroha was Owen's answer to his father's *Friendship*: a two-storey, 27-tonne launch he'd commissioned and christened with Avenal's middle name. It means love in Māori and her peripatetic parents gave it to her as a permanent mark of New Zealand, should they or she need to leave it – a common enough convention at the time. *Aroha* was the only way to get out to their place.

Owen would park the car near *Aroha*'s berth and go on board to start opening up: removing covers, turning on generators, switching off alarms. He'd change his suit coat for a blue pullover, put on a captain's hat – a proper one with black shiny peak, a white crown and a pennant badge of the Royal New Zealand Yacht Squadron. Then he'd set about tinkering with the engines, testing and checking, raising a flag up the aft mast, polishing here, scrubbing there.

Avenal took to the galley, dusting, putting away supplies and getting ready for afternoon tea while the rest of us trudged up and down the wharf's planks, like sappers with sandbags, making sure that every box or tin or bottle was moved from the car to the boat.

Aroha felt like a floating hotel. Inside everything was teak, silence and comfort. The staterooms had sheets embroidered with the vessel's name. There was a copy of the front page of the Christchurch paper reporting on its delivery to Lyttelton. In the accompanying photo, Owen stands at the door to the bridge, berthing *Aroha* in reverse. He was asked about the cost. He said it was adequate. He had strict conventions with adjectives. Speed was adequate, time to get something done was adequate. Any other quantity – pudding or beef or length of nap – was always ample.

Suddenly it would be bells ringing then thumping as the engines ignited and we'd start the journey. Owen had to turn two keys, one each to start the two giant engines buried below the saloon. I can hear those sirens now and feel the throb, a giant heartbeat muffled by heavy doors, but reassuring as we sat at the dining table. Avenal, of course, would serve tea, having removed her mohair cardigan to reveal a dress of nautical aspiration if not outright design: white with blue piping and epaulettes perhaps, or with a stylised pattern of anchors and ropes.

Owen captained from a high bench in the pilot house with a timber ship's wheel, jagged with handles and almost a yard across. My brother, sister and I would all haul ourselves up to sit beside him, jostling and bumping, Owen making room for us without murmur. *Aroha* cruised at 8½ knots and the passage out to Arapawa Island took an hour and a quarter. I can be precise

The author and his younger brother on Owen's launch, *Aroha*.

because the co-ordinates and travel time were inscribed on a small panel on the dashboard.

The trip took us past the Snout that separates Picton Harbour from Waikawa, past the southern bays, Point Dieffenbach and Tory Channel. On Arapawa Island theirs was the third inlet along, opposite the Bay of Many Coves with Snake Point and beyond it the prominent bulk of Mt Stokes. It might be getting on to dusk as we finally turned out of the main sound and slowed to chug the last few hundred yards to the jetty while Owen swept the bay with a spotlight and the radar blipped green.

Behind the house were more hills, 450m straight up to the top. It was a tough climb in the hot sun, scrabbling on all fours in parts, being scratched by gorse and listening out for the sounds of wild pigs. At the top, though, a view in all directions. Down the other side of the island into Tory Channel, where the water always looked more teal than navy. West right down the sound to the outline of the Richmond Range. And to the north, one of the world's last great geographical discoveries.

Captain Cook himself allegedly came this way on the afternoon of 23 January 1770, three days after he and Joseph Banks bought a preserved head (a mokomokai) from a party of Māori in a waka that came alongside *Endeavour*. From about this point Cook saw the eastern edge of the strait that now bears his name. It confirmed that he'd found two narrow islands, not one, and that no great hidden landmass existed to the east. Cook complained about 'impenetrable woods' on the hills. I'm sympathetic.

Looking down the hill, the way you'd come, miles below it seemed, *Aroha* still and gleaming white at the jetty, the wide lawn by the beach and people sitting on the deck or snoozing beneath a *National Geographic*.

I don't know how many summers we spent here, but it felt like all of them. There are photos of me there from at least the age of four, sitting between Owen's legs on a red mower as he cut the lawns. He tried to teach me to sail, too, in a yellow P-class that I managed not to capsize, though I found the rigging, basic as it was, incomprehensible. He also showed us how to fish, but his method was idiosyncratic and not easily replicable. He'd take *Aroha* at a speed just above neutral to set drift nets across the bay and then haul the whole thing up onto the beach. I'm pretty sure that's illegal now but it wasn't then and if I'd asked him, he would have chuckled and shaken his head or claimed it was efficient. It was also the best way of using his boat to fish without actually getting the catch on board and making everything messy.

Being on a remote island meant no electricity. This gave Owen the opportunity to fiddle with a sooty generator and coax it into action each stay. Or there was that red ride-on lawnmower. Or a motorbike with trailer, which he used to retrieve baggage from the jetty. Or even his own bulldozer, which was how he gardened. Often we'd get rides on this too, sharing the earmuffs with him. He'd get to use about ten machines a day if he wanted.

Isolation didn't prevent Owen and Avenal from performing their usual religious offices. At Easter or any other high holiday they would host divine worship in the main room. The observant boated in from other bays; I remember most of the men had beards. Owen played the organ. He wasn't as musical as Beryl but he could play hymns. Afterwards there'd be morning tea. Later in life Owen and Avenal took to inviting their vicar up for holidays. He and his family would stay on *Aroha*, moored in the bay, and we'd all play cricket on the lawn. They were about the only people other than family who ever stayed.

There was a sense of an orderly home, echoing life in Christchurch: similar furniture, similar structure to the days; the kitchen was even carpeted in the same mesmerising pattern. It wasn't exactly what people would expect if you told them it was a beach house, miles by water from the nearest settlement.

It was possibly this migration of chattels from Christchurch that was responsible for an old record in a brown paper cover that I once found in among the albums of classical music. I pulled it from its sheath and saw it had 'Beryl, 1945' written in her hand on the label in the centre. I put it on the turntable and the recording crackled to life with a male announcer, a clipped but scratchy voice perfect for the year. You could just imagine him broadcasting the death of a king or the fall of Berlin. But his news was not so grave. He told me that I was about to hear from the three finalists in that year's national opera competition. The second, introduced by name when her turn came, was Beryl, delivering an aria in an impressive soprano.

5

At the age of 13 I followed Owen not on holiday but to board at his old school. This was Christ's College, founded by the Canterbury Association and named by FitzGerald for his old Cambridge college to balance out Godley's use of his Oxford one for the name of the city itself. The Pilgrims even brought out their own headmaster on the First Four Ships, the Reverend Henry Jacobs, formerly of Charterhouse and a fellow of Queen's College, Oxford. The rumour was that classes started on board on the journey out. The school began in a Lyttelton barracks in 1851 before moving the following year to the parsonage of St Michael's in the city. Its coat of arms came to bear four shells, one for each of the first ships, as well as the rose of Christ Church College, Oxford, and the lion of Cambridge University.

Christ's College ended up being built around a quadrangle on what was then part of Antigua Street but later became Rolleston Avenue, a few blocks west of the cathedral. On one side are the Botanic Gardens, on the other, Hagley Park. Whenever Owen drove us into town we'd pass the school's black iron gates. There were traffic lights and as often as not we'd be stopped for a few moments and could look through to the billiard-table lawn and its circle of castles. The boys were prominent too. They belted across the road in front of us, ties trailing, or ambled about Cashel Mall wearing black and white striped blazers in summer or dark grey suits and stiff collars in winter.

• • •

My parents often had to live abroad for work and if they needed to move once more, boarding would allow continuity. I took up the plan with enthusiasm. I liked the idea of the tradition. Around Owen and Avenal's house were photos of Owen in school uniform, and an old college boater used to appear in wardrobes or hang on bedroom door hooks. There were exercise books with the school coat of arms on the cover and black stripes, and Owen's copies of the school's annual *Register* going back to the 1930s, with photos showing buildings I already knew by sight.

I even had a copy of a magazine in which the school appeared. The cover story proclaimed it the country's most splendid school and I used to take it to primary school and show my friends photos of the heroic life I would live: boys in shorts and long socks, prefects in suits and silk ties, athletes

The entrance to Christ's College in the 1930s. STEFFANO WEBB COLLECTION, 1/1-005189-F, ALEXANDER TURNBULL LIBRARY, WELLINGTON

Owen, right, and two friends in Cathedral Square on the way to school. They have probably just got off the tram from Sumner.

wandering through the gardens in whites and blazers and striped cricket caps; boys lounging under cloisters or laughing in panelled common rooms; stacks of tuck boxes named in thick black paint; rugby and cricket on enormous playing fields; candlelit chapel services; the communal jollity of mealtimes in that great, flag-draped, hammer-beamed stone chamber of the dining hall; and very young boys carrying wobbling stacks of books against the background of the school's Gothic façades.

Owen started in 1934 just after a new headmaster had been appointed, a veteran of the Western Front and former prisoner of war called Reginald Richards, who vowed not to change any of the old traditions. The school history tells me that two years before Owen got there, a pair of first-year boys were punished by being stripped naked, covered all over with boot polish and made to parade around the junior common room. A famous air force pilot and international cricketer who was a near contemporary of Owen remembers the lack of privacy and the difficulty of knowing no one. He found solace in the chapel and 'when the boys said the prayers for their homes he would weep into his cassock'.

A prominent historian, looking back on his own arrival 30 years later, noted that dayboys 'were looked down upon as a rather inferior species … predominantly sons of city businessmen or of urban professionals'. Owen's father, for all he became, was a merchant.

The school focus in Owen's day was on cadets and rugby, mostly. Did Owen have to polish a rifle? Go camping? Decline Latin nouns? Run around Hagley three winter mornings a week in the frost? He never spoke to me of his time there, and I never asked. That should have told me something. Before I arrived I was so partisan it never entered my head that Owen might not have enjoyed his time at Christ's College. Then, after I'd begun, I didn't want to talk much about school, either. I'd heard that Owen had once been caned across the face. It didn't put me off. I was told it had been a mistake and his sons benefited from the credits so earned when they turned up to find the same master still teaching the same class.

There's a book known as the School List. It's thick, hard covered and the latest edition is scarlet with silver embossing. It records every boy who has ever attended, numbered in order. Owen was number 4486. I was 11,465. Despite the gap of 60 years and 7000 boys, we had the same uniforms, the same hymns. The children of some of Owen's teachers were to teach me. Even the exercise books were the same: white covers, black and white stripes top and bottom, the school's coat of arms in the centre.

The night before my first term began we stayed with Owen and Avenal. The next afternoon my father drove me to the school. I'd been through those gates once before, for the entrance exams. Then we had stood in the lobby of the hall without the lights on. Several squadrons of boys in matching uniforms; only a few, like me, in mufti with their parents. Then a giant in a black robe opened the doors and bade us sit at a desk. There was line after line of them. It was first exam I'd ever taken.

On the afternoon of arrival there was an introductory tea of sorts with the housemaster, and games in his garden to build camaraderie. Upstairs we saw our dormitory for the first time. The external walls were sliding glass windows; in winter you could see your breath.

Then Dad and I walked down the concrete staircase and back out to the quadrangle. I watched him drive out through the gates. I was alone, standing in a canyon of dark buildings that no longer looked as welcoming as in the photographs. I turned and walked into Jacobs House, on my own for the first time. The door was heavy and riveted, like a drawbridge. I went upstairs and knelt by my tiny bedside locker and packed and repacked into it, for want of anything else private to do, keeping my head down the while. Then the first night in that strange cold bed, far from home.

On the first morning we made our way to the music school. It was down an alleyway, under the hall, past the bike sheds, right by the river. At the top of the stairs was the head of music, who had strong and dark features and wore a gown when he played the organ in chapel. We sat down in rows. He called us forward letter by letter.

'Can you sing, boy?'

'No, sir.'

'Sing this note.'

For a capable few, the piano key might elicit a sweet equal in reply. There were several in our class who'd come from the cathedral choir school. Their talent was predictable. For the rest, it was a first and last solo performance. I was among the rest. We each had several attempts, just in case one's initial flat monotone had been bad luck or subterfuge.

'Now this one.'

There was no escape.

'That's enough. Sit down, please.'

The reward for success was the choir, which seemed of equivocal value: formal recognition of a high-pitched voice, regular practices stretching into the forever and the obvious femininity of cassock and surplice. Choir or not, we all had chapel three mornings a week, evensong every second Sunday and congregational practice on Fridays, with the music master charging the aisle exhorting the lazy sods to look up from their books and sing in the manner the College was famous for.

As with all our little foot pilgrimages in that first week or two, we moved en masse. Floppy, low-rise centurions in blazered formation, folders for shields. From the music rooms we wound back to the wider school, coming out upon the great emerald tablecloth of the quadrangle, around which the rest of life was arrayed. Masters could sweep across it in their robes but it was otherwise untouchable.

We needed to head for the far corner, diagonally opposite, to an old wooden building that sat on what used to be the college's fighting ground. This was the main school sport until about 1900. Future Cabinet minister William Pember Reeves once fought an older boy here every day for a week, the teachers looking on.

We had to hurry. The five-minute gaps between lessons didn't accommodate ignorance. The building was musty and rotting and on the ground floor even the prefects deferred to the rats. Up the steep, stale staircase was Latin, where an imposingly sized master (weren't they all imposing?) presided over a cramped room that smelt of leaking windows. He'd been a boy at the school in the misty past and returned to this job straight from university in London. His father had taught here too, and a grandfather. His mother had been born literally on the school grounds, when each housemaster had four indoor servants.

When we were seated the master pushed himself, gown and bulk, out of his chair. Pointing towards the wall, he said, 'Do you know what this is?'

Silence.

'It's a cupboard, isn't it?' He walked over and opened it. 'But look at it. Look, it's empty.'

A theme was emerging in our responses.

'Do you know why it's empty?'

Shaking of 20 heads.

'Because I'm not allowed to cane you any more.' He continued, 'There's no cane,' looking around, 'is there?'

Heads shook again, some muttered imprecations, and he sat down. The cane had been outlawed 18 months before. We were only the second intake to avoid it altogether, but it was axiomatic that there was a causal link between effete punishment mechanisms and the perceived degraded moral fibre of the year ahead of us. Boys in our year who'd been caned all through prep school claimed they preferred it. Got the punishment over and done with, they said, knowing they'd never have to face it again.

This master, we were to learn, kept little sweets by his elbow. These would be thrown from his desk in waves of justice or injustice, depending on your point of view, depending on your ability, in response to correct answers. Not many came from me in those early days. The class was ab initio but everyone else, it seemed, had been doing Latin since birth. We also had to underline all our headings and sub-headings in house colours; difficult for those in Julius, which is white, or the then new Rolleston house, which sported maroon.

From Latin we went to English. To get there we had to criss-cross cobblestones and duck among slender mammoths with venturesome fists. Above the Little Theatre was a crisply accented ascetic who was to be our form master. His rooms overlooked the mythic field of Upper, where the school's Olympians had trained and played since 1852. It was also the scene of annual compulsory athletics, known as Standards, and the licensed violence of house rugby.

It would have been after English that we had our first proper lunch in the dining hall, squeezing through the massive oak doors to stand in silence by our places. Each house had five tables, allocated by year group, but the last few pairs of first-year boys to arrive had to ornament the ends of the older tables and ensure all slops were tidied up.

We were to eat every meal here, every day, many of us for five years in a row beneath the vaultings, the flags of the Allies on the far wall, portraits of benefactors, soldiers, bishops, former headmasters and other worthies on the others. There was one, only one, of a woman – dark haired and alabaster skinned, in Victorian dress against a classicised background. Her name was Maria Somes. Her late ship-owning husband Joseph had made a fortune and she endowed the school's scholarships, of which I was a beneficiary. This provided no great distinction, studies being popularly perceived as an unfortunate distraction, if not an outright encumbrance.

As we stood and waited the masters came in, last of all the headmaster, who took his seat centrally on an oak throne. The high table filled with prefects and one of these paladins shouted a simple grace into the silence, every day the same and it comes easily to me now, ending with 'For Christ's sake, Amen.'

Grace was followed by thunder. Forty heavy wooden benches, forms, heaved across the floor as 250 boys hurried to sit down and assault whatever was on the tables. Twenty minutes and it was all over. We stood again in silence. The same prefect came forward to a carved case holding the Book of Memories, with the names of the dead from the Great War. Over 300 old boys were wounded and 149 killed. Thirty-four died just in the first three months of Gallipoli, all from a roll of about 300 in any given year. The prefect turned a page and reclosed the glass lid before stepping back up to the dais to turn and face us all. Then the final prayer: 'For these and all His mercies, may God's Holy Name be praised.'

And where else that first day? Maths was in the so-called open-air classrooms, as were other languages – we had German that term, I think – and then our housemaster for chemistry. The chaplain taught us divinity, thinly rebranded as life skills. Social studies was in the Chapman Block, now demolished, with a teacher who sported a moustache and modelled dressing gowns for Ballantynes in the catalogues our mothers received.

After school was sport. Everyone had to try out for cricket, even if you were a natural rower. We all changed into whites, put our striped college blazers back on and made our first uniformed walk in a shambling black and

Masters stand under the school clock at Christ's College, the quadrangle and dining hall in the background, 1950. CREATIVE COMMONS

white caterpillar through the Botanic Gardens to the college's playing fields in South Hagley Park. Then back quickly for showers and dinner, the dining hall again, 20 minutes to eat as much as you could from a tray. It always seemed to be hogget, which I'd never heard of before. We had to be quick to be seated in set places for two hours of notionally silent prep, overseen by some low-voiced giant from the fifth year.

These house prefects had more interest in the anthropology of our subordinate status than in their own studies. I suppose they could stay up all night and we were, after all, almost another life form. A popular punishment – among both the gaolers and, Vichy-like, the prisoners too – was to stand the perpetrator on a pew, arms stretched out sideways, palms up, an encyclopaedia resting on each. If the arms began to droop, something was thrown at you. It was the only time these books were used.

Even on that first night, two hours wasn't enough for prep. A boy on his first day was in no position to judge what could be safely avoided. To work late, though, required a special permission, given on sufferance as proactive reclusion from communal life was suspicious. There was, anyway, only a space of 45 minutes before bed. There was a television that first-year boys had no rights to watch, and a single telephone, the queue for which was equally impenetrable to us. The phone also stood in the middle of the hall, a small sheet of plywood the only concession to privacy.

By 9.15 it was lights out; about 25 of us in a long room of pine beds separated by bedside lockers the size of a piece of carry-on luggage. We were allowed our own duvet covers at least, to make up for the scratchy army issue grey blankets. And then I was lying there, in the darkness, surrounded but alone and at last back in control, even if only of my own thoughts: Where am I? I can't do this for five years. I can't do this for a week. Around me dozed the true sons of that Canterbury dream. I remember in those first few days the contraband conversation (punishment was severe for talking after lights out) moved to silage. One of the boys' farms possessed the largest silage pit in the South Island. Silage, silage, what is silage?

And then, before you knew it, the bells. Again and again and again. Ringing like a fire alarm from the walls, but one of our number marching through our dorm in his dressing gown, clanging a handbell, to really make sure. It was our daily Angelus. It meant we started everything over again: race into slippers, down the three flights (don't slip), grab a towel and out the front door for our daily trudge to the far end of Upper, where the artesian swimming baths had been getting colder and colder every day since the 1880s. Names were checked as we immersed ourselves, only gravity taking us into the water – our breath pushed out by fear and chill.

Back to the dorm. Quick dressing. Always this press of time. Cold hands putting studs into collars. Can I borrow a stud? Mine's broken. How do you do this? Who's taken my tie? How can that be the bell already? Get to the dining hall, the crush of entry, to stand again by our tables and wait for the grace. Then house jobs – fagging was out but first years did all the same tasks under guise of a different naming system – and mayhem sweeping and cleaning and fetching and polishing and trying to be efficient and not get blamed before the school bells rang, again, and everyone, all 600 of us, gathered by the chapel doors for two hymns and 15 minutes of equality before God.

6

We were allowed out three times a term, for a night at a time. Owen and Avenal would call for me at noon on Saturday and wait in their car, which was as old as me, until I was released. I would round into the quadrangle from class or sport, passing under the great black and gold school clock, like something out of Prague, and see them sitting there, the car – also gold – glowing against the dark stone. Owen behind the wheel in a suit and hat, Avenal beside him with a cross around her neck.

It would take me a few minutes to dash into the boarding house, change out of uniform and reappear with a little bag. I would slip into the back seat and it would be warm and quiet and private. The door clunked shut. Then Owen would start the car and we would glide quietly out the college gates, Avenal smiling back at me over her shoulder.

Their house, so familiar, was a different world now, just 10 minutes' drive away. The car whirred as it made the turn through the gates and onto the drive, where the crunch of gravel marked arrival and the start of a weekend of freedom and peace and comfort.

Avenal would have lunch prepared and as we pulled up I would see the table laid in the dining room: bone-handled cutlery, china, juice in a crystal jug with a crocheted cover. The clock would peal a welcome. We'd eat straight away, Owen at the head, Avenal to his right and me on the left, with my back to the armoire and the silverware. Owen said grace with, behind him, above the fireplace, a portrait of Joan of Arc at the moment of her passion, eyes heavenward in supplication.

I have trouble recalling our precise conversations at those lunches, on those weekends, but I know I didn't want to talk about school. I wanted to focus on the unimaginable luxury of almost 30 hours of cosseted indolence that stretched ahead of me. The last intruder I wanted here was the world I had escaped.

Owen was happy with this. He spoke mostly in smiles and chuckles and winks, or would mutter 'Jolly good' if he felt a verbal answer was required. Avenal was more inquisitive. She had been taken to France for a year as a sort of finishing, and as something of an escape for her mother after her father died. She had a good grasp of Latin (far better than my own), had gained a masters in philosophy and literature and had been the first female to edit the Auckland university student paper. John Mulgan, of *Man Alone* fame, had been the editor seven years earlier. Avenal's classical education was antagonised by the cutlery we used, and I remember her commenting on it one day, flattering me perhaps that I might be up to the task of understanding. There was an engraved crest with a motto underneath.

Avenal as a graduate, late 1930s.

'I can't believe they got it wrong,' Avenal said, shaking her head, a fork in her hand.

'Who?' I asked.

'Your great-grandfather.'

Tracy, I guessed, who else? But I was a bit lost.

'What did he get wrong?'

'The cutlery.'

I looked at the fork in my hand. Four prongs? Was that standard? When had I ever counted prongs on a fork? Did formal cutlery have five?

'He had it engraved incorrectly,' Avenal continued, 'or the engravers got it wrong.'

I was still lost. 'What do you mean, wrong?'

'The Latin. All of it. They got the motto wrong. It should be "Domat Omnia Virtus". Do you know what that means?'

I looked at the fork once more. I got on well with the Latin master and enjoyed his classes but my actual Latin let us both down.

'Something about all the virtue?'

'Virtue conquers all. But look what they've got instead – "Fides et Justitia", faith and justice. It's not even a motto, there's no verb. It's just two nouns.' She shook her head again. I did too.

'It was Tracy's crest?' I asked.

'He seems to have borrowed it from Sir Matthew Gough.'

'Who was he?'

'An ancestor, possibly, supposedly. He fought in the Hundred Years' War and was knighted on the field of battle. He was mentioned in Shakespeare, too.'

She went off and came back with a book and a single sheet of paper. The book was entitled *Heraldry in Shakespeare* or something similar.

Years later I looked up the Shakespeare reference. He appears in *Henry VI, Part 2*, in the opening of Act 4, Scene 7. It's during Jack Cade's rebellion and Matthew, back only a month from years of war in France, is sent to suppress it. The scene in question reads:

Smithfield, London:
Alarums. MATTHEW GOFFE is slain, and all the rest.

It's not a big role, is it? But if one has to be slain at Smithfield, it's as well to have it remarked by Shakespeare.

Avenal opened her book and pointed to Matthew's coat of arms. She went on, part reading, part from memory: 'Matthew fought with Henry V and Henry VI. He was at Le Mans alongside Sir John Fastolf and also with Lord Warwick; William Herbert, first Earl of Pembroke; Lord Salisbury; John Talbot, Earl of Shrewsbury; the Duke of Somerset; Sir Robert de Vere. He even defended a town called Beaugency against Joan of Arc,' nodding to the painting.

'Sir Matthew was taken prisoner once for three years, but he made friends. The French called him Mathago. The English made him baron of Coulonces and Tillières. He was one of the only people to escape the massacre of the English army at Formigny, having had his life saved by Pembroke. He fought right to the end and handed over the keys of Bayeaux to the French in April 1450.

'He had four children and they moved out of the Welsh Marches into western England, into Shropshire and Staffordshire and eventually to Birmingham. His sons married and they had children. They became cloth merchants' – the wool trade was very big in the west of England, Avenal interpolated – 'and then inherited lands through marriage. One was knighted and then another was ennobled. Their estates were at Perry Hall and Edgbaston.'

'Like the cricket ground?' This was something I could grasp.

'Yes, that's there now too. When they developed the area during the

Industrial Revolution, I believe they wouldn't allow factories or warehouses. It made it an attractive place to live.'

'This was all Tracy's family?' I asked.

Avenal did not shrug but her words produced the same effect. 'Your great-great-grandfather came from the same area, from Birmingham, and shared the same surname. He thought there was a connection. So did Uncle Wilfrid.'

I'd never heard of Uncle Wilfrid, but the name sounded perfect for a dedicated family genealogist.

The sheet of paper she held showed a family tree with that same coat of arms in the top left corner. Names and birth dates were calligraphed below. It looked wonderful.

'This is what Uncle Wilfrid researched and prepared.'

'Who was he again, sorry?' I asked.

'Wilfrid? Tracy's brother-in-law. He married Tracy's younger sister.'

'Right. Of course.'

I had a close look at the document. It seemed to show two lines of descent, one grand, one not; this latter held the names I recognised. The two lines did not intersect; there was just common location and similar timing.

'I'm not sure I can see the link,' I said, 'or at least it doesn't seem very strong.'

'Well, Tracy believed in it and so had this cutlery reflect it.'

'Well, it's rather nice anyway.'

'It is.'

I'm not sure how seriously Avenal took it all. We once went together on holiday to northern France, our family and Owen and Avenal. We rented an old presbytery in a one-shop village out of Proust and drove all over Normandy and Brittany and the Loire. Owen drank Beaujolais for a sore throat. We ate galettes. We visited St Malo, the Mont-Saint-Michel and saw the battlement Chateaubriand had to navigate to visit the loo at night (it reminded me of school). But we never did any hunting for relics of the alleged ancestor Sir Matthew.

I did years later find a visitors' guide to Edgbaston Old Church among Owen and Avenal's belongings. The brochure showed the historical ownership of pews by the various local families – how parish churches used to be funded. It mentioned a family namesake as having paid for the church's eighteenth-century restoration. So I guess they'd gone there once to look, but Avenal never mentioned it.

· · ·

After lunch we'd move to the library with the eternal fire burning in the grate and ready ourselves to pass the afternoon in a medley of sedentary activities. Owen would take up his seat in the slanting sun. Avenal and I would sit either side of the fireplace.

For someone who spent a lot of time in this library, Owen read little. He preferred chess – which he won if he wanted, smiling all the way and barely looking at his moves. His mind was alert, but practical. By the time I was arriving on these brief leaves from school, Avenal was borrowing large-print detective novels for him from the library. He would pick one up from time to time but rarely breached more than a few polite pages. Then, when Avenal was out of the room once more, he would return it to the tea table, refold his hands over his waistcoat, sit back, smile and close his eyes.

Avenal's armchair abutted her shelves of Christian literature, with a little kidney-shaped table for tea by her side. She had a wide range of intellectual interests and the library catered to them more than to Owen's. If you lent Avenal a book she was the sort of person who would come back a few weeks later with her notes written up, ready to compare them with you.

There were shelves of poetry, Romantics mostly, and unfashionable Victorian novelists – all in tiny, crumbling leatherbound volumes; books on art and architecture; several different encyclopaedias; history, politics, the usual literary classics; travelogues. Despite this, Avenal read the Bible as often as not. King James – leather cover, burgundy, soft like gloves.

I would read too. I'm afraid my tastes were – still are – more materialistic than spiritual. I might reach for one of their lavishly illustrated volumes on country houses, or one of the folios on the Old Masters or architecture that filled the bottom shelves. They were heavy, big books and across my lap they buckled me into my armchair. Grateful for my sanctuary, I would imagine myself to a still more delicate world.

From time to time Owen might stand up, press his suit coat and trousers with his hands and take the wicker wood-basket out to replenish the logs, and I might yet help him. This was about the most athletic we would get. Owen kept the fire alive with the same dedication that Avenal showed towards her books.

Time away from boarding school existed in some different, compressed dimension. It would pass faster than time elsewhere, as if in some inverted Narnia. The minutes disappeared as I sat in my chair, every quarter-hour interval recorded by the clock in the hall. By the time darkness had fallen and dinner was finished, the idea of tomorrow had already begun its unavoidable slide from improbability to reality. This made bedtime less a retreat than a watershed, marking the transformation of today's celebration into tomorrow's melancholy, with the return to the rigour of cold rooms and discipline.

We would head upstairs early, with hot water bottles. Here on my own, not competing with other siblings, I'd be entitled to sleep in my mother's blue bedroom with the white furniture. Owen and Avenal kept all the beds coated in thick blankets and feather counterpanes. The layers felt heavy, almost claustrophobic, but the density made for great warmth. Getting in was a tussle, getting out even harder.

I was warm, I was comfortable and I was well fed. At night in the dormitory I might dream of lying here, in this bed. I should have slept easily but the return to school the next day made it difficult. As I lay awake the clock below me would chart my restlessness, but not unkindly. It rang clear at night, unchallenged by the sounds of daily life, the curving stairwell lifting the chimes to the bedrooms like an amphitheatre. I might listen to it announce 11, 12 and then back to one again before I drifted off, so that by morning I was still bleary and tired – that perpetual tiredness of the institutionalised – while Owen and Avenal got up and dressed for church.

School was seen as worshipful enough that I didn't have to go with them, and Avenal was always polite enough never to burden me with outright refusal. Owen would bring the car out of the garage and around to the front door. You could hear it emerging and then the thud of the idling engine as he sat waiting for Avenal to descend. If it was raining she wore a Burberry that she'd had lined with fur and a matching brimless fur hat that could have come from Moscow. I would hear them leave and, grateful for this reprieve, wallow longer amid the blankets and breadcrumbs.

They had abandoned beautiful stone St Barnabas, virtually at the end of their road, and started attending a more exuberant congregation a few miles away. I once asked my grandmother about this choice. It seemed a long way to drive when salvation was so close. The vicar at St Barnabas hadn't been *charismatic* enough, Avenal had replied. I was 12, maybe 13, and I nodded as if I knew what she meant. She was saying, I told myself, that one needed a charming vicar; and I thought yes, quite right, no one likes a bore.

I bought a copy of that same vicar's memoirs not long ago, found, of course, in a church-run book fair. He loved sports, enjoyed socialising, wrote in an avuncular style, did broadcast sports commentary on the side. He described St Barnabas as a good parish. I know how Avenal responded: a church with whitewashed concrete-block walls, a metal roof and a reputation for percussive liturgy that was a long way from evensong. Charismatic, I learnt, meant hands in the air.

Sometime after they'd driven off I, in no hurry, would push back the blankets and plod through the hall and across the stairs to the bathroom with the view over the back garden. Here was that private green landscape enclosed by trees and dappled in the morning sun, but it was only mine for a few more hours. Then a shower, hot water and as long as I wanted. And I can remember so clearly being all cleaned and dressed, in clothes I barely recognised as I had little chance to wear them, walking downstairs, seeing myself in that huge wall of sparkling mirrors and thinking I was lucky, and it was not all so bad.

I tried to slow those Sundays down. Surely doing nothing would cause time to droop, to drag. But it was no help and the days slipped past me, no matter how tightly I closed my eyes or how far into that armchair I burrowed.

Before long Owen and Avenal would be back from church, then it would be lunch – my last full meal and so another watershed. Then back to my chair in the library, more time sitting there enjoying the peace, reading a page at a time before drowsing. Finally, a rushed supper, the drive back to college, through the door of the boarding house, just in time for roll call and to be swept up once more in the shouting, the fighting, the slamming of doors.

7

That first year at school went slowly, but it went. I once answered a prefect's maths question correctly during prep. Then I had some success with the cricket ball. And so inch by inch I claimed some humanity within the institution. We went to chapel. We tied our ties. We stood in line. We did our prep. We polished our shoes, we lowered our heads. And, month by month, year by year, life improved. Freedom increased. The skills to navigate the system sharpened. We grew from dorms into cubicles, private spaces with our own desk and wardrobe.

We memorised Wilfred Owen – 'What passing-bells for these who die as cattle?' – and could empathise with hasty orisons, we studied the Tudors, we analysed *King Lear*. 'It's about filial piety,' our English master told us, 'and how ruinous it is to expect it.' We talked about the theme of hypocrisy in D.H. Lawrence. There was spare time during the day. There were trips into town. There was the promise of a senior blazer. Winter sport was trundling a golf bag around Hagley Park, chatting with friends.

In my penultimate year someone, my mother I guess, decided I was old enough to attend a meeting at the family company, Tracy's one. It clearly had a big role in my mother's family but I had given little thought to its mechanics, and not having grown up in Christchurch gave me distance from any prominence it might have once enjoyed. Other than during the war, Owen had worked there his whole life. His three sons, my uncles, had followed him but by now had all left and were on their own trajectories. The only one who hadn't worked there was my mother. After university she left for London to study art history at the Courtauld, where Anthony Blunt was impolite about colonials while hiding his Russian treachery. She met my father – newly arrived too, but to the London School of Economics – and never lived in Christchurch again.

On the day of my visit I got a special leave from school. Owen and Avenal collected me. With the school day in full swing, their distinctive car gathered more attention than it would on Saturday mornings. I got into the back as I always did, this time wearing my dark school suit and black and white tie.

The company's offices had occupied a series of buildings on the high east bank of the Avon River, just a few minutes' walk from the school gates. Nearby was the Bridge of Remembrance, erected to the city's Great War dead in 1924. But by the 1970s the company needed more space. The original buildings were sold – to my mother and her brothers, displaying what I've learnt is the family's pervasive sentimentalism – and the company headed to the industrial suburbs to build afresh. Owen was chairman at the time, and Avenal's influence meant the new headquarters were built as a Greek cross. I just thought it funny that the front door seemed to be jammed between two right-angled wings, and put it down to the eccentricities of that period's architecture.

This is where we headed, to the south side of town near the railway tracks and surrounded by factories. The drive from school that day took us past Wigram, the air force base where Owen had served for three years of the war. When we arrived Owen parked at the front of the building alongside shiny new vehicles driven by his sons.

Family members didn't visit the company often and as we came through the front doors it felt silent. There was a long reception desk where four people sat. We stood there, waiting, until someone arrived to usher us into the boardroom, largely filled by a table the size and shininess of a ballroom floor. A lot of people were already gathered, few of whom I recognised.

I sidled towards the tea and coffee and plates of pastries and sandwiches and noticed that the catering was by the same firm that made our school meals, which were widely derided. It seemed the wages of commerce were not what I'd been led to believe. But aside from my grandparents, it was the most familiar part of the whole day.

Just to the right of the refreshments was a portrait: grey suit, white hair, glasses. This was Tracy. It was the first time I'd seen his image but he was enough like Owen to be recognisable, and, after all, who else would it be? Owen had finer features and less flesh. Tracy looked lumpy, with rounding shoulders.

It looked as though the picture had been whipped up for someone in a hurry. *What sort of portrait? Just a portrait, didn't you hear me? Get it done.* One-dimensional, both the picture and the subject, and I thought about that. It often means painted from a photograph, not life. That would make

Tracy Thomas Gough
c. 1932, a few years
before buying Mona Vale.

sense. The picture looked new to me. The paint was too bright, too fresh; the frame simple and modern in varnished pine. The background was lavender, like Beryl's carpet, like 1980s curtains; not a colour that would have been used for the background of a businessman's portrait in the 1940s. It was a narrative piece, and it did that job. The chairman of the board presiding. It was the only portrait in the room, a pantheon of one: 'make no mention of the name of other gods, neither let it be heard out of thy mouth'.

I took a sandwich from underneath Tracy and tried to fade into the edge of the room. Not far away an array of businessmen in dark suits smiled at one another, then smiled and introduced themselves to us. To Owen and Avenal first, but it was hard not to include me, a trailing adolescent intensely aware of how irrelevant I was in this dimension of the grown-up universe.

The businessmen looked old to me but young beside my grandparents. I rarely saw Owen and Avenal interact with people they didn't know well, or outside their daily habitat. They seemed almost shy. Maybe they could sense that their conversation was, in the politest way, no longer coveted by people more interested in current events than past. I doubt Owen and Avenal thought about it like this and if they had, I doubt they would have minded. It suited them to stand quietly, and it suited me. It meant I had people to be near to.

Off to another side, talking to the chairman, were people called the trustees. There were three of them, and their suits looked more expensive than those of the managers and directors. The trustees tended to be lawyers but they acted more like powerful bishops at a mediaeval court, or barons at Runnymede, and would incline their heads in greeting. They appointed the directors, made decisions about how income was distributed and, on the side, managed the inevitable tensions that these decisions caused. It was their letters that would appear with regularity, announcing news good and bad.

The number three was a precise distillation of a complex story, most of which I was not aware of at the time. You see, Tracy married twice, I knew that much. And thus there was one trustee for Tracy's first family, Owen's family, my family; and one trustee for the other. An independent chair was there to keep them apart.

It's hard, now, to recall accurately how little I knew then. I suppose we all encounter this in life – so-called wisdom one of the rare welcome companions of age. But looking back on that day, I feel the channel between me and what was around me was at its broadest. There were these trustees and, more surprising again, a group of strangers who shared my mother's maiden name.

It's harder still to explain why I didn't think this discovery worth further inquiry, either then or in the months or years that followed. Perhaps because it's hard to question when no one else is. If I'd been a child and had a child's courage I might have asked why or how. But in adolescence one's world can grow smaller, sometimes never to expand again.

And so I stayed silent as people with cups in hand twirled from one small group to another until I was brought face to face with a man who looked familiar but wasn't. His name was Blair and he was Owen's half-brother. This was the first time I'd met him, though I think I'd heard his name before. Blair resembled my uncles, but his eyes were like Owen's. They had the same twinkle: mirth or warmth or welcome. Blair, who had a beard reminiscent of a Romanov or a later George, said hello with a handshake and a smile and asked me about school.

After meeting Blair, I spoke to Robert, the only trustee I knew. He was from our side, as I'd heard older relatives say. Often as not it was Robert on the telephone to my mother after those letters had arrived or convening meetings that occurred behind closed doors. Robert never laughed but was always funny. He spoke in memoranda, parsed to resemble crossword clues or inexpensive telegrams. He always sounded bored, or nonplussed. Or he was never either of these and what I actually heard in his voice was a sharp brain interested in the world but communicating within a compact register. Robert was courteous, and I was grateful for it. It was a relief to have another friendly compass point. I'd never have thought somewhere with so much family could feel so foreign.

'Your first visit?' Robert asked me.

I nodded.

'What do you make of it?' His tone never modulated. It wasn't flat, but it was even.

'Not sure I think much of the food,' I said, or something along these lines, trying to smile; trying to learn how to flash a rapier like these others, but failing, flailing.

Robert looked at the tea and sandwiches, then back at me. He didn't smile.

'It should be interesting.' He nodded and moved to talk to someone else.

It wasn't. But it was at least decorous. We had a little to eat and then we stood listening to speeches, perhaps to make it less formal, or to emphasise that the addresses would be short. But it was more formal, and some guest executive or other spoke for a long time in what our English master would call jargon or cliché or both.

I knew standing would be uncomfortable for Owen and Avenal, but they didn't want to cause a fuss and rare is the person who likes being offered a seat due to age. About halfway through, however, Owen was overcome by coughing. He couldn't stop. I was too far away to help without adding even more disruption. Avenal patted him on the back before eventually leading him to the side. The speeches continued, filled with concepts and figures that meant nothing to me. As I listened, I looked at Owen and thought, he's getting really old.

8

By the fifth and final year at Christ's College, doubtless at any traditional boys' school, you joined the paladins yourself. You could dawdle out of bed, take long hot showers, lounge in age-graded common rooms and go wherever you wanted beyond the school gates without a master needing to sign a red booklet the size of a visiting card.

I found myself going for walks most afternoons. Often not far, just straight down Gloucester Street to the central library a few blocks away. They had a reading room, behind glass doors on the first floor, where they kept the older and special edition books. I enjoyed borrowing volumes on Canterbury's history and architecture: homesteads, churches, chambers, colleges. I would then walk these books back past some of those very buildings and lie on my bed in my own study and browse through the pages, reading about this world of the imagination while surrounded by its reality.

Looking at photos, it was easy to grant this world authenticity – easier, perhaps, because at the end of the twentieth century its echo seemed so faint. The aspirations had been formed in England and then realised in a hurry in southern stone, but just as quickly, it seemed, had disappeared. Many of the grand old mansions – once on the outskirts but now subsumed into the city – had been broken up into bedsits or B&Bs. Some had been turned into schools. On wide streets running east of Cathedral Square, lines of grand Italianate buildings built for commerce were mostly empty, often run down. And the last thing you wanted to be caught wearing in the square itself was the uniform of my particular Anglican school. Even around where I lay in my study I knew that every citadel was only one stone thick: every side you couldn't see was brick.

Perhaps parts of Christchurch were already moving to self-parody and had been for years? Its boundary with nostalgia is porous. The pub that had the most lenient attitude towards underage boys from my school was called

His Lordship's. The antique bartender who served was no taller than many of her young patrons and she prosecuted her duty of care by limiting the very smallest to four drinks. Maybe we were the comics? There were several layers to balance: What was it meant to be like? What was it actually like? What did that mean now? I saw townhouses where walled gardens had been, concrete block where there'd been Gothic arches. I lived in an institution formed to bring boys closer to God – and I knew how that had worked out. Among all this I kept a fondness for what remained. I'd like to say it was a wry, knowing, worldly fondness, but a fondness all the same; one that could see many faults but gave credit for effort.

So I would read about this old Christchurch and think about it and it didn't matter if I dozed off and turned up later for dinner. There was no need to rush back to the boarding house for supervised prep at a tiny desk. There was time to talk at length and toy with food and get a second pudding if you wanted. Then at the end, when you'd run out of excuses and gossip, you stepped into the evening light, with the sun clipping the tops of these grey castles that by this time had been my home for years. They were still imperious but at least now familiar.

Dusk brought silence to the whole school. Except on a Friday, except for the chapel, where the choir would be practising for evensong. It would go through the dinner service and in the summer term they left the doors open. Last – or at least it suits my memory to tell myself it was always last – they sang the Nunc dimittis and it would drift with the twilight over the quad, unchallenged by fighting or scolding or yelling or the other daily proclamations of a large boys' school. Always the same setting too, Dyson in C minor – I have put it on now as a I write – very slow, like a lullaby:

Lord, now lettest thou thy servant depart in peace: according to thy word.
For mine eyes have seen thy salvation,
Which thou hast prepared before the face of all people;
To be a light to lighten the Gentiles and to be the glory of thy people Israel.

• • •

While I'd been getting more comfortable, Owen and Avenal had gone in the other direction. They were less mobile now, coming up for 80, but rather than moving house, they were fortunate to be able to stay put with the help of people to look after them. A Belgian named Marc, who'd buttled at the

The cloisters and quadrangle at Christ's College. SAMUEL HEATH HEAD PHOTO, 1/1-007127-G, ALEXANDER TURNBULL LIBRARY, WELLINGTON

Dutch embassy, came to stay. He moved into one of the bedrooms and made multi-course meals with lavish sauces. There was a sense that an Anglo-Saxon approach to flavour had been replaced by a European one.

Marc rightly encouraged Owen to start drinking the good wine in the cellar. Avenal pursed her lips but did not object, perhaps an oblique recognition of mortality. When I visited one weekend Marc was carefully cleaning the chandelier, crystal by crystal, in a bucket of hot soapy water. He, and others, would also go up to the Sounds, sitting in the back as I once had and helping with the endless ropes and varnishing and moving of boxes.

Owen and Avenal changed the house slightly. The Fun Room under the stairs was turned into a study. I don't know where they put Owen's hats and coats. A long-term but younger friend of theirs, Eleanor, used the new room as her base when she came to help them manage the bills and maintenance and chequebook reconciliations that were all becoming a bit too much.

In this way, Owen and Avenal were able to extend the rhythm of their lives beyond what their bodies would have allowed. They kept their world intact. Maybe this was why, when change came, it felt so sudden?

Older, enjoying school, with no need for solace, I sought less the refuge of Owen and Avenal's. I'd become more self-conscious about such visits too. Seventeen-year-olds didn't take weekend leaves with their grandparents. Their home became a place for brief visits, calling in for tea rather than staying overnight. Or sometimes I'd just meet them in town at lunchtime. I would find them sitting quietly side by side in an uncle's office, hats and coats on, as if waiting for a train. We'd eat, often in the café at Ballantynes, and I'd wander back in time for afternoon classes.

What I most remember about visiting Owen and Avenal in that final year of school was using their library. I was thinking about university and became drawn to the idea of Cambridge. It was the original, after all, of what they'd tried to create in Canterbury. It turned out that Christ's College had addicted me to quadrangles and crumbling stonework.

From so far away it wasn't easy to gather information on how to apply. The school careers adviser didn't have Cambridge on her books. I phoned England instead and asked if they wouldn't mind sending a prospectus to Christchurch.

I was also lucky that one of our English teachers had been at Cambridge. He recommended trying for a college with playing fields nearby.

'I'm not much of a sportsman,' I said.

'Not the point,' he replied, 'It shows they're wealthy. That means they'll look after their students well.'

It was a wise insight but there were still gaps, and to fill them I started returning to Owen and Avenal's and a red-bound children's encyclopaedia set that they had from the 1920s. Each college had its own entry and I'd sit there with several volumes open on the sofas or across my lap, comparing sepia photographs of great courts and stained glass and working out which one might be convinced to accept me; or which one had looked the best 70 years before. In the end I plumped for St John's, the college of Samuel Butler and George Selwyn, as it happened. St John's let me in, though I didn't find out till months later. I think Owen and Avenal were pleased.

And then it was all over. Summer term, exams, the end of uniforms. I found myself realising that I would miss it, the buildings, the masters, the classes, the traditions; cricket, the park, the chapel. I would miss it all. Owen and Avenal came to my final end-of-year service, when the whole school walked through town to the cathedral and filled the nave for one last bout of hymns to wish us all well and encourage us not to let ourselves down too badly. Owen and Avenal sat at the back, by the west door. As a leaving present

The drawing of Jacobs House, Christ's College, by Rodney Wells, given to the author by Owen and Avenal.

they gave me a drawing they'd commissioned of the little corner room that had been my private quarters that last year.

Not long before I left the gates for the final time the Latin master stopped me. I'd got to know him well. He coached me at rugby, took me for Classics. In our later years, I and others had gone to his place for pizza and cards. He was a friend.

'My mother,' he said, 'remembers your grandmother from school. She's always said to me she thought her a true lady.'

Another master was more forthright.

'They're a rum lot, your family. What do you think of them?'

'Which ones, sir?'

'Mother's family.'

What do you say?

'Well, they're family, sir.'

'I suppose there's that,' he allowed. 'Problem is the money. No one ever says anything to them, even if they're wrong. Rum, very rum. Something not right there.'

9

In September of the next year, 1997, at the age of 19, I left for England and university. I had tried walking into the P&O office in Wellington to ask them if they had a ship I could take. I rather liked the idea of arriving with a steamer trunk in tow. An uncle had travelled this way in the 1970s. The P&O people looked at me as if I'd asked for a ticket to space and said that the last scheduled liner for England had left decades earlier. I went by plane. My mother came with me, all the way to Cambridge, where she stayed in a hotel for a few nights while I, thanks to a drinks party of unexpected popularity, managed to get myself a personal introduction to the dean after being there for just 12 hours.

At Cambridge, Christchurch all but disappeared altogether, the way Owen and Avenal's had in those last years at school. Christchurch was a distant part of the outside world, ignored without malice or intent as I found that the original overshadowed the imposter. I had swapped one picturesque, all-consuming world for another.

In my first two years at university I thought of Christchurch perhaps twice. Once when a former teacher arrived and we had a couple of pints at the Eagle, followed by a Chinese meal, and once when a Christchurch QC, whose name I recognised but whom I had never met, got in touch asking for my approval of an increase in the annuity that Tracy's trust paid Great-Auntie Beryl.

This inversion of the generational hierarchy felt indecent. I didn't understand why I should suddenly have a view on anything, let alone my great-aunt's income. The explanation lay in my having been transferred a few shares in the company, which I didn't even remember happening. I think it was linked to some supposedly advancing maturity which, in the College Bar or the Maypole, seemed as distant as Christchurch itself. After much confusion I eventually sent my approval, feeling sorry for poor old Beryl that a lowly student had any say at all.

In my third and final year I moved into a terrace house with five friends, on Park Parade overlooking Jesus Green. I was as independent as I'd ever been. At the same time, back home, Owen had a stroke, a severe one, and was immobilised. He lost all power of speech but retained full comprehension. He could no longer move more than an arm or a single hand. He relied on people to push him in a chair around a world now much diminished.

Despite Owen and Avenal's efforts to maintain their life together, Owen had to be moved. I know how ghastly, and how sad, they would both have found this. They chose the closest rest home they could, a place called St Winifred's. Avenal remained in the house, alone there for the first time since 1952. Each day she would get up, dress, descend past the giant mirror and then walk down to see Owen. She would push him back the short distance to the house, tracing the path of her former perambulations with the barrows of pears. This was the extent of Owen's travels now and a ramp was installed to get him up the front steps onto the porch. The gravel driveway didn't help.

After lunch Avenal would push Owen into the library where they would sit together as they had always done. Owen had never been talkative but now the silence must have felt like misery, not comfort. And I can imagine how the clock stamped time for them both, but particularly for Owen, as his afternoons now chimed towards departure. Before it got too dark and cold, especially in autumn and winter, Avenal would have to push him down the road again in time for dinner at his new home. Then, for the fourth time in a day, she would walk back up, alone, to a quiet house.

When I visited, over Christmas perhaps or the long summer break, I still stayed in my old small bedroom and Avenal still filled me a hot water bottle at night. It almost felt odd, the two of us alone in the house. We took to living in just two or three rooms. She would still make me breakfast but we'd eat it downstairs together, in the kitchen, not the dining room.

I wish I'd spoken to her more about her life, their life – but I never would have. Even if I were magically the age I am now and knew what I know now, it just wouldn't have suited the way we were. People tell you things if they want to, even if you're not listening. But sometimes if they want to confide in someone, a stranger or a blank page is easier than a child or a grandson.

I was home straight after graduation: summer in the north, bright blue, snow-capped winter in the south. Back in Christchurch I saw that Owen had deteriorated further. He'd been moved to another complex, no longer within walking distance but not far away, in Merivale. Here the residents dressed in tweed, the women wore pearls and there were drinks before dinner.

Mona Vale in the 1940s.

Here, too, Owen could be watched by a nurse throughout the day. It was harder for Avenal to visit though: she needed to be driven and she shied from imposition.

Then she got sick, too. She had kept the cancer growing inside her a secret while she tended Owen, not wanting to divert attention from his needs. She kept it secret until it became physically impossible to do so. She must have known that each day's delay reduced her options until she had none. By the time she owned up, the doctor told her to rest. There was nothing else to be done.

If there was any good in this, it was that it cut their separation short. Avenal joined Owen. At short notice she couldn't get a room near his, but she couldn't wait. She took one at the opposite end of the corridor, in a separate wing. At least they both looked out on the same garden, and on a sequence of bright winter days you could swing the doors open and make your way directly between them, choosing a path of grass and sunshine rather than detouring around bridge players and newspaper readers in the sitting area. Avenal could now see Owen every day, under her own steam. He remained immobile.

Because most of their furniture was too large to fit in their new bedsits, we bought Avenal a single bed and took just a dresser from her bedroom, a small red carpet and some paintings to try to make her new surroundings feel familiar. Avenal liked to return home every few days, though. She'd swap pictures around to liven up her little room, or pick up small mementoes or trinkets to give to people; old friends coming to visit might find something pressed into their hand on leaving. She knew what was coming even if no one else did.

I think Avenal just liked to see the house too, to be inside it and to walk around the garden. It was, after all, the home she and Owen had lived in continuously for 50 years, even though poor health was making her a mere visitor to her own life. I believe we all felt guilty about this, staying in their home and enjoying it while we visited them in their pair of small rooms.

I drove her back to the house once. It must have been no more than three weeks before she died. It was just the two of us and I used Owen's car. When we arrived I waited downstairs while Avenal went up to their bedroom. Then she asked me

Avenal, 1950s.

to come upstairs and help her take a watercolour off the wall. I did as bid and she told me to keep it. It was a street view of stone and timber terraced buildings; she had painted it herself. For years I thought it must be in France. It is only lately that I have realised it shows Canterbury's Provincial Council Chambers, admired by Nikolaus Pevsner as one of the best examples of high Gothic outside Europe. The fault was not with the picture, which is a fine reflection. It's more that I took for granted something I'd seen a hundred times before. I lived with it without really looking.

We were at the top of the stairs, where the rainbows danced in the mornings. She burst into tears and I hugged her. I was so much taller than her now. She was a little embarrassed. She hated knowing that every visit might be her last but I think this one was. We went downstairs together, shut the door and drove back. The painting now hangs in my son's room.

Soon after this Avenal became bed-ridden, her abdomen distended and painful. She was hungry and thirsty but barely able to eat or drink. Family began to congregate, keeping her company as she weakened. The house

Owen and the children at Akaroa, c. mid-1950s.

became something of a dormitory, and we started a roster of staying overnight in her new room – someone on a late shift; someone on an early one.

After a couple of weeks of near constant vigil we decided an afternoon away in the sunshine might do everyone good, and so we headed to Akaroa Harbour, about an hour from Christchurch. The drive over Banks Peninsula is slow and winding, past a string of settlements and then climbing up the sides of the old volcano. At the top is a view of the harbour, sheltered and bright blue with hills on all sides; brown, bare hills for farming. Tracy had raced his yachts here, and Owen too, small ones as a youth when he was known for never capsizing. Then he'd taken the children to teach them the same.

We headed to a house that belonged to an uncle but had once been Owen and Avenal's. It sat in a small bay called Lushington's, west of Takamatua, with two others belonging to old family friends. Avenal was always chuffed that, during their 1977 tour, the Queen and Prince Philip had gone there for lunch with one of the neighbours. I've tried to confirm this but have never been able to. Fact-checking is maybe not in the spirit of family storytelling but it's a habit I've fallen into. Further around the harbour was Akaroa village itself, once home to French migrants, the first of whom arrived a week after British rule had been declared.

My uncle launched his little boat and we headed out to sea, seven or eight of us packed tightly. We went way out beyond the heads of Akaroa Harbour

Avenal and her daughter, the author's mother, c. 1950.

and bounced up and down on the ocean rollers, failing to find the seals rumoured to live there. The weather changed to winter and it felt exposed and dangerous on our 5 metres of fibreglass made for a calm American lake. The boating party lost some of its zest and we headed back into shelter, pulling back up at Lushington's in the late afternoon. We dropped a few people off at the jetty and I helped my uncle put the boat up on the trailer, deforming the propeller on the rocky seafloor in the process. As we came at last to the house my mother, wearing sunglasses, emerged onto the verandah.

There are moments when you know something is about to happen, or just has. My mother had received a message from the doctor. Avenal had taken the chance of her first day alone in several weeks to slip away.

• • •

Owen could communicate only in small noises and nods, or through his bright blue eyes, heightened further by the pallor of his skin. It was hard to believe he understood when he could never answer. But he did, and you could see the heartbreak streaming down his cheeks when we told him about his wife. We took him into Avenal's room and he sat there beside her body as the same vicar they'd hosted over summers in the Sounds prayed. We were all in a circle around the bed, the priest by Avenal's head, Owen at the foot in his wheelchair. I wondered if he wanted us there. If I'd been him, I'm not sure I would have.

Avenal's funeral was at the crematorium. She didn't want to be buried, which I remember thinking was unusual given her visceral Christianity. Only family went, followed by an interment that was smaller again: just Owen and his children.

10

I returned to the northern hemisphere not long after Avenal's funeral to attend a university in France. I'd convinced myself, and my parents, that I needed at least one more year at a mediaeval institution to prepare myself for the modern world.

I lived in a flat with one window looking over a cobbled lane that felt like a ravine. The high walls on either side blocked the sun but managed to trap the Provençal heat. One morning when I'd slept all night with the window open but the shutter down, the phone rang. It was maybe six. No one ever rang. All my friends lived within a few hundred metres of me and they were never up at that time. Besides, we saw each other in the same bars and cafés almost every day. It was unusual enough that I actually got out of bed and answered. It was my mother, calling to say that Beryl had died.

Somehow, though generally expected, the news was still a surprise. Beryl had also been getting weaker and was, anyway, Owen's senior by three years. But she'd never been ill or sick. The news coming disembodied down the line made it seem even more artificial. In the prosaic, offhand way you think of people a lifetime older, I told myself she'd had a good life and this was an expected end. It had been comfortable. She'd been born into a fortunate family and hadn't had to live with the pressure of daily work. As deaths went, not that I was familiar with them then, it didn't feel too tragic.

The funeral was to happen quickly and getting back would be complicated. Travel then meant a visit to an agent, a paper ticket issued a few days later, an itinerary, a plastic wallet full of documents. As it was, even had I left that minute, I couldn't have made it back in time. Others went, everyone who was home. I stayed in the south of France, not thinking enough of Beryl, not realising that this meant Owen was on his own for the first time in his life. The last of his tribe.

Beryl, Owen and Avenal at a twenty-first birthday for one of the author's uncles, 1967.

Over the months and years that followed everyone in the family tried to make sure Owen was never long without visitors. Other relatives and I would come and stay a few nights in the house and spend the days with Owen, in his little room, trying not to do or say anything that reminded him of Avenal. I'm not sure it worked. I came across some old Christmas photos recently; it must have been the first without Avenal. I was flicking through them, my sister beside me. 'He looks so sad in every one,' she said, and he did.

Films became a favourite, and easy, pastime. He developed an appreciation for slapstick and it seemed sensible to keep the entertainment light. We'd watch comedies and he would shake with silent laughter. We also tried a few games of chess. He'd always enjoyed it and had taught me how to play in their library when I was small, learning its simple calculus: weak king, strong queen, powerful bishops. He always beat me, even if trying not to. That might have been easy enough but others, grown-ups, used to talk about what a proficient player he was. It was the only classically intellectual activity Owen undertook. He still had an agile mind, even if it had never dressed in academical robes.

I realise now how much the teaching showed about Owen's patience. My eldest daughter likes to play chess. It's maybe the only activity for which she chooses me over her mother. She's getting good. I can last a game, maybe two in a row. Thankfully that's her limit too. Owen never wavered: me, then my brother, back to me, then my brother again. Always happy to play, adding smiles and humour for good measure. In his dotage and illness, though, Owen couldn't control his arms. He would look straight at me, all shining eyes and innocence as a heavy wrist swept through lines of pawns in a single army-eviscerating move while his queen moved into pole position. Then he'd chortle.

Dressing Owen challenged the nurses each morning, and if you wanted to take him out he needed further coverings to keep him warm. A suit was too much but we could still get his overcoat on and place a hat on his head. We might go just into the garden to sit at a wrought-iron table in the sun. Or a walk to the village shops for coffee, or sometimes to a church service at nearby St Mary's.

One afternoon I wanted to try something different. I thought I'd take him for a drive, in his car. It was sunny but I got Owen into a coat and trilby all the same, against the cold and the risk to dignity of appearing in public underdressed. I wheeled him to the car door then levered his dead weight into the passenger seat, while he chuckled at my exertions and his own inability to help. He knew what a nightmare he was to move around and as I puffed and heaved, he laughed until the tears ran.

I drove around the neighbourhood, the Fendalton and Merivale in which Owen had spent almost all his life. It was good for the car and it was good to be away from his small room. I'd got used to being the only one talking, taking the movement in Owen's eyes as response. In the car it was harder, not looking at him, more like talking to myself. There was no evidence that his mind or his memory were impaired but it's easy to miscompute muteness and I found myself slipping into guided tour inanity about familiar landmarks he knew better than I did. Here's Fendalton Road. Do you remember St Barnabas? Here's Hagley Park, and so on. I'm not sure young adults are ever that good at talking, meaningfully, to the very sick or the very old. I wasn't.

I avoided their road for fear of invoking the sadness of Avenal's death. Trying to think of accessible attractions, I headed for that gatehouse by the railway tracks and the entrance to Mona Vale. Perhaps seeing what I thought of as his childhood home might recall happy memories without touching on recent sad ones.

We came from the direction of the park, as we'd done on the day of Beryl's wedding, and turned left into the long drive. It was early autumn, but I seem to remember it was all still green and leafy so you couldn't see the house until you were right upon it. Maybe Owen didn't guess where we were going? Maybe he no longer recognised it? I doubt it was either, but there was little reaction until the house hove into view. He was tranquil as we traced the line of the river, looking across to large, looming modern homes. As we saw the house, I turned to give Owen the obvious news of where we were. He'd started weeping, silently. I'd planned to stop here and push him around the grounds, over bridges and by the river. The tears discombobulated me. I drove straight on without pausing, past the house, the rear lodge and out the back gates. Then I took Owen back to his little room. The outing was over.

Later, I mentioned the incident to my mother. She put her lips together in the sort of smile you give a child who's just dropped a newly bought ice cream.

'I think he's always seen Mona Vale as a sad house,' she said.

• • •

We lowered Owen into the ground on a cold day in early autumn. His death reduced us to two generations and so we were a small group, standing there around the grave. My mother, and my father, of course, my mother's three brothers, several cousins. The soft rain on dark overcoats gave off the scent of hand-washed woollens. As the casket descended, sextons straining at the straps, our heads followed it in automatic supplication.

They work in a strange way, family graves. They're covered with loose gravel as they wait to be filled up. Then when the last silent resident arrives they're finally sealed with cement and covered with marble. Owen was this last; the first was his mother, in 1941. For 62 years this grave had been waiting to become dormant, like its rows and rows of neighbours.

But I wasn't being so profound at the time. I was looking around for distraction, a mental pinching of the skin to stave off worse thoughts. I looked at the grave. It was the first time I'd seen it but all I noticed was the plain black slab at the top with the family surname stencilled in clean gold capitals, not the ostentation I'd feared. I rather liked it, if you can say that about a grave.

If I'd known, there was more information there for me, but my mind took in little from the eyes and anyway the vicar was intoning the committal of Owen to the fellowship of the saints and the abundance of the kingdom of heaven. Then a shovel-load of finality was thrown in. And the drizzle mingled on the cheek with the sorrow that only the last view of a casket can evoke. Because no matter what a churchman might say, this is an end, if not the end. We broke the cemetery's silence with a convoy of cars and headed back to Owen and Avenal's home.

The funeral had been at Owen and Avenal's usual church, the more progressive, modern one that I'd often avoided when on leaves from school. I had driven Owen's car once more along the route he had taken every Sunday. And when we arrived and pulled into the asphalt carpark, my brother and I got out and stood either side of our mother in our black suits, both much taller than her, and each held a hand. My father took a photo, then we all walked inside.

Close family oscillated near the doors to welcome Owen's wider sea of friends and associates. It was unusual for all my mother's siblings to be in one place, but who else was there? Maybe some school friends? Sailing friends, old colleagues. Friends from families who seem to link at each generation. Owen's godchildren were there; a lot of people from this parish; most of my uncles' ex-wives. There was Douglas, quiet, like Owen, who tended the

Owen aged about 20.

garden and fruit trees for decades and was well into his seventies himself. Eleanor I knew too, from her long friendship with Owen, Avenal and Beryl.

Also present, I saw, were some of the apparatus of the commercial patriarch, recognised from rare visits to the company. It was funny still to think of Owen as a businessman, but I guess that's what he'd been, and was likely how he'd be remembered. The company delegation were men in dark suits that almost matched and who talked to one another and had to leave promptly. Their presence was appreciated, but I felt sorry for them, having to attend to the rituals of a stranger's death as part of their jobs.

One of my uncles was worried about the undertaker's preparations: not enough service sheets printed. He thought hundreds would attend, but it's hard to draw large crowds of friends when you die in your eighties. In the end the turnout was adequate, and there were enough pew sheets. In fact I have a spare one near me now, fallen out of a book borrowed from my parents. There were four hymns: 'Lead Us, Heav'nly Father Lead Us', 'O God, Our Help in Ages Past', 'Eternal Father, Strong to Save' and, of course, 'Jerusalem'.

After the service, there was the protocol of tea and coffee to formalise consolation and discuss the recently dead. In the narthex with the linoleum floor, over a hot drink in a brown glass mug, I spoke to more distant relations.

And I spoke again to Robert. He was there with Gareth, one of the other trustees, two senators standing in a corner.

That day Robert, slightly shorter than me, wore a navy suit, striped shirt, red tie. His white hair was neatly combed. When I turned 21 my mother had taken me to see him to formalise a will. Robert might have come close to smirking as I failed to decide, sitting there in his office with a view of the ocean, who would get my cricket bats, my books, my suits and my fountain pens. He explained to me that his usual practice, with aged spinsters and others who had trouble allocating minor items, was to attach a chattels schedule to the will that could be easily changed, since family members might wax and wane in favour. He spoke carefully, each word placed down after the other, as if laying a table for a grand dinner. There was always something of the ritual with Robert, and of the riddle too.

Then he looked at me, eyes level, silent, and awaited my response. I thanked him for this advice – with, I like to think, the austere dignity of a man contemplating his own mortality – and said I would consider the options.

At the funeral I'm sure Robert would have liked to talk more about the past or more about the future but he probably knew I had little of substance to offer. Thankfully he also enjoyed court intrigue and for this I was better prepared. I lived among the family and so had currency to spare. I played guttersnipe to his Richelieu. Anything more would have required a knowledge I didn't even know existed.

'Who's your uncle with?' Robert asked, indicating one of the three. My mother's were the only wedding vows that had remained intact.

'I am pretty sure that's her there,' and I nodded. 'I didn't catch her name.'

He indicated the uncle known for his car collection. 'What did he come in?'

'Just a station wagon, I think. Grey.'

'Restrained.'

'He's in mourning.'

His baser instincts indulged, Robert pointed to the distinctive Edwardian beard. 'Blair's here.'

'Yes, I thought I recognised him,' I said, 'But I think I've only met him once or twice. Nice of him to come.'

'They were brothers, after all,' said Robert.

'I guess,' I shrugged, 'but quite an age difference.'

'You know by how much?'

I shook my head. 'Twenty years?'

'Twenty-six,' said Robert.

'Hard to be too close then, isn't it? I mean, they didn't exactly grow up together.'

'I think there were other things going on too.' Robert sipped some more tea, looking at me.

Standing near Blair were his children, whom I knew by name but, then, not well by sight. They're not much older than me, these sort of uncles and aunts, and so they muddle the generations. I can't remember if I spoke to them that day.

• • •

The service sheet reminds me that I was a pallbearer. I thought it had just been my brother. How could I forget? I remember the eulogy, though. I delivered one on my mother's behalf. I was up all night writing it. I sat at the table in the kitchen of Owen's house with a small heater by my feet. A table I had known all my life. White Formica, black steel base, surprisingly heavy.

I sat there and thought and dawdled and scratched out and tried to summon back the essence, as I'm trying to do now. And all night the clock in the hall reminded me from chime to chime that I had 15 fewer minutes now than when I'd last put my head in my hands.

How to summarise any life in a few lines? I could describe Owen's face or his smile or his sense of humour. I knew the way he would set aside a book and wink, and then nap (or pretend to). The chess, the boats, the suits. I had a grandson's view, my own memories, but they were as much about me as about Owen and placing them in any wider context was difficult. His birth date was memorable. I knew where he'd gone to secondary school and where he'd worked; the air force; his marriage, who his children were. But even these fundamentals were hazy and the need to write something cohesive sharpened my curiosity.

In the end I had my mother's nocturnalism to thank for helping me. Hers was a dilute version of Beryl's, but the common ancestry was clear. In the quiet of the night she wandered, looking at the final days of this home, still the same as when she'd grown up there but not for much longer. Her habit was to end at the kitchen, fill a hot water bottle as her mother had done, and have tea.

This time she found me there, tapping a pen on a piece of paper and thinking to myself that this was much harder than the university essays I had habitually left to the last minute. I was still only on Owen's very early days.

'I think I remember you saying that he left school early?' I asked.

'Yes. At the end of sixth form.'

'Because he wanted to join his father's company?'

'That's what he did,' she was filling the kettle at the sink behind me, 'but I think he also felt he might've been a burden.'

'A burden?' I asked.

'The school fees. He thought he needed to get out and pay his own way.'

'How could he possibly have thought that?' I asked. 'Weren't they living at Mona Vale?'

'That was a little later, a year or two,' she said.

'Still, it doesn't make much sense. If Tracy was shortly to buy it, he can't have been hard up.'

'Well, it was Julia really.'

'Julia?'

'Dad's mummy. I think she had a worrying sort of temperament – given to worry as they say. People used to tell her she was bad with money and so she worried about it an awful lot. Then Dad worried for her.'

I was jotting down notes as she spoke, among the doodles and spirals. My mother sipped her tea.

'Mummy and Beryl used to say Julia was the gentlest person in the world. Very sensitive, very artistic. They were so sad when she died. Dad too, of course. He was very young.'

'I can imagine,' and I could.

'Then there was Alison too.'

I was writing this down. 'Alison?'

'Their elder sister,' my mother said.

'What do you mean?'

'There were three of them: Alison was the eldest, Beryl, then Dad.'

'I've never even heard of her.'

'She died young, I never knew her either. It was before I was born.'

I might have asked more about this but it was late already and I had a deadline as unavoidable as an iceberg. So instead my mother and I spoke of Owen's time in the air force (she worried the engines had made him deaf, and that's what made him shy), his life afterwards, his work, the company, the move to their home, even that story about meeting Avenal at the Selwyn River. I was scribbling the whole time.

Having drunk her tea, she drifted off as she'd come. It would have been midnight by then. I had just hours to go and decades to cover. I was alone with the buzz of the shoebox-sized heater. The kitchen was a small room but it was a smaller heater and I only remember my feet being warm, even with the doors shut. There was a large curtainless window behind me and I could feel its inky coldness on my back.

I managed to complete a few simple pages. It was hard, I wrote, to separate Owen from the environments he inhabited. To young eyes, he defined them and they him. I would speak, in a few hours' time, about him tending the fire in the library, about the man winding the clock, about the smiles for grandchildren. I would remember holidays, summers in the Marlborough Sounds. My earliest photo with Owen is a black and white image, recently refound, outside the Peninsula Hotel in Hong Kong. I'm in my mother's arms, waving to the camera. I must be about 14 months old. Luggage indicates that we're leaving or arriving. Owen stands beside us in a pale safari suit that I now possess and have latterly tried to wear, without great success. Owen was always svelte, you see.

What else, what else? An overwhelming benevolence of spirit that made everything happy and kind and welcoming. Courtly was a word I used too, in the eulogy. His seemed an ideal life that I didn't mind idealising. The imperfections in the story of this fortunate man hadn't properly registered.

As morning broke my mother appeared again, to make toast on the day she was to bury her father. I'd just finished something I thought I could say out loud. But then I had to start worrying about typing it up and where to get it printed; after all my crossings out and arrows, I needed something legible to read from the lectern.

And it was still cold, or at least I was cold, and I would have liked to return to bed with a hot water bottle but it was time to get into mourning uniform. All dressed, I went downstairs past the huge mirror and looked at myself. I'd walked this way many times before, knowing I was to leave this house to do something I didn't want to do.

• • •

The three uncles speak first, each in turn, and then I stand up and deliver the jumble of words I finished five hours earlier.

I try to discipline the free-form nostalgia of images and memories and stories. I leave out the last illness and those swathes of life that a grandson

The author, carried by his mother, with his father and Owen (in safari suit),
Hong Kong, 1979.

would never have witnessed and so wouldn't know. I don't mean to edit the historical background, it's just that Owen's early life evades me, barely occurs to me – it's not the sort of thing that matters when you're six and just wanting to ride on the red mower or help steer the boat; nor has it yet started mattering when you're 13 and hibernating, even if only overnight, from school.

I don't go into it, but I imagine, or rather I worry, that a lot of Owen's contemporaries might have thought him dull. Or misinterpreted his state of silence as aloofness rather than a preference for peacefulness. But he was shy really, and incredibly gentle. When he did speak, there was never anything unsuitable for a drawing room.

I could go on. But mine is the fourth essay on Owen the mourners will hear that day, and they will all have their own memories.

At last, the recessional. It is Psalm 8, which I know so well from Christ's College and which Owen would have known too, from renditions on the same pews, in the same chapel. We used to sing it in the round, with the nave in the lead and the choir following. That old setting stays with me and plays without prompting in my head as a I read the words:

Oh Lord our Governor,
How excellent is Thy name
In all the world.

Owen, Avenal and children at home, c. 1953.

When all the tea was drained and the sandwiches had turned to crumbs, we left for the cemetery in Bromley. It was my first time there and I almost got lost. When it was over various of the family went back to the house. I remember staying up very late, until the early hours of the morning, discussing family history on the stairs with an uncle. We went all the way back to the Hundred Years' War again. These old family myths. Later, very kindly, he sent me a history of it, the references to Sir Matthew bookmarked by orange tabs.

11

The day after the burial my mother and her brothers began the sacred task of dismantling Owen and Avenal's home. They held a conclave in the dining room, the four of them. They shut the door, but we could see them through the paned glass, seated around the table, muttering and passing papers back and forth. In the end the broad breakdown was thus: my mother would keep the house, the valuable treasures would go in order to balance the equation.

To this effect they would create an inventory of every possession, appraise it, then divide it. That was the plan, but a stocktake of sentiment is complex and it wasn't long before the dining room door reopened and the formalities were abandoned. The bereaved negotiators began to move around the house, seeking visual inspiration for souvenirs, or just to confirm what was there.

They recalled provenances as they circulated. Everything seemed to carry a story or the shadow of one, and as I eavesdropped I realised these often stretched back to Tracy. If my mother had been five when Tracy died, then her two eldest brothers would've been around 10 and eight, their memories developed enough to have held an image or a comment. Mona Vale, the grandfather lying in bed: it felt like the sort of thing you would remember clearly.

A pair of portraits of Māori elders by C.F. Goldie – one male, one female – dominated Owen and Avenal's hallway. They were somehow out of place: their size made them grandiose where the rest of the home was restrained. Their black frames stood stark against white walls. But they'd always been there to greet you, their faces twice, three times the size of life, as you stepped through the front door. Goldie's style is photo-realist, orientalist some might say, but whatever you think of it, the images are arresting. One was drowsy, the other watched your every move. Now their time was up.

'They were at Mona Vale, weren't they?' an uncle asked.

Another uncle nodded: 'He had masses of them. Hung them frame to frame up the stairs.' And I imagined that Mona Vale hall, further dimmed by these pictures in their pitch-edged barricades, watching as you crept past. It turned out half a dozen had made it to Owen and Avenal's, including that Joan of Arc in the dining room.

The four siblings wandered along the hall to the drawing room, entered so rarely in my childhood that I could almost count the occasions. Once, a friend came to tea and Owen set the fire. Later, their golden wedding anniversary, for the family photos. They'd posed in the same place for their silver anniversary too. But long periods of standing at the doors looking in at the sea of scarlet carpet swirling around islands of gilt furniture mean I can remember precisely how the room was arranged. The piano was in the far corner, the organ beyond the fireplace. The piano went, the organ stayed.

On the walls, clockwise from the door, there was first a portrait of my mother aged 17 and painted by gangly, liberal, innovative Robert Nettleton Field. He'd studied alongside Barbara Hepworth and Henry Moore before emigrating to Dunedin in 1925 to take up a teaching job. He wore baggy trousers, sandals and a beret and used a small listening trumpet while painting my mother. He also kindly painted some stage decoration for the school play she was directing, *The Widow of Ephesus* by Petronius, a comedy despite the title. The set pieces were, and are, still in the attic. My mother's portrait stayed where it was.

Next along was a work by British impressionist Henry Fidler, of Clydesdales doing a heavy day's work in the sun, rendered in thick sloshy strokes. Hanging by the organ was a dark-haired nude seated on a chaise longue, leaning onto a table or pillar, her legs and torso twisted sideways in contrived modesty. I can't remember where she went, but I remember the discussion as the siblings stood before it.

'Dad had so much trouble getting this from the estate,' someone said.

'He wrote to the trustees to say that Julia had bought it years before TT died.' TT was Tracy, Tracy Thomas. He was often called TT by the family. 'Dad really wanted it as a souvenir.'

'But they didn't believe him,' someone else added, 'said it was more recent.'

'But he found their engagement photo, with this,' a gesture towards the painting, 'hanging in the background.'

They mused on this, as did I. They could only have been referring to Owen and Avenal's engagement.

'New Year's Eve, 1940.'

'Well before TT married again.'

They moved on. Above the fireplace was a large oil of cows lying down in a field, the sky blazing above them. Then an outdoor tea party glimpsed through a green picket gate left ajar for the next visitor; and finally, above an old bureau, a cutter sailing on an indigo sea off Valparaiso. All but the garden party had previously hung at Mona Vale. These were all memorials, I realised, not just indulgences that Owen and Avenal had spent money on. Likewise the ormolu furniture – heavy lacquered cabinets and armoires and vitrines with complicated brass inlays; a French gilt furniture suite; a marble statue of a bird landing on a girl's outstretched hand and much else besides. It had all been Tracy's.

Back in the hallway, a vast nineteenth-century bucolic scene hung at the bottom of the stairs. In its ornate gilt frame it must have been over 2 metres tall. It too had come from Mona Vale. It showed a family outing to a willow-crowded riverbank. A restoration a few years earlier had revealed a little girl by the water's edge. She'd been painted out long after the rest of the work was finished, the restorer said, given that the covering layer could be easily separated from those below. We had all wondered what tragedy or scandal caused her to be excised.

Before long the dreamy system of reminiscence began to succumb to the reality of the job at hand and the car in the drive. It was one thing to discuss memories, it was another to document, and picking up the vase or the book or the piece of silver and placing it in the boot was easier than ploughing through what felt like administration.

Thus the most portable objects disappeared first. Tracy's old cutlery was wrapped in tissue paper and removed. The same happened to the collection of weapons, also Tracy's, that hung in the library. Their loss left the walls looking like the back of a broken transistor radio, little tufts of wire sticking out everywhere. Some of my favourite books – Owen's tales of adventure and exploration and some of those great architectural picture books that Avenal would have purchased – were noted to be first editions. They were boxed up and taken away, leaving the lower shelves looking toothless.

I watched for a while. None of it was mine and it was not my place to decide what went where. But it was still sad to witness the hollowing, the picking over of the bones. I went up to that tiny sunporch and lay on my bed, aged in my twenties and sulking in a pinstripe suit.

I'm embarrassed by this performance now. My rights, if I had any, were the least of anyone's. The four in the generation above me were mourning their father and the end of their time as a family. This was their childhood home. These possessions no longer belonged to the house, they no longer even belonged to Owen and Avenal. It was the right, if not the obligation, of their children to come and pack them up and take them away as their keepsakes. I would have done the same. I would have wanted to scoop up those beautiful items made the more luminous by sorrow and the fact that someone now lost had once valued them. And I know now that in their shoes I would be furious if I were trying to salvage some memento of my mother or father and someone more distant tried to stake a stronger claim, even if only passively and silently.

But while I realise it wasn't justified, I can still understand my response. 'Decorating is autobiography,' Gloria Vanderbilt said, and I suppose it felt like the house was having its personality stripped. It probably made the others sad too, but it just had to be done.

The diaspora took about a week all told, ending at dusk then resuming the next day. I began keeping out of the way. I stayed lying in my room, alternately reading and despairing. I looked out the window at a garden that didn't change, while below me the rooms did. I'd emerge late afternoon or evening, once the day had receded and the gravel had been churned for the final time that day by cars heading out the gates. Then I'd wander around and survey what had changed, what had moved, what had disappeared.

Actually, a lot stayed put, stayed as it had been. Other than those few first editions, the rest of the library was considered uninteresting – neither Owen's detective novels nor Avenal's evangelical polemics had many suitors. The encyclopaedia that had helped me into university stayed put. Abstruse volumes on English country house decoration weren't in demand. The attic wasn't touched. Any furniture that was more functional than decorative stayed. No one wanted that heavy kitchen table, for instance. Nor the funny old chairs.

Grown sons didn't want their mother's furs or their father's suits, which were all in three outdated pieces and too small to boot. The kitchen's old pots and pans stayed, as did the tools and boxes of screws and bolts in the workshop. The rusty toys were allowed to remain, dozing in the slatted boxes they'd been calling home since the 1960s. The linen and towels stayed in the cupboard, the sheets on the beds.

It was less a draining of the house than a straining of its contents through a fine and discriminating filter. The bulk of life's daily, simple chattels stayed but also some of the most important items: the portraits of Owen and Avenal still hung above the stairs, the clock kept sounding its music beneath them and the car remained in the garage. The last thing to go was the chandelier that had showered every morning in rainbows. It was lowered by its winch – the pulley was hidden above the ceiling in the attic – and taken away. A glass replacement was substituted. It doesn't send out nearly so many coloured shards, and they're the wrong shape too: rounder, less elegant.

Over the days that followed, the dwindling numbers of us who remained in the house got used to living with shadows. In the end it was just my mother and me. We used odd knives and forks. We found some old furniture to sit on and we rearranged the pictures to fill the gaps. The effect wasn't bad, I thought. It still felt like the home I knew, just with some jewels missing. After about 10 days it was done. We locked the door one last time and left, the clock still chiming.

12

I was living in China when Owen died. Always on the hunt for ways to escape reality, I'd gone there to travel in 2001, returned in 2002 and ended up staying. I spent some time at a university in Beijing and then managed to convert the most fragile of Mandarin skills into a job in finance, advising people how to do things. Though I knew little enough myself.

I lived 30 floors above Beijing with a couple of friends. We were three men and a cat suspended in a mustard sky. As high as we were, the sound was a constant: drills and demolition, traffic and shouting. It was the rumble of millions of people in action; a city crunching gears into high speed, no matter what the consequences.

The road to our apartment building was brand new. Months earlier it had been an old neighbourhood of grey brick houses and lanes as wide as two bicycles. Now it been cleared, sealed and named and was already filled with cars, trucks, limousines, vans, taxis and workers' trikes. The view to our north was disappearing at the rate of a floor a day. We might have a beer in a bar on a Saturday and by Wednesday it was rubble and a shrug. Green grass was a painted affectation, blue sky a political event, and Beijing's famous courtyard houses were succumbing block after block to the new China dream, already 20 years old but only now coming to the world's attention.

The city had a pace far removed from the old Mandarin capital. Many Western reports of Peking before the communist takeover noted scenes of civilised languor amid squalor: generals breeding blue-tipped butterflies; white-robed scholars reading in drifting skiffs on the Northern Lake; the filth of the hutongs; the polluted creeks; the fog-thick yellow dust storms thundering in from the Gobi every spring, covering the tapering eaves of temples, palaces and even the Forbidden City. 'Looking back on those days,' wrote former fighter ace and author Cecil Lewis, 'I retain an overall sense of peace and quietness of heart. There was no hurry. Time was not the whip of life.'

The opposite now seemed true, but being there was exciting. And there was no more brutal testament to the pace and scope of the national project than Beijing itself, becoming the future at a rate of square kilometres per day. It felt like the least nostalgic city on earth. There were countless stories of private anguish as another thousand households were demolished and their inhabitants sent to the outer darkness of Huairou to make room for a condo, but there was little public reflection. And it wasn't my place to judge. Yet it was hard not to think about what had gone before. Were all the old ways discarded during the 50 years of war and revolution it took to emerge from the Qing into the People's Republic? Of course not. Rejection was selective. There were relics, physical and customary, and in my attraction to them I saw no contradiction, no hypocrisy, even though it was the modernisation that attracted me and countless others, and let us stay.

The whole city was a testament to decline and resurrection. Millennia of imperial rule, the capital of the Son of Heaven, dynastic collapse, war, famine, precariousness and strife – Beijing had passed through it all and re-emerged stronger than ever. Beijing, if not all of China, seemed to have used loss as motivation, and triumphed. A lot of what the past had wrought came tumbling down: the palaces, the temples, the specialised merchant streets. Ever since Mao razed the Ming-era city walls – from one gate of which camel caravans still left for Turkestan until the late 1930s – the old face of the city had been changing. But loss sharpens the need for a boundary, for a before and an after, and we all took it for granted that we stood at this threshold as the demolitions escalated.

Sinophile John Blofeld called his memoir of 1930s Peking *City of Lingering Splendour*. At that time the city was dealing with what felt like even more momentous change – the loss of the imperial dynasty and their expulsion a few years earlier from the Forbidden City. He acknowledged that 'the gaiety, charm, good living and old-world fragrance of that [Qing] era went hand in hand with wretched poverty and many other human ills'. But Blofeld also remarked that the city still drew its rhythms from the extinguished life of the old imperial court. He talked of the lacquered doorways, the marbled moon bridges, the vast palaces 'tiled with gold porcelain, and green or blue-roofed temples with scarlet pillars and intricately painted eaves. Multi-roofed ceremonial archways spanned tree-lined boulevards', even then partially hidden. The palace might be empty, but if you looked hard enough you could see the old influence told through the life of the people.

Likewise my friends and I saw wrecking balls, car-clogged ring roads and trees dying from smog, but there was an ancient skeleton beneath the new skin. One historian has described Beijing, Peking, as a city of palaces and temples. It was hard to believe this, but amid all the traffic at the centre of the universe sat the greatest palace of them all: the Forbidden City, a vast empty home, now a public museum stripped of treasures that had all been moved to Taipei.

Parts of the oldest and grandest quarters of Beijing still survived, encircling the Forbidden City. Nanchizi Street, the hutongs springing from the moat and spreading either side of Earthly Peace Avenue. North, too, along the spine of the old Imperial City that ran from Tiananmen through Coal Hill and up to the lakes of Shichahai, the Drum Tower, Pipe Alley.

When the communists took over in 1949, every work unit and agency and state organ worth its salt grabbed an old palace as its headquarters. Powerful residents ensured these areas were either purposely protected or somehow overlooked. This was the China the tourists came to see. It was also the Beijing that its people loved, unless they had to live in a hutong house with four other families, no proper plumbing and no heating.

We enjoyed sitting in a tiny lean-to bar with no name. It overlooked Silver Ingot Bridge, which crossed the narrow confluence between Front Lake and Back Lake. In summer you could watch as people took rented wooden skiffs onto the water with a meal from one of the lakeside restaurants and – for the ostentatious antiquarians – perhaps someone plucking the horizontal strings of a guqin. At Mid-Autumn Festival the lake would fill with tea lights floating on red paper.

In winter the lakes would be frozen and the bar door became layers of quilted bedcover that you'd push through, into the blinding darkness and pungent heat from an ancient iron stove. In the height of summer – intense, bone dry – we might buy large bottles of Yanjing beer for one kuai each, and rest against the walls of the Bell Tower, a few steps to the north, Peking's official timepiece from the fifteenth century until November 1924 when the last Manchu emperor, in the middle of eating an apple, was expelled from his realm, ending the Celestial Empire for ever.

We'd watch Beijing men, their vests rolled up to rest on their stomachs, one trouser leg always raised above a sock, squawking and hawking as they illegally gambled at majiang or Chinese checkers, or a card game called Resist the Landlord, which came with loud slapping of cards on rickety tables. Meanwhile their matrons circled them on evening constitutionals in groups of two or three, often sporting the red armbands that indicated their skill as neighbourhood gossip was officially recognised and they had a duty to report upwards as a member of one of China's pervasive neighbourhood committees of retired aunties and uncles.

Only metres away were sleek cars and sleeker buildings, but this collision, the unlikeliness, was part of the attraction. Such islands of the past were hard to find amid Beijing's bustle into the future but were the more satisfying for that. An abandoned temple in a land of abandoned temples is commonplace but finding one where you least expect it is a victory. Turning off a clogged thoroughfare, going down a lane, past stray cats and piles of concrete and rubbish, pushing open a loose gate in a high steel fence and seeing an old wangfu, palace, with the peeling red paint of the expat's imagination, glass towers rising beyond and a growling tenant who knows its story – that felt like discovery.

• • •

As I know from my scrawls on its inside cover, and from my own memory, one of my favourite books at the time was *In Ruins* by Christopher Woodward. I bought it the month Owen died. Woodward opens – and this may be why I remember it so well – with the image of an 1872 engraving by Gustave Doré of a hooded 'New Zealander' sketching the ruins of London. At the time, New Zealander meant Māori, and the idea was to show the people of some future ascendent civilisation coming to view the remnants of the old, as Englishmen toured Rome or Athens. It was intended as a warning of hubris: this, too, can happen to us. Woodward uses the image to illustrate that when we contemplate ruins, we are examining not just the past but our own future.

The book journeys through history, promoting the values – the attraction even, dark though it may be – of the broken down, the crumbling, the picturesque. It was an argument I adopted in full and tried to outline, stutteringly, awfully, to my Chinese teacher Tian Xue, which means Heavenly Snows. Tian Xue had a brother living in Rome, another in a semi-underground rock band, and one of her jobs was sourcing Chinese books for European publishers. The attraction of collapse and loss was not as incomprehensible to her as it might be to many others in China, sensitive to implications that they should now accept less than the best.

Tian Xue and I used to meet in Sun Altar Park. It was quiet and retained a lot of its Ming design. In the mornings the park's darkness would fill with groups of ballroom dancers, tai qi aficionados or sword wielders, all generally

Temple of the Ancient Monarchs, Beijing.

accompanied by their own transistors. Later in the day you could get a coffee at the Stone Boat, a café built of rocks at the edge of an ornamental lake like a miniature of the empress dowager Cixi's colossal marble version at the new Summer Palace.

Tian Xue interrupted my contortions by introducing a new word, mo luo. It meant to decline, or to wane. The first character means 'not to have' and is commonly used in daily speech, albeit with a different pronunciation. The second character means to descend, like an aeroplane, but it has a second meaning, as here, which is settlement, or place to gather or to stay. So the character by character translation, which is not the way anyone but a foreigner would approach it, is 'waning home'.

Mo luo, Tian Xue explained, was frequently used in modern China, normally prefixed to enemies like feudal society or landlords in works that dealt with the official version of history. This amused me and my amusement amused Tian Xue. I rolled the word around and applied it to different nouns. Waning sunshine? No. Waning fortunes? A shake of the head. Waning families? A nod, and from then on she called me Moluo, and still does.

She and I talked about the Old Summer Palace, the one razed in 1860 by the English and French armies in return for the torture of their negotiators. It had been designed by Giuseppe Castiglione in the 1740s with baroque façades, shuttered windows and Chinese roofs, but now sat in huge white marble chunks scattered over a wooded park. It was one of my favourite spots in Beijing, though you couldn't tell many people this. Its name had been made synonymous with Western brutality and Chinese disgrace and to say – particularly in accident-prone attempts at Mandarin as bad as mine – that you liked wandering among its ruins might horrify. They'd assume it was to revel in the destruction by the Foreign Armies. Its real attraction was that it was unvarnished and, in a city of landmarks, overlooked and quiet.

Another spot with similar claims to calm amid confusion was the Temple of the Ancient Monarchs. It sits west of the Forbidden City, just near one of the Catholic cathedrals that came under the most intense shelling during the Boxer Rebellion of 1900. The temple exists to venerate ancient kings of China, but it's obscure compared with its neighbours, which again is the charm. One travel writer summarises it as having 'overall the atmosphere of a cast-off chunk of the Forbidden City'. This is a compliment, and it feels true. The main building is a virtual miniature of the Hall of Supreme Harmony, the gold tiles affirming its imperial use. It was dusty and empty when I visited and inside, arrayed over a long table, were dozens of shiny red and gold tablets, like lacquer tombstones. Each carried a former emperor's name. Never the emperor's image, mind; that was seen as ghoulish, as I found when I tried to hunt down old scroll-like ancestor portraits for sale. Most people thought it uncouth, at best, to seek out images of other people's dead relatives, but I liked their stylised perspective and their distinctiveness, immediately fixable in space and time to Qing China.

Even for family, such images would only have been unrolled and hung once a year for the act of reverence known as Qingming, or grave sweeping in English. This is not so much ancestor worship as filial piety and reverence, consistent with Confucian values. There are screeds written on the Chinese attitude to aging, dying, death and the dead, but at a simple level it felt in China as though obeisance was paid and in return the ancestors watched over you. My attitude to my predecessors felt more backward, less dynamic – where had they gone? In China the traditions seemed to reinforce a sense of unbroken lineage. In the West death felt like a boundary, an indelible marker. 'The end of an era,' a sympathetic mourner might say, as you squinted into your teacup.

Remnants of this ancient, ritualised world lay everywhere beneath the new Xanadu. Oddly, I was interested in them, to which I had no connection, but remained uninterested in my own world, that of Owen and Avenal and Christchurch. It had been rolled up and put into an attic, along with so much else. I reflected on my past as little as public Beijing seemed to, and instead got distracted by bars and temples, decay and development in one of the world's oldest cities, far from my own. And I read *In Ruins*. At the start of the third chapter Woodward quotes a translated excerpt from a Chinese poem, just known as 'Old Poem', from the first century AD:

That over there is your house,
All covered over with trees and bushes.
Rabbits had run in at the dog-hole,
Pheasants flew down from the beams of the roof.
In the courtyard was growing some wild grain;
And by the well, some wild mallows.
I'll boil the grain and make porridge,
I'll pluck the mallows and make soup.
Soup and porridge are both cooked,
But there is no-one to eat them with.
I went out and looked towards the east,
While tears fell and wetted my clothes.

• • •

I had remained in touch with Robert while abroad. He'd retired from his law partnership but carried on in the trustee role for the family. It seemed an eccentric choice; there must have been easier sinecures. So-called family meetings attracted emotion like clouds to a mountaintop. I guess wherever there is stuff worth arguing over, there will be arguments, and that's what lawyers train for. Still, it looked like hard work and no one was ever entirely happy – such is the lot of an adjudicator. Why did he choose to carry on? 'I like your uncles,' he replied. 'They're real individuals.' And maybe, on some level he was unwilling to admit, he enjoyed the theatrics? They were a far cry from his own sobriety. Maybe he enjoyed the drama of the history – a history he remained closer to than I did.

Part of Robert's trustee role was keeping the family up to date on trust business. This included me, it seemed, now that I wore a suit most days and worked in an office and could perhaps be taken seriously. And so I began to receive the latest updates, quarterly letters of a page or two. They gave little away. Sometimes, though, Robert might interpolate a polite inquiry after my own news, or that of my brother and sister. I was fine, thank you, I'd say. China was fascinating. Work was confusing.

In this way our correspondence morphed into more general musings. I might try and draw it towards my mother's family and its unusual arrangements: separate divisions, mutually exclusive groupings, professional trustees, notionally informal meetings where minutes were taken. I can't pretend I was thinking of clever ways to ask, 'Come, tell me how it all began.' I didn't think of it as having a beginning. It just was and if I was interested in anything, it was the current situation: the company, its business, who did what.

I felt I understood the rules of the game well enough: never sound too curious, never ask a direct question. Robert left doors open and floodlit but never took me through them himself. He was too discreet and professional for that. But conversely they would slam if I ran straight at them. I learnt to tread carefully while he remained elusive and allusive. Once I went too far – I think I asked why it was this way at all – and Robert rewarded my gaucheness with a few lines from Lewis Carroll, typed out in Wellington and delivered electronically to my desk in Beijing:

'The time has come,' the Walrus said,
'To talk of many things:
Of shoes – and ships – and sealing-wax –
Of cabbages – and kings –'

13

One day a girl arrived in Beijing, from England. She stood in the sun at the airport, holding a copy of Lampedusa's *The Leopard*. It was my favourite novel, though I didn't tell her that at the time. She'd come for sight-seeing and a break from work. We knew each other from university and a mutual friend had put us back in touch. 'Contact him in Beijing,' he'd said. 'He'll show you around.' I took her to the Summer Palace and we walked the Long Corridor. I took her to that café in Sun Altar Park, and to Sanlitun for cheap drinks, sitting on a tiny stool outside Black Sun in the old South Bar Street while the cars cranked past centimetres away.

We had Peking Duck at Little Wang's. I ordered without looking at the menu. She was impressed. I'd memorised the names of several dishes. You speak Chinese, she asked? A little, I shrugged, and when I didn't understand the waiter's question, I just asked for beer and said thank you. We went to a friend's birthday party. She wore a white dress. I collected her from her smart hotel in Beijing's most malodorous taxi, the car's engine choking and spewing on the forecourt. Both the driver and I were surprised to be there, like an ex-smoker on a futile jog finding himself leaning against the gates of Wimbledon.

After a few days the girl left, back to London and a new job in the City. She wrote some time later. She didn't like the new firm. She was thinking about taking a year out, maybe studying. Maybe Chinese. That's a splendid idea. Can't recommend it highly enough.

Within the year she was back and this time she stayed.

By then I'd been in China on and off for around four years and, as happens, I was already starting to think of other places. I found the language interesting. I found the history stimulating, and the people. Everything about it, in fact. But other things I missed. Beijing was grey and dusty; sometimes I missed the green and blue lightness of home. The smog made your eyes run. Friends were always sick. Every trip to work was an adventure or an argument. There'd been SARS, which had emptied the Beijing streets, and bird flu was coming, we heard. There was formaldehyde in the beer. There was coal in the air. Whenever a holiday came, foreign friends flew far away to places that were cleaner and quieter. This seemed illogical. If, as a foreigner, you wanted to leave Beijing, then no one was making you stay. If I felt I needed the same luxury – to be away – then why did I stay?

With this thought in mind, she and I took off one winter, just for a holiday – home to Christchurch. We landed in the afternoon and took a taxi straight to Owen and Avenal's house. The route was simple, unchanged from the hundreds of times I'd driven it before. Straight from the airport onto Memorial Avenue, past the golf course on one side and grazing horses on the other. Memorial Avenue becomes Fendalton Road and not long after it's left into Glandovey Road before the final turn that gave me the view of that jutting stone wall buttressed by bushes. The black iron gates had never been shut and we pulled through them onto the drive – the sights, the sound of the gravel all so familiar. The house was still, the windows dark and silent. How long since the last visit? Four years? Four years since Owen's funeral?

'Nice place,' the driver said, as we pulled up.

'It's not really mine.'

'You live here, though?' he asked.

'We're just visiting.'

I got the luggage out and put it on the porch and then stood there, looking through the front door, hand on the key, key in the lock.

I could see straight down the hall to where the stairs curved to the upper floor, the mirror glinting the light back at me. With my nose almost to the glass, I told myself I could smell the house, that combination of log fires, roasts cooking, clean cold linen, wool blankets, camphor, grass clippings, old books, the diesel from the furnace, scrubbed surfaces, fresh flowers, wood polish, clipped roses, rich sauces. Inside it was cool and dusty, like an empty temple you might stumble across in the Western Hills near Beijing.

'It's freezing,' she said.

'Nice after the heat, though?' I suggested. It was high summer. I brought the bags in and shut the door.

She shivered. 'It's a lot warmer outside. I think we should keep the door open,' she said with a smile.

Outside the Canterbury sun was turning the grass to straw and we took shelter at a yellow table that was always used for afternoon tea, sitting in the shade of a silver birch, toes tugging at the grass. Beside us was a giant black-green urn, also from Mona Vale but too heavy to move elsewhere.

We only had a few nights to stay but it still gave us time to see some old friends. They came to visit and we sat around together on long evenings with cool drinks and clean air.

'I didn't realise you still knew anyone here. I thought they all moved away?' she asked.

'People like it. They like living here. Some stayed, some have come back.'

'You left?'

'That was a while ago,' I said.

Beyond the gates, everywhere was holiday. The city smelt fresh. The sky was a blue that in Beijing you almost didn't know existed. If you walked to the end of the driveway and stood by the road, it might be minutes before a car passed. It was quiet, it was suburban, and after the noise and suffocation of Beijing, it was bliss.

'I like it here,' she said.

'We could live here,' I replied. 'We could move in.'

A few months later we did. We left China for the wide skies of the south. There were parties and farewells and sadness at a closure, as there always is. On the last night, to a small group of old friends, I used a Chinese phrase I'd looked up and tried to learn. I said we were returning to 'the edge of heaven and the corner of the oceans' – to the faraway lands. It felt suitably bombastic. I'm pretty sure I mispronounced it.

It was autumn in Christchurch, the autumn of 2007. We followed the same road and arrived to find the green had faded and the trees were laying a blanket of red and gold over the lawns as the garden readied for winter. We stood on the same porch and opened the same door to the same wave of memories.

Before we did anything this time I walked down the hall to the longcase clock and wound it, as Owen used to do. It answered atonally, the gonging and the chiming concurrent and clashing. It took several hours to clear its throat. Once the rhythm came though, it didn't matter what else was missing. The house sounded the same.

In summer we'd stayed just a few days, most of them spent outside. Now we were here for good we took the time to look around the place properly. Browning outlines on the cream walls recalled the paintings. Dents in the drawing room's carpet mapped where furniture had stood for decades. The library looked the same, with the brass fire irons standing on the hearth beside a basket full of wood and newspapers.

Portraits of Avenal and Owen by R.N. Field.

The study beneath the stairs still had diaries and chequebook stubs in the drawers. Grey ringbinders of bank statements and invoices were organised by year and ranged on the shelves. The laundry had six cupboards full of vases in every size, material and colour. I don't think I realised that where I saw memories, other might see a museum of curiosity, at best.

As you climbed the stairs, Owen and Avenal remained smiling at each other across the void. I'd been told the story of why the portraits didn't match. They were supposed to be formal but Owen had refused to get dressed up. He thought it ridiculous to wear a white tie in the middle of the day. I found this amusing and retold it then, standing on the lower steps.

'See, she's in a ballgown and long gloves and a cape but he's not dressed up at all. He's just in a suit,' I say, swooping my arm from Avenal to Owen and back again.

'That's the funny thing?' she asked.

We moved on upstairs, holding the bannister. It still shone. At the top of the stairs the bedrooms were all as before. Last time we'd stayed in one but left the others undisturbed, unopened, but this was home now. In my grandparents' squash-court-sized bedroom Avenal's favourite photos, her hairbrushes and her hand mirror lay on her dressing table. Her jewellery, wrapped in tissue paper, was sitting in a brown cardboard box on the floor. It took me a moment to realise that she must have had this with her, in her little room, when she died. Someone would have packed it up and left it here and it hadn't moved since.

Owen's two gold pens, always clipped into his inside suit coat pocket, sat on his dresser, with his watch. His handkerchiefs and his socks were in the drawers below. Some socks were named – had he had these since school? No, I remembered, a retirement home is just another institution. You need name tags there too. The wardrobes were full of their clothes. Avenal's Bible was on her bedside table. Their bed was made up with the same pale-blue cover we used to slide off.

We chose a bedroom overlooking the drive. It had the emptiest wardrobes. I tried to get the heating working but there wasn't a sound, not even a failed spark. This didn't surprise me. Instead, we lit a fire in the library. I didn't think about it at the time but the logs I threw on would've been put there by Owen. Finally, I phoned my mother to tell her we'd arrived safely.

'What's it like to be back for good?' she asked.

'It's nice. It's nice to be here.' And we were glad. Leaving a giant city for a quiet town lets layers of concerns melt off you, before others emerge to take their place.

'And how is the house?' she asked.

'Feels strange to think we'll be living here.'

The phone sat on the hall table and as we spoke I thumbed the drawer open. Inside was a diary from 1974, a roll of Sellotape, some business cards and a collection of blunt pencils.

'I guess there'll be things to get used to,' I continued.

'Such as?'

'There's still a lot of clutter around.'

'We cleared out quite a lot,' my mother said with some emphasis, maybe indignant.

'I found food in the kitchen that seems to predate telephone numbers.'

'I did the kitchen myself. The only items there are things that would last.'

'Demonstrably. I think the custard powder came in war rations.'

'Don't be silly,' she said.

'But it's eight years since anyone was here,' I said. 'We left it as if people might be here regularly. It just feels a little unlived in, despite all the stuff.'

'Have you got Mephistopheles working?'

'He's broken. Or the tank might be empty. I'll call for more fuel tomorrow.'

'The name and number of the repairman are written on the side. He was at school with Dad, you know.'

'I know. I remember him.' I'd already tried. 'The number's disconnected. He may've died too.'

'There's an old column heater you could use. Put it in the bedroom.'

'I found that. It must be 50 years old. It's got a cloth cable. I'm not sure it's a good bet in an old wooden house.'

'Well, there are plenty of blankets. And you know where the hot water bottles are? Upstairs in the linen cupboard.'

Avenal and the author's
mother, late 1960s.

'I remember.'

'And otherwise?'

The clock made the quarter-hour.

'Oh, but I hear the clock,' she said. 'You've got it working at least. That's something.

In retrospect I wasn't being sensitive enough to what the house meant. My mother had left Christchurch and this house when young, before it became burdened with the cares of adulthood. The home was her childhood; it was her parents. I think she'd always hoped one of her children would move in to help keep the status quo. Even acknowledging this, it still felt like stepping into that Auden poem, 'As I Walked Out One Evening':

The glacier knocks in the cupboard,
The desert sighs in the bed,
And the crack in the tea-cup opens
A lane to the land of the dead.

By the time I was off the phone, night had fallen and we hadn't managed to get any food. Owen's car was there but the battery was flat. I started it using mains power and then let it pant and heave in the driveway like a large hound. Like the clock, it needed time to shudder itself awake and after a few minutes filling the night air with smoke – me nonchalant, this was normal – we slid out into the streets.

Left or right? I thought there was a takeaway place to the right and we headed that way first. It was a Tuesday, I think, and about nine o'clock. After a few loops we realised there was nothing open. The lambswool seats and the car's heater made a nice change from inside the house so we carried on driving. I know where to go, I said, the darkness hiding the fact that I was already retracing steps.

Several blocks away a sign announced fish and chips. We stopped. I said nothing, by which I hoped to imply I'd been aiming for here all along. We went inside and ordered, waited and then took the warm bundle back to the car. I turned the key. It wouldn't start. I hadn't driven for long enough to properly charge the battery. I rang for assistance and was told it would be about an hour. So we sat there, side by side, becalmed on a deserted street in a town I thought I'd left for good a decade ago. We ate the fish and chips straight from the paper, the car windows steaming up with the heat and tried not to get greasy hands on the woodwork.

That was our first night back.

• • •

I looked around the garden the next morning. It was overgrown, untended. The roses alongside the old pool were being threatened by some sort of freakish botanical experimentation taking place within. A pyre of rotting fruit was building at the base of the pear tree. Acorn Cottage was covered in creeper.

The view from the far end of the garden back to the house was as it had been when I was at school – the world blocked out on all sides by walls of green in summer, reds and browns now. It would soon be leafless and melancholy, and in winter sometimes covered in snow. The trees would become a lattice of bony wooden fingers and the whole garden would adopt the haggard grey pallor of one who has truly lived the summer party to its end and perhaps now regrets it a little.

I poked my head into the back garage last. Opening the old, solid wooden doors took a huge effort, like pushing a tyre uphill. The railings they slid upon were full of dirt and screeched in resistance. Inside was a graveyard of domestic machinery. There were four lawnmowers of varying vintages, two pushbikes, masses of boxes, at least a hundred bicycle inner tubes, Owen's old hospital bed, his mobility scooter, his shower chair. Hanging from the ceiling on a pulley was a vast model landscape in papier-mâché that had once been the proving ground for my uncles' Hornby trains.

Even my mother's first car was there, way down beyond the gloaming and so small that at first I almost missed it. It had one door, one seat and wasn't much more than a metre long. My mother used it to get to university, with Marcus Aurelius, their 70-kilogram St Bernard, often catching a lift. He would arrange himself around my mother like a standing shawl, head one end, hindquarters the other. Then his head would be pushed out the side window, giving other motorists a fright at the lights. One time my mother was running late to lectures and parked the car on Montreal Street. There was no time for anything else so she lashed Marcus to the bumper and ran off. A thumping sound followed her and, turning around to check, she saw Marcus dragging the car down the pavement after her.

I shook my head, shut the garage door and went back inside. I did this easily. Despite ungrateful whingeing to my mother, I wasn't a campaigner for change. This was the house as I knew it and expected it. It didn't occur to me that anything different was rational, let alone possible. I might have thought it was chaotic, but it was the chaos that I knew.

I enjoyed the idea of the lost world behind the locked door, the more unfashionable the better. I've read that when Prince Charles first inherited his grandmother's Scottish estate of Birkhall, he left it exactly as he found it, down to her mackintosh on a peg. And so I could close a cupboard door on shelfloads of antique lightbulbs and tell myself all was fine. I could mask complacency with respect: it is thus, thus it should remain. Anyway, we lived among it all, and we were happy.

• • •

In those first weeks and months back I had Owen's car properly repaired – the cost still makes me wince – and we unpacked our clothes into the one empty wardrobe. We used the old counterpanes but added plenty of blankets. I took my mother's advice and we deployed the hot water bottles too, boiling the water in a rusty kettle Owen and Avenal had been given for their golden wedding anniversary, with 'Drink Deeply of God's Love' engraved on the lid.

Old friends visited. Where I saw newly minted suburban squire, they saw comedy and anachronism.

We had tea in here with my parents in third form.

I remember that. It had felt formal. You wore a navy rugby jersey and Chelsea boots.

Some pretty fruity books here, you know?

This about the shelves of Avenal's religious works.

Is there still carpet in all the bathrooms?

Don't tell me you don't have this at your home?

You must still have the old car?

Of course.

Do you think you'll update anything?

Why? It all works fine.

The pink cupboards are, ah, interesting.

It's coming back in, just you wait.

Who plays the organ?

It's not working.

You know this wiring is technically illegal?

I'd rather pretend I didn't hear that.

We settled into life at Owen and Avenal's. We got comfortable. Despite, maybe because of, the house's idiosyncrasies it worked well for festivities. People enjoyed the time capsule. It gave everyone a sense of lived-in comfort. We didn't often start fiestas at home, but they frequently ended there. We'd return late at night from the pub or someone else's place, friends in tow and, emboldened, open the drawing room doors. A record would go on the turntable, hymns or swing music played so loud it split the room. Bottles would go missing from the cellar. Someone might add to the mayhem by trying the organ (it never worked). Someone else would wander upstairs to the hat cupboard and bring accessories down for everyone just as a guest wobbled out the French doors and into the nasturtiums. And all the while we'd be trying not to spill too much claret on what remained of Owen and Avenal's cream silk furniture.

One day we came across some snapshots tucked behind something on a mantelpiece. They were colour photos and both the saturation and the outfits suggested the 1960s or early 1970s. Not that the main subject wore anything: just a shaggy coat in white and copper. This was Marcus. There was a photo of him sitting bolt upright in a dinghy while a bronzed uncle strained at the oars. Another of Marcus sitting beside Owen at the dining

Avenal with two of her children on the balcony at home, c. 1965.

table, their heads next to one another on an almost equal plane, Marcus looking at the camera straight on. Finally, Avenal, in teal twinset and turban, standing beside Marcus on the front lawn. He's a sphinx, tongue out, posing once more, and she leans down and pats his head.

We looked at these photos and thought, this is what the house needs, a replacement St Bernard. And so we acquired Daphne. She was mammoth, but a lady. Unlike my friends and me, she respected the drawing room. She would lie in the hall and watch us, jowls on paws, sad eyes under enormous eyebrows, trying to sleep but also somehow acting as guardian of the house's previous incarnation.

Her performance wasn't always perfect. She chewed the Chinese hall table and left big teeth marks on the stairs. The house took possession of a distinctive aroma and a layer of fur. Our friends shook their heads. It confirmed to them that our embrace of the anachronistic bordered on the unwell. It wasn't just regression, it was time travel.

14

For me the rhythms of Christchurch are inseparable from its seasonal intensities, and these in turn always took me back to school years when I'd last lived here, when I felt more exposed to the elements. The bright summer is the first day of school. It's third form cricket trials. It's shorts and long socks and finding your way around. It's long evenings with the light low over Upper and the sun setting in the dining hall's high windows. It's a morning caravan of dressing gowns and slippers from a stone doorway on the quad to a frigid dip at the far end of the school.

Or it's fifth form and lying on a brick terrace as if it's the Lido, but the only water's in the shower block beneath us and the sun's hot enough to melt asphalt. Two boys are thumping each other silently while a third carves a name into the stone balustrade with a screwdriver. We should all be inside in the shadows studying for exams but the heat is both unbearable and deeply attractive to adolescents put in charge of their own time for a couple of weeks.

Autumn. We changed into long trousers and suits. The timber guardians of every Christchurch garden and park turned to grey. The decorations were discarded and the trunks stood bare, almost humiliated. Their hibernation left a landscape of desolation that was predictable, but no less depressing for it. It was just the same now, the season of our return, watching the old deciduous trees that make the city feel so ripe and fresh when in leaf begin to abandon us. You saw it out every window.

Then winter coming in, and fast. The mornings became dark and frostbitten. The arc of daylight was bent sharply, like a thick wire turned back on itself: the sun rose late and quickly, a brief apex, then crashed down with the same speed. Winter was the regulated vigour of hands trembling to catch a rugby ball in the snow and then trying to warm them by grasping the narrow pipes that carried hot water around the boarding house and holding on for as long as possible. Winter was seeing breath in the dorms at night behind glass like paper. It was grey army surplus blankets, as thick as a tissue and as soft as stubble.

From time to time, now, we'd awake to a city enveloped in mist so dense you'd swear it contained men in opera cloaks and voluminous whiskers swinging sinister canes. I imagined myself, bowler hatted, walking across Hagley Park through the murk. I never made it, though. I stayed in bed instead. It was too dark and cold, and reminded me too much of running around the park in the frigid blackness before breakfast.

Winter is curtains drawn and private spaces. We nurtured the fire in the library and it made me think of sitting there on Sundays, trying to hide from time. I used to resent finishing the weekend in suit and stiff collar, sitting with 20 others on a wooden pew. But the habits were grooved deep and Sunday evenings began to find me at the cathedral where they still used the old Book of Common Prayer, as they had at school, the cadences as familiar as the clock in the hall or the rumbling furnace.

Evensong was an hour of sitting by a stone pillar, eyes down in supplication or head up in recitation. I could recall the whole sequence without trouble: the Magnificat, the Nunc dimittis, each followed by the Gloria, then the priest calling unaccompanied to the choir who chanted their responses. The Apostles' Creed, too, came back to me in full, the single opening word suggesting all that follows, like glimpsing a tiny corner of a well-known painting: I believe.

At the end of the service I enjoyed wandering the cathedral's aisles to the sound of the postlude, past the chapel of St Michael and St George, reading the memorials on the walls or in stained glass – to families, settlers, founders; colonists, farmers, soldiers. It was like colonial cathedrals the world over, in its way, only here I knew many of the names from school.

At the ice-white marble effigy of the city's first bishop I'd turn and head back for the Great West Door. In the porch, around the benchmark, was a chiselled record of all the original members of the Canterbury Association as well as stones from Canterbury Cathedral, Christchurch Priory, Tintern Abbey, Glastonbury Abbey, Herod's Temple, St Paul's Cathedral and the original Christ Church, Oxford. Then out onto the steps where Beryl had had her wedding photos taken. From there the view was straight across the square, almost empty, and down Worcester Boulevard. At the end the Canterbury Museum, Botanic Gardens on one side, Christ's College on the other.

Winter was the best time for evensong as it couldn't help but be dark when the service ended. You could almost smell the dew as it waited to settle into frost. The only movement was worshippers, retreating from the cathedral's spilled light to make their journeys home, trailing white breath. I'd get into Owen's old car and trace my own way back via the landmarks I knew best: over the Avon, past the school gates, a glimpse of my old room, Hagley Park, Fendalton Road, Mona Vale's gatehouse, more gates, a driveway, home.

• • •

Then it was spring. Its start always coincided with my birthday, but more vividly I associated it with returning to Christchurch for each year's third and final term. Owen and Avenal would meet me off the plane from Wellington and drive me to school. The cherries would be in blossom down Harper Avenue and I would brood on the back seat about the unfairness of a world bursting back into life just as I was to be shut behind iron gates for 12 more weeks.

That first spring back in Christchurch carried no such burden for me, but I did go back in time. I returned to Great-Auntie Beryl's place in the Cashmere Hills. It was also as she'd left it. The family, it seemed, had a soft spot for letting homes calcify into museums. At Beryl's, though, there was method in it. Her will had required the house be kept in case her husband Peter – seriously ill since many years before Beryl died – returned. He never did. His recent death meant that the place needed to be dismantled.

This task fell to my mother, who flew down one week to take it on. Beryl had no children but my mother was her god-daughter and, of the remaining family, the closest to her in temperament and sensibility. Where others might have seen Beryl's evangelism as dottiness, my mother was alert to its central kindness and gentleness. The clear-out promised to be a monumental task. It was to be the two of us and Eleanor who, much as she had for Owen and Avenal, had cajoled and organised Beryl. They were close to be being best friends by the time of Beryl's death. Eleanor would have seen her almost every day.

We arranged to gather at Beryl's one morning to begin. I drove my mother across town in Owen's car, and it felt just like a childhood visit. Eleanor was already there, sorting papers and stacking them in disciplined piles: music, letters, magazines and newspapers, miscellaneous. The shelves either side of the drawing room fireplace were empty for the first time in decades. Dust floated in the sunlight. There was an air of shabbiness, which wasn't Beryl, but also of progress, which arguably wasn't her either. Still, our arrival was a good excuse to pause for tea and a briefing. Eleanor, my mother and I sat in the small conservatory with a view over the city and the plains, baking in the familiar magnified heat.

'Everything here's either for your mother to take or it's to go to the Sallies,' Eleanor said. 'No one else is interested in it.' The best, of course, had gone, distributed in accordance with Beryl's will. Included was a small number of Goldies, which had to be auctioned. I was surprised when an uncle, who'd loved them, bought them all back.

Eleanor had completed a manifest of the remains. As at Owen and Avenal's, these represented Beryl's, simple, real life once the luxury and inheritance had been boiled away. But if I'd found my grandparents' house cluttered, then Beryl's was an apotheosis of accumulation. Furniture, all large and heavy and wooden; every cupboard (and there were plenty, including down narrow corridors I'd never seen before) stuffed, every drawer too. Flat surfaces were covered, piles everywhere. Papers, bundles of letters tied with waxy string, records, music, knitwear catalogues.

There were odd collections everywhere of the sort characteristic of the Depression generation: broken electronics, boxes of cassettes, dozens of cake tins, old envelopes, pens, pencils a couple of centimetres long, paperclips, rubber bands, balls of string; pictures, cards, books, batteries. There were ornaments, statuettes; crockery, more furniture.

A few days before, an estate agent who knew my mother from primary school had looked around the house to assess it for sale. Then he'd driven to Owen and Avenal's to talk to us. He was kindly and gentle and mostly retired. We sat in the library as he told us he'd seen a lot of houses but Beryl's was 'the most complete testament to a life concluded that I've ever seen'. He probably just meant 'bursting', but it was a nice way of putting it.

There was Beryl's grand piano with the ivory coming off the keys and the woodwork sunbeaten. It had been left to my sister – she had played the cello and Beryl obviously remembered – and so it was stickered to be moved to Owen and Avenal's. None of us are musical but taking the piano meant we felt compelled to look at the sheet music too. There was folio after folio, sitting stacked on a low table with legs shaped like lyres and its varnish peeling to match the piano. Beryl would have played it all once and we kept it, along with the table and the piano stool.

And once we had the piano and the music, it seemed silly to leave the records. We had a turntable, after all. Flicking through, it appeared Beryl's tastes were less sacred than I'd have expected. It wasn't just Masses and hymns,

The author's mother, aged around 16, in Napier with Beryl. Beryl has likely taken her on an outing from boarding school in Havelock North.

there was Mendelssohn and Brahms and Mozart and Haydn, arranged in maroon cases, each weighing as much as an oven. We already needed a van for the piano so we shrugged and took these too. In this way, in a series of small gestures, small decisions, sentiment began to triumph over sense.

There was the fold-down escritoire where Beryl had written her copious letters late into the night. It held her envelopes and stamps and address books, which we left in place and decided we would take too. Ditto her walnut sofas. They were valueless and probably uncomfortable but would match what was left at Owen and Avenal's. The same went for a set of balloon-back dining chairs. Then there were Beryl's books – beautiful (unread) sets by the metre with gilt embossed covers: red for novels, blue for science, green for antiquity.

There was a giant oak sideboard in the dining room. It would be silly to keep it, given its size, and it was bulky rather than attractive, with what seemed an odd mixture of motifs – geometric Art Deco above barley-twist legs. I pulled open a drawer, saw it stuffed with debris and shut it. I opened the next. It had Beryl's smart cutlery, for entertaining, arranged in compartments, each labelled in Beryl's cursive handwriting. Actually, we couldn't give this away, I thought, and that was as well as my mother mentioned that the sideboard had come from Mona Vale. There it was again, looming in the background.

Many pictures of lower quality remained on the walls: a scratchy, dubious landscape in a dull bronze frame; some watercolours; a French impressionist work of a punt moored at the edge of a pond overhung by trees. The painting itself was covered in dust and its frame was rotting and spongy to the touch. Despite appearances, Beryl wasn't a materialist; she just had a lot of objects that held her memories. For this reason we weakened again and kept a lot of the paintings – and they, my mother said, had come from Mona Vale. One of the watercolours showed a brick house, steps and deep crimson flowers flowing from stone urns. My mother thought it might have been Mona Vale; it didn't look quite right but we saved it as well. It was by the well-known artist W. (for William) Menzies Gibb.

There was Beryl's own portrait, painted by Field at the same time as those of my mother and her parents. Beryl's just into her fifties, blond and aquiline. She's seated against a blue background, wearing a blue skirt and holding a single lily stem diagonally across her white blouse. No one else wanted it. We took her to join the others. Our pile of keepsakes had grown to the size of a fortress; a monument to my monumental weakness.

• • •

We spent several days up at Beryl's. Eleanor had more discipline than my mother and I and so, despite our obstructions, room by room the house emptied. Almost at the end I found a photograph hiding behind a door that had always stood open. The photo, obviously taken in a studio, was black and white, the frame was gold, the subject was a young woman wearing a ballgown and long gloves. Her hair was crimped.

'That's Alison,' said my mother, as if it would mean something. It had been years, though, and I'd forgotten.

'Who?'

'Auntie Alison, Dad and Beryl's sister.'

'But you said she died young?' I asked.

'She did.'

'I thought you meant like a baby or something.' I'd imagined diphtheria or smallpox or some other ghastly disease since outlawed by science; a child, a tiny coffin, a life never lived. This was a debutante, an adult sister.

'No, but it wouldn't have been long after that photo. Long before I was born.'

Alison looked happy, pretty and graceful. She was slender. Now that I knew who it was, what to look for, I thought she looked more like Owen than Beryl: fine features but not too sharp; face a shade wider than Owen's, rounder. Her smile matched too – wide and semi-private, mouth mostly shut.

Alison Mavis Gough, c. 1924.

Alison made one more appearance that day. There was Beryl's dressing table, kidney-shaped, draped in cream silk and with a triptych mirror on a glass top. My mother had a matching one at home.

'Tracy bought the pair in America,' she explained. 'One for Beryl, one for Alison. The silk used to be pink,' she added. 'Mine used to be Alison's.' My sister was to get Beryl's.

15

With us living in Christchurch and Owen and Avenal's house once more inhabited, my parents took to visiting regularly again. It must have felt odd for my mother to skip a generation, to visit her son here now, not her parents. As if to make up for time lost by the house to emptiness, they'd invite old friends and relatives over, people they might not have seen for years. One of those who visited was a cousin of my mother's. His name was Luke and his grandfather was Tracy's brother, Edgar. He and his wife lived nearby. They came for tea and we sat in the library while the afternoon sun came in.

Luke was just back from America. He'd been on a dutiful family pilgrimage of his own, visiting an elderly great-aunt, one of Edgar's daughters. She'd lived in Boston most of her life, was approaching 80 and Luke thought this would be his last chance to see her. We talked about her Christchurch childhood, her move abroad, her memories. Luke mentioned he'd photographed a painting that she'd taken with her from Christchurch more than 50 years earlier.

'I thought it would be the last time I'd see it,' he explained as he showed us a copy. The picture was a watercolour of a house: pink brick, purple and blue flowers, lawn, steps. It was immediately recognisable. 'That's Leeham,' he added.

I recognised the picture immediately but not the name.

'Leeham?' I asked.

'Charles' house,' he said.

'Charles?' I was struggling.

'Tracy's father. Your great-great-grandfather. He lived in this wonderful home. It had a lovely garden apparently.'

'We've got almost exactly the same picture,' I said and went and fetched the watercolour from Beryl's house. Her version was painted from a different angle, less of the garden, more of the house. Same artist, though.

I'd thought Tracy had bootstrapped his way up from nothing. but this was rather grand, having a series of paintings done of your home, and a lovely home it was. I mentioned as much to Luke.

'Charles was certainly successful, at least for a while. But I think he was rather spendthrift. My grandfather,' by which Luke meant Edgar, 'was very careful with money. I often heard it said that this was because his father had had such ups and downs.'

I briefly considered my own spending habits. Maybe I could blame genetics?

'They'd come from a very modest background, though,' Luke continued.

'I thought they were supposed to be linked into the local lairds? Edgbaston and all that?' I asked.

Luke smiled. 'I think that might be just a story. They came from Birmingham – from Edgbaston – but I'm not sure there was much more in it. I've done some work on the family history.' He had been retired several years. 'I've gone back several hundred years and it's pretty ordinary.'

'Such as?' I asked.

'Well, Charles' father was a master grocer, then a mason. Thomas's father, Charles' grandfather, was a maltster.'

'He made beer?'

'Ingredients for it, probably. Most likely he would've worked for a brewer, a small part of the chain.'

Luke had done a lot of work: he talked me through it then, and later sent me what he'd compiled. Charles' parents, so Tracy's grandparents and my great-great-great-grandparents, were called Thomas and Elizabeth. They'd lived in little red-brick terrace house, one room wide and two storeys high, on a nondescript street in Birmingham. There can't have been much room for the seven children they eventually came to have.

The street where Charles was born was close to the aristocratic landscape that Avenal had outlined to me years earlier. One of the estates of the famous family with the same surname, Perry Hall, was two miles (3km) north. The other, Edgbaston estate, was the same distance south. But the closest the family got to either of them seems to have been on 30 March 1884 when Charles, my great-great-grandfather, married another Elizabeth, Elizabeth Duval, at the Edgbaston parish church (the one that Avenal and Owen visited on a trip to England). At his marriage Charles gave his calling as cabinet maker.

'Oh, but I remember Elizabeth,' my mother said. 'She died when I was a child. We used to visit her. Everyone called her Tiny Granny.' She was also the source of my mother's middle name.

'If you remember her, she must've been like a thousand years old!' I said.
'I think she died in 1955,' said Luke. 'She would have been about 90.'
'And Charles?' I asked.

'He died much earlier,' said Luke. 'Around 1930. But he'd been born in 1863 after all.'

Shortly after their marriage Charles and Elizabeth left Birmingham for good. There doesn't seem to have been any obvious event that drove them: no one had been sent to gaol, their parents were still alive, no major economic event. You never know, of course. Charles could have lost his job but he was young and Birmingham in the 1880s was non-conformist, progressive, technological, industrial, growing. It just wasn't as great a source of migrants as Ireland, say, or the East End of London.

Charles and Elizabeth headed to Australia, very likely attracted by the prospect of an assisted passage. About a year before they set off, the Archdeacon of Grafton, a pastoral area in northern New South Wales, gave a lecture on 'emigration to Australia' in the Birmingham town hall. Later that year, in December, the New South Wales agent-general in London, a businessman and politician called Sir Saul Samuel, spoke to a similar meeting in nearby Worcester. Charles – or one of his mates or even his future brothers-in-law – might have sat in the town hall and listened to stories of open landscapes and opportunities.

I'm not sure Charles and Elizabeth's motivations would have been different from those of any other working-class emigrants from British industrial cities – a new start, adventure and so on. And in this case two of Elizabeth's brothers, Thomas (five years older) and George (three), left at the same time. They were the three eldest of eight surviving siblings. Most emigrants in this era would never see their family again. To all intents and purposes, departure had the same effect as death. Elizabeth's parents lost three children to the same horizon, on the same day.

They stopped first, it appears, in Western Australia – many vessels made landfall at Fremantle before continuing to Sydney. It takes just a few seconds to record this journey on paper, but it would have taken them three months. They were so young: Charles and Elizabeth both around 21. This may have meant that the adventure shone brighter to them than the risk, but still. They had almost certainly never left Birmingham before. In fact the records show that they and their families had lived in the same narrow, working-class area of the city for generations.

The life that awaited Charles and Elizabeth doesn't seem so different from what they'd left. Warmer, surely. Stranger fauna, yes, but still a growing, thriving industrial city. They lived on Shepherd Street in Darlington, the area around the University of Sydney. Rapid subdivision had followed the university's foundation and when the young couple arrived Darlington was the most densely populated suburb in the city and widely regarded as a slum. It would have attracted those fresh off the ship.

It was busy too. According to one history, industries operating at the time included an iron foundry, a zinc and brass works and factories making jam, cordial, boots and portmanteaus. There were also two cabinet factories. Perhaps Charles found work here? Cabinetmaker was still the occupation he listed when, around three years after they arrived, the couple's first child was born, on 3 May 1887. This was Tracy Thomas Gough.

• • •

According to his birth certificate, Tracy's life began at 94 Regent Street, in Redfern, also a migrant entrepôt and not far from where his parents lived. Present at his birth were a Dr West and a Mrs Donovan. The latter might have been a midwife working from home; the doctor might have been summoned if the birth was difficult, or expected to be.

Tracy's Christian name, improbable though it might be, has stuck and been reused like a talisman through the generations. Since my days of repeating to incredulous friends that the name is a French relic, I've found it can be Irish too, meaning warrior-like. No Irish connection in the family, alas, but it would have been an easier sell in the schoolyard. The French version is derived from Thrace, the ancient name for the very southeastern corner of Europe now occupied by Bulgaria, Greece and Turkey. Thrace has disappeared as a political construct but Tracy exists in the names of several villages in Normandy. Maybe courtesy of a homesick centurion in the age of Asterix, sent to battle on the empire's northern borders.

It was Tiny Granny who used to tell Avenal stories of her alleged French heritage. Maybe it was her doing? Her maiden name, Duval – 'of the valley' gives some superficial credence and had helped support ideas of fleeing Huguenot refugees. But I know Elizabeth Duval is English, Birmingham born. If the story were true – about the origins of Tracy's name – perhaps the link was back via Tiny Granny's mother? Maybe her maiden name was Tracy?

It wasn't. Her mother's name was Miller. She'd been born in 1838, was an illiterate shoe binder and signed her marriage certificate with an X. Her Christian name was Kezia. It's unusual and exotic today but was fashionable in the nineteenth century. Kezia was one of the girls in Katherine Mansfield's *The Doll's House*, for instance. French? No, it's Hebrew. As far back as it was possible to look, there seemed no real French connection in this direction.

As Birmingham maltsters, grocers, masons and cabinet makers, the family had abounded in Charleses, Thomases or Davids and Georges. Now a new son is born on the other side of the world and called Tracy. The coincidence with the old Norman stomping ground of Sir Matthew seems too neat.

Permanent migrants often crave souvenirs of their heritage. Some go further. New arrivals can find it easier to reinvent. Physical distance can tempt elaboration. At 15,000 steam-powered miles (24,000km) from home, there's a reduced accounting for authenticity. The migrant with the romantic but wilfully elusive background is a familiar character: the White Russian noblewoman in the Shanghai nightclub, the Austro-Hungarian baron driving a cab in 1920s Paris; French gentry waiting tables on the Riviera; the Count of Monte Cristo; Jean Valjean. Around the time of Luke's visit I happened to be reading Tom Reiss's *The Orientalist*, which charts the transformation of Lev Nussimbaum, a young Jewish boy of Baku, into famed Muslim orientalist Kurban Said of Berlin and New York. There's even an aria on the theme in *Madame Butterfly*.

There's a type of person who enjoys the storytelling for the flamboyance, for the story itself, which I find somehow more forgivable than outright lying. They're not pretending to be more than they are, just that they once might have been or even just that they can tell a good tale. I wonder whether 'Tracy' was a signal to Charles and Elizabeth's inner-city Sydney neighbours of the sort of dashing lineage whose claims made their way down to me? In one word they'd be creating a story. It's speculation, but I find it compelling. It implies a decorative instinct that I recognise in the generations above me, and in myself. It fits, too, with what I later came to learn of Tracy.

Maybe I'm overthinking it all and it was just a trend? In a 1930s *Who's Who* entry for Tracy, the man who follows him, a Gould, carries the middle name de Tracy, as does his father.

• • •

'How long did they stay in Sydney?' I asked Luke.

'I think they left around 1899. I'm not certain. But they were in Christchurch early in the century. I'm not sure. There's just not much more on them in Sydney.'

Spurred on by Luke, I later found a reference to Tracy attending school in Sydney. This jarred too, like Charles' house. We'd always been told Tracy had had no formal education. It was part of the story, the implication being that his success was all his own.

It wasn't just any school, either, but fancy-sounding St Aloysius. It's become prominent now (a recent Australian prime minister is an old boy) and sits across the harbour from its original location, but in Tracy's day it was in Darlinghurst, a mile or two from their family home. It was also relatively new, private and Jesuit.

Birmingham wasn't the most loyal pocket of the established church in England but the family was Anglican and had been as far back as one could look: weddings always in C of E parishes. I'm inclined to think they were drawn to the Jesuits' famed ceremonialism, and that being a newer foundation than private Sydney Grammar School or state Sydney Boys' High School made it more approachable. St Aloysius grew fast in the 1890s so many others might have felt this way.

Taken with Luke's story about the later, lovely home, I felt I'd underestimated Charles. He might have been successful in his own right, making me think more about whether Tracy's was less of a singular triumph. If Charles had arrived in Sydney as a cabinet maker, by 1896 at the latest he was in the footwear trade: importing trunks of boots from the UK. The link might have been Elizabeth. Her father, most of her family and apparently most of her ancestors were in that business.

Potentially Charles made enough to afford fees. As Anglicans I doubt they would've been offered a free ride at a Roman Catholic foundation. Tracy could have gained a scholarship but again it felt unlikely that these would have been offered evenly to people of all faiths. Could you dissemble your way in? Young Tracy, bright as a button, Catholic son of France via Birmingham? It feels improbable.

I wrote to the school's part-time archivist, who replied straight away – yes, they did have a Tracy Gough. He was registered as being there in 1898. Apologies but no records for other years. Yes, this might indicate he stayed only one year, but equally the records might be incomplete. From what Luke had said, it seemed Tracy would have had two years at the school at most.

The record was only Tracy's name and that year. It wasn't conclusive that Tracy hadn't been a scholar, say, but then he left. To start Tracy at a private school – a huge leap for this working-class Brummie family – and then move after one year implied a compact dramatic arc. I wondered if something had happened to Charles and his fortunes.

It could be that Charles spied better opportunities somewhere new, as he may have done when deciding to leave England in the first place. In Australia, the boom that had started with the gold rushes was ebbing by the early 1890s and with it came bank failures and labour unrest. There might have been enough uncertainty in late 1890s Sydney to consider making yet another new life. Like many migrants then and today, Charles and Elizabeth might have had friends who'd already moved and sung seductively, and perhaps selectively, of the new country's charms. The encouragement didn't come from family: one of Elizabeth's brothers returned to England and I believe the other stayed in New South Wales. I'm inclined to think that something went wrong, financially, and a new move seemed a good idea. At the very least it indicated a spontaneity not often associated with financial stability.

No matter how much I speculate on the causes, what I am left with is that by 1900 the family were 2400 kilometres further south and east, in Christchurch.

As thousands of migrants had done before them, Charles, Elizabeth and their now three (of what would be four) children – Tracy, Edith and Edgar – would have sailed into Lyttelton Harbour. The port settlement now hosted some 4000 souls and there were better ways to reach the plains. The planned coast road via Evans Pass and then down into Sumner and on to town had been opened in 1857, but they would have taken the train: there had been a rail tunnel through the Port Hills – the first in the world to be built through an extinct volcano – since 1867.

They found in Christchurch a prosperous settlement of about 55,000 people, including various outlying boroughs and suburbs, where all the traffic was still horse drawn. Even the trams, introduced in 1880, were powered by horse or steam, though they were electrified shortly thereafter. In the 50 years since the Pilgrims had landed, the vision of the Canterbury Association had largely been realised, with its parks and squares and turrets and towers. The Christchurch they found was reasonably similar to the town I came to know.

Mark Twain had visited Christchurch in 1895 on his world tour, lecturing his way out of bankruptcy. It was, he wrote, 'Junior England all the way to

Christchurch – in fact, just a garden. And Christchurch is an English town, with an English-park annex, and a winding English brook … It is a settled old community, with all the serenities, the graces, the conveniences, and the comforts of the ideal home-life. If it had an established Church and social inequality it would be England over again with hardly a lack.'

New Zealand had not escaped the Long Depression of the 1880s, but by the early 1890s Christchurch was taking off once more. The Canterbury Plains and beyond had been turned into a vast and vastly productive farming hinterland. Refrigerated shipping and pastoral farming efficiency had helped to stoke an export boom in higher-value produce being sent to Britain, where farming suffered. Christchurch served this economy, and benefited.

Queen Victoria's Diamond Jubilee had been celebrated enthusiastically worldwide in 1897, especially so in Christchurch. In 1899 the wealthy surrounding province of Canterbury was one of the biggest contributors of self-funding volunteer troops to the war in South Africa. My school alone sent 99 old boys, about 1.5 percent of the more than 6500 soldiers sent from New Zealand.

The future King George V and Queen Mary visited in June 1901, and a few months later Captain Robert Falcon Scott left from Lyttelton on his way to Antarctica. The town has had a link with the frozen continent ever since. The longstanding US Operation Deep Freeze is based in Christchurch and the cathedral would hold a special service at the start of every summer season to pray for those who were heading to the ice. Among these, many years ago, was Owen, sent to see if he could fix American tractors that were otherwise left on ice floes to disappear into the depths. A statue of Scott, carved by his widow as a replica of one in London, stands today on the banks of the Avon. A plaque beneath quotes his diary: 'I do not regret this journey.'

Nineteen hundred was also Christchurch's, and Canterbury's, fiftieth anniversary. All the surviving Pilgrims, several dozen of them, met for photographs, arranged by ship. The celebrations included an exhibition reflecting on the province's achievements, a military parade, the signing of Te Deum and a speech from the governor. As historian Geoffrey Rice has noted, by this time, 'The central city was … almost fully built up and there were no "slums", as that term was understood in London or New York … Christchurch had a better drainage system than any other New Zealand city, and typhoid was now virtually a disease of the past.' Christchurch workers were, it was said, the best fed and housed in the country. 'A high proportion of its citizens owned their own homes, or were paying off mortgages rather

Charles' boot shop, High Street, Christchurch, early 1900s.

Inside Charles' shop.

than paying rent … Edwardian Christchurch was an elegant colonial city …' Overall Christchurch was distant, small and isolated but also spacious, well-off, confident. Maybe that was enough for Charles, Elizabeth and their family.

Charles established himself in boot selling. The first evidence I could find of their arrival was the advertisements he started taking out in the local paper, beginning on 12 July 1900: 'The Nugget boot-polisher, which is now universally used, can be obtained from C.D. Gough, Armagh St.' Those same 16 words appeared around 100 times at regular intervals over nine months, before they stopped completely early in May 1901. Another abrupt change, but the business appears to have continued.

The electoral rolls told me that, over 1905–06, Charles was living on Fitzgerald Avenue, one of the four that enclosed the original Christchurch. It was right on the corner of Armagh Street, so possibly the same address. He was listed as a bootmaker. By 1907 Charles was advertising again, this time for further staff, and his shop was in High Street. Good news. By the 1911 election the family had moved further south and west, this time to Bealey Avenue. Charles called himself a boot retailer. By 1912 it was different again. Charles was established. He was living at 34 Stratford Street in Fendalton. A nice street, a nice address, a fine house. This, I believe, was Leeham, where Luke and I had started.

16

As the loads of souvenirs from Beryl's swayed up the driveway to Owen and Avenal's, I put my head in my hands and wondered what to do with it all. I squeezed as much furniture as I could into the drawing room, some items stacked on top of others: chairs on a chest, chest on a day bed. The piano went in here too, along with the music, the records. Above them I hung the picture of the punt on the lake. Beryl's Meissen figures, kept on someone else's whim, were placed with those of my grandparents to form a well-dressed porcelain army, magnified many times by the mirrored glass of the cabinet that formed their barracks. The bulkiest items, like that sideboard, I had to put in the garage. I covered them with blankets (Beryl's) and a tarpaulin (Owen's) and pulled the door shut on my greed.

Among the bric-a-brac that, through exhaustion, I'd left scattered on the floor was a rattan bag of Beryl's – possibly a souvenir of missionary work in the Pacific – full of framed pictures and photos, and a jumble of old papers. The photos included a wooden-framed, black and white one about the size of a paperback, of two young people posed by a table. Tracy, standing four square, chin jutting forward, his dark suit – am I imagining this? – a little too large. In front of him, seated, must be my great-grandmother, Julia. I could see in her something of the Alison I now knew. Julia is close enough for Tracy to rest a hand on her shoulder but instead he's shot one into his pocket. On the dark tablecloth is an open book, pages twirled by Julia, and a sprig of foliage that looks as though it's done years of good service in this studio. Looking at the proportions of the composition, I'd say that even if it hadn't been the convention for the man to stand, Tracy's height might have led him to prefer it. He looks as if he takes himself seriously and wants others to, also. It's a photo from the time of their wedding, my mother told me.

It was my first view of Julia too, and belatedly this made me realise that, as with Tracy, she didn't appear anywhere in Owen and Avenal's home. She's

Tracy and Julia around the time of their wedding, 1912.

24, her face soft and delicate, her hair up. She wears a dark-coloured dress. It looks severe for a celebration. She seems thoughtful, whereas Tracy appears almost cross, or impatient. They seem to be looking in slightly different directions.

Julia's family name was Philpott. Her parents were Noah and Jane and her grandparents came out to Canterbury on the *Randolph*. The First Four Ships have always meant something in Canterbury. As late as 125 years after their arrival, memorial plaques were erected in Cathedral Square, recording the names of all those initial Pilgrims, arranged by ship and ordered by class. Not far from these is the statue of Godley, coat over one arm, hat in the other hand. I have a feeling it was the sort of thing that might have meant something to Tracy, too.

The Philpotts were not the most conventional colonists. Nonconformist grandfather Isaac and his wife and mother had almost been forcibly disembarked while still only in the English Channel for singing Wesleyan hymns, ironically some of the best-liked among Anglicans today. The captain threatened to turn the ship around and drop them back in Plymouth Sound. I think that kept them quiet for the 99 days it took to reach Lyttelton, or Port Victoria as it then was.

After arriving in Canterbury Isaac worked felling trees, then took his family away from the centre of settlement to swampier St Albans, a kilometre or two to the north. Several nonconformists moved this way too. It was micro-sectarianism, but the land was also cheaper and Isaac was one of the first Europeans to start breaking it in. He cleared and drained it, then farmed it. The approximate location is today a football ground.

Julia and Tracy were married in 1912 at St Matthew's, the Anglican parish church of St Albans. The convention has always been to have the wedding on the bride's territory, so after Isaac's death in 1896 the Methodist Philpotts might have begun to adhere to Canterbury's conventional faith. As farmers (albeit smaller scale) and Pilgrims (albeit immigrant class), the Philpotts represented something different from Charles and his Australian children who would've stepped off the boat in 1900.

At the time of his wedding Tracy seems to have been working in the same trade as his father, on what we'd now call the sales side. I don't know how Tracy and Julia might have met. From the looks of that photo she is a young farmer's daughter – in a town where that meant something – and Tracy is the confident commercial chappie.

132

On the wedding certificate Tracy is listed as 'salesman', Charles as 'bootseller'. I know from electoral rolls that Tracy by now had left home, but he gave his father's fancy Fendalton address for the record. I was still getting used to the idea of Tracy as anything but a Fendalton squire. It seems he thought the same. The only attendees I know of for sure are those on the marriage certificate: Tracy's mother, his younger brother Edgar, the bride's father Noah and a 'traveller' – travelling salesman – named G.E. Williamson, most likely a pal of Tracy's. There was no engagement announcement and the marriage notice didn't appear till a couple of months after the event.

I could imagine Tracy seeing Julia as fitting. I already thought of him as a man in a hurry. But I think these lenses underestimate a commonality of tastes that might have existed between them. Both Tracy and Julia inclined towards the artistic: he was interested in interiors, in art, in furniture (the influence of his father's early profession?) – or at least, in later life, in accumulating these with an educated eye; Julia in art and music. I hope they were both happy. Could I imagine Tracy as a romantic? It was difficult in that human sense, but everyone has a sentimental side and it would be unfair to discount it completely.

I wonder what Julia's parents thought? Noah Philpott was a farmer of 60 by the time he gave his daughter away. His age, his profession and his name make it hard for me to imagine him in anything other than Old Testament terms. Julia's mother Jane, whom Noah had married in the same Anglican church as their daughter, died four years later. Noah lived until 1941.

Tracy and Julia's union was blessed within the year. This was the long-lost Alison, Alison Mavis, the first of what I now knew to be three children. Alison was born in 1913 in the suburb of Fendalton, at Dreumagh Avenue. The street name was changed in 1915, which made it hard to pinpoint, but I found it was now called Tui Street, not far from Stratford Street. Tracy and Julia's second child, Beryl, came along three years later, in August 1916, and then finally there was Owen, in 1919 – their baby boy born for Christmas.

One day at home I found Owen's christening certificate in a drawer in the sewing room. It had frilly edges like a doily and told me that, unlike the rest of the family, he'd been born in what was then the breezy seaside village of Sumner and christened at the parish church of All Saints.

I knew Sumner and had sometimes gone there on weekend day leaves from school, but it had to be hot enough to be worth the bother. On a Sunday – Saturday was cricket – it took 45 minutes from Cathedral Square, with the sun turning the bus into a glasshouse all the way. A narrowing road

Tracy with baby Owen, c. 1920.

heads east towards the coast. It winds over a causeway and through several other small settlements, now suburbs – Mount Pleasant, Redcliffs, Moncks Bay, Clifton – before coming up against sharp bluffs on one side, silver sand and bulky rounded waves on the other.

Sumner sits in a small V formed by hills that back away from the sea. A wide road fronts the beach, and its larger houses, built to catch the view, incidentally protect the more modest streets behind from the eastern winds that whip sand and chill everywhere and can turn the surf treacherous. To the north there is a broad but shallow tidal estuary. This is sheltered by a long, low sand bar permitting only the narrowest outlet to the sea, almost crossable on foot at low tide. There was sailing in the salty, shallow estuary or swimming at the beach with hundreds of others. Swimming and splashing were followed by a bag of hot chips, sitting on bollards as the sun escaped and the wind crept up. Then at last a bus back to town with a bag of wet togs, the quadrangle at twilight, the boarding house and changing into suits for evensong.

Sumner was dignified with the family name of the Archbishop of Canterbury himself, but it remained a village of winds and waves. At the time Owen was born Sumner had only recently got electricity, had a population of around 3000, a pub, a hall and a local school. It was fancier by the time I would visit from school, with large and often new houses along the Esplanade, the sort with more window than wall. It was, and still is, especially popular with people who value the dream of living between the sea and the city. Locals know the drawbacks: the choked road access; the vicious easterly that thumps in off the Pacific, rattling windows and spraying sand up the lanes and roads; the cold sea, refreshing only when the sand's too hot to get to it.

It remains a lovely place to visit – we regularly took Daphne out here on weekends, especially when my parents were in town – but it didn't have the grandeur, the flash that I associated with the later squire of Mona Vale. It didn't feel *formal* enough. Tracy's addresses over his adult life were Fendalton, Fendalton, Sumner, Fendalton. Even statistically Fendalton seemed more Tracy's natural home and I wondered if there was anything to the move.

Those tottering forests of papers from Beryl's helped me here. They sat, uncatalogued, at Owen and Avenal's, but I had noticed among them two illustrated papers from the 1920s. Something of a newspaper keeper and clipper-outer myself, I assumed there must have been some reason for their retention – though Beryl's policies on this were clearly even more liberal than mine.

I can't remember the name of the first one I picked up but it had a dusty pink cover and over 100 pages. I put it on a table and it immediately fell open at a glossy photographic double-page spread in the centre. In front of me sat Tracy. I was familiar by then with his shape and face. He's older than at the wedding, but already with the rounded shoulders and slumpiness of later life. The same round face too, young-looking, the hair still dark. I snuck a look at the date – 1923, I think it was. Tracy would have been 36.

If the photos are to be believed, he should be fit. He's been deerstalking with a group of friends, who fill the pages either side of him. They're all in short sleeves and braces, Tracy alone is in a singlet. They're talking and laughing. Damp fringes hang over eyes or flop back from foreheads. Guns are scattered over what looks like the stony edge of a riverbed, and the victims of the expedition are spread in the foreground. This is the boys in the wild, picturesquely captured.

Tracy is more alive than I've seen him before. He's jovial, laughing – not stern businessman or sterner bridegroom. I'd never thought of him as a sportsman before, either. He looks virile and also as though he has a taste – and a talent? – for expensive gentlemen's pastimes. He is, however, wide enough about the waist to imply that hunting through the steep Canterbury hills was not a regular pastime, or not regular enough.

I picked up the second publication, *The Ladies' Mirror*. It had a glossy cover and was from a year later – September 1924. Its subtitle reassured me that it was the journal of fashionable New Zealand ladies. It was with no real surprise now that I found, among 'A Romance of the Latin Quarter of Paris' and a story on ladies' golf, a page devoted to Tracy and Julia's Sumner home.

It's presented as a typical example of a better-class New Zealand home, 'where good taste is never allowed to degenerate into pretentiousness', built in the then popular California bungalow style: clinker-cut weatherboards, stone (local, volcanic) foundations, heavy gabling and deep porches. It was a style that had appeared in New Zealand in large numbers since the end of the Great War. Their garden is pretty if not grand – plenty of hydrangeas, large lawn.

It amused me that the airy, modern look was external only. Inside it looked more like what I'd expect from the owner of Mona Vale, more to the taste that, rightly or wrongly, I associated with Tracy. I'd call it Edwardian: dark panelling, heavy Axminster carpet (shades of Beryl), vases of flowers. There was a clearer line from this to a carved entrance hall and ormolu furniture than from a seaside bungalow.

It all made me realise I'd never given much thought to Owen and Beryl's early lives. Tracy and the world he bequeathed loomed so bright that anything before was formless, almost void. Tracy was success and Mona Vale, and that's unconsciously where I placed his children too. Here though was their actual childhood home, and it looked pleasant, normal. A great place to grow up: Owen salty and sandy and unfussed, Beryl singing at the piano, in a drawing room dim against the ocean light.

• • •

Inspired by my discovery in *The Ladies' Mirror*, I tried researching other newspapers from the period. Tracy's unusual name made searching easier. I found a sequence of press reports from 1925, the first one headed: 'Motors Collide – Claim for Damages'. The story told was of a car, a large American-made Packard. It was in the news for smashing into another vehicle on the Lees Valley road in the Ashley Gorge, north of Christchurch.

The Packard belonged to Tracy's father Charles, and would have cost as much as a house. Tracy, then in his late thirties, was at the wheel. The whole family was out for a drive. Unfortunately, Tracy took a bend in the wrong lane. Even more unfortunately, the car he crashed into contained a noted barrister. The force of the impact pushed the other vehicle some 25 feet (8m) downhill. Among those injured in the other car, I learnt from the court report, was Martha Hill, who was permanently incapacitated, and cried on impact: 'You fool, you've killed me!' Everyone with a car knew one another in those days.

The accident went to jury trial at the Supreme Court. This was serious for a traffic incident. Tracy's defence was that in the west of the country, where he'd spent a lot of time, it was commonplace to crash rather than risk going around the outside on a hill road. He didn't want to endanger his children by such a manoeuvre. He was quoted as saying as much at the scene: 'I saw that a collision had to take place, and rather than go on the outside, I took you head-on …' The judge dismissed this as nonsense, saying there was no evidence that this was a convention, and that it wouldn't be justification anyway.

The trial lasted two days and was reported nationwide. Tracy was found guilty, but not before informing the court that all the statements made by the plaintiffs were untrue. The jury took only half an hour to disagree with him. Total fines and damages awarded came to just over £1400, of which Martha Hill got some £800. It was a considerable sum: several hundred thousand dollars in today's money for this family outing. Father and son did not appeal; the fines were paid. It all sounded reckless but by the end of the reportage I felt slightly sorry for Tracy, despite his braggadocio. He was criticised for speed but the evidence, which doesn't seem to have been disputed, was that he was only going 8 miles an hour (12kph).

The whole episode reminded me a little of one of my mother's brothers and his racing machines. Straight after school he had built his own motor cars from scratch. They were beautiful, curving creations in iridescent blue. I was at a wedding not long ago and sat next to a woman who had been at school with my mother. 'Your uncle,' she said, 'always used to turn up for your mother in the most amazing cars. We were always so impressed.' I can just imagine.

When I was at school he had dozens of vehicles. On my infrequent visits I might get to select a favourite and be taken for a drive. We took a black Lamborghini out once and he swung it out towards Sumner, of all places, and

Family car journey, 1920s, on Banks Peninsula.

let it go like a rocket on a long stretch of straight road. Once, though, after I'd been visiting during the day and was safely back at school, he crashed his motorbike. Things quietened down after that.

• • •

Tracy's lovely, almost fawned-upon home, his family's ability to drive such a car, to absorb such colossal fines (though I don't know what hardship paying them might have caused): it was clear that he, and his father, were enjoying a comfortable life. That, too, was a revelation to me. As I said, I had no conception of Tracy other than as Mona Value plutocrat. His success was immaculate.

It meant Tracy didn't belong anywhere else. Seeing him other than in his natural, opulent habitat felt indecent. The Sumner house might have been comfortable but it was inconsistent with my image of him and, in the way of the self-centred, this didn't make me think my view of Tracy needed to change. Instead I thought he didn't fit here. The facts of his life didn't align with my third-hand, inherited narrative, so I wondered what oddity had caused him to deviate from the trajectory I'd extrapolated backwards for him without asking. I developed three loose theories.

The first was that Tracy followed fashion. Sumner was becoming more popular. After the Great War the country's most famous architect was Samuel Hurst Seager. He'd been appointed to design all the New Zealand battlefield memorials in Europe. Beforehand he lived on a hillside over Sumner way. He turned developer, creating eight cottages and, with some publicity, selling them off as The Spur. This was advertised as the finest housing development in Canterbury's history, with the best views. Each house was an expression of the English domestic revival style that Seager had been promoting since the 1880s. Possibly a man about town, or an aspirant one, might have been attracted to it. Charles himself moved that way, ultimately acquiring one of The Spur's dwellings, but that seems to have been a later acquisition than Tracy's.

My second theory is that Tracy liked the area. He liked boats, yachts, the water. He had some sporting tendencies, if not outright hobbies. Perhaps, like so many of us, he just craved the wide blue horizon of a place by the shore. Because it appears their stay there wasn't fleeting; they lived in at least two houses in the area.

A sales brochure for The Spur, Sumner, the property of S. Hurst Seager. COURTESY OF CHRISTCHURCH CITY LIBRARIES

My third possible explanation is the most speculative but also the most flattering to Tracy. The impact of the Spanish influenza pandemic that swept the globe at the end of World War I and hit New Zealand in October and November 1918 remains overshadowed by the war itself, but it was more insidious. It infiltrated your neighbour's house. You couldn't see it; you couldn't hear it. It scared people and put them off living in built-up areas. They became nervous about low-lying, damp or swampy ground such as the Pilgrims chose for Christchurch. It was thought that so-called foul air helped to spread the disease.

Tracy moved after Beryl's birth but before Owen's, so sometime between mid-1916 and late 1919. Given the sort of house they moved to, I get the sense that by now Tracy was in control of his destiny, able to set his own timings. Julia would have been obviously pregnant from late June 1919. A move might already have been in train, but I doubt it would have been initiated subsequently. Hence I think it's reasonable to assume they had moved by, say, August 1919. Likewise, I doubt they would have moved while Beryl was new. So let's say early 1917 to mid-1919.

That's still two and a half years with the flu in the middle. It's not likely that they moved to avoid the disease before it hit Christchurch, but I think it's a possibility that they shifted after its coming and that by then Sumner was perceived as a healthier, breezier place and this helped them to make the decision. It might not have formally played Fiesole to Christchurch's Florence but it could have seemed a good bet.

None of these theories is evidenced by anything more than circumstance and supposition. I record them as each gives a different slant on Tracy, with whose character I was later to spend much time wrestling. Explained or not, the result was the same: by the early 1920s Tracy was enjoying a comfortable life. Mona Vale did not come out of nowhere.

In one of the many coincidences that has emerged during the years this family jigsaw puzzle has been covering the coffee table of my life, I happened to watch Sir Peter Jackson's film, *They Shall Not Grow Old*. Near the start is a shot of one of the early recruitment posters, which shows a middle-aged man in an armchair, surrounded by children. The man's hairstyle is just like Tracy's. The caption asks, 'Daddy, what did YOU do in the Great War?' I had a similar question.

The personnel files of all World War I soldiers are publicly accessible and provide a series of predictable and basic details on age, military activity, next of kin and so on. I couldn't, however, find such a file for Tracy and this made me curious. He was the right age, was apparently healthy and – at least a few years later – seemed to enjoy using a gun.

Tracy was 27 at war's outbreak in August 1914 when, all over the British Empire, volunteering was enthusiastic. There was another surge, surprisingly, after the disaster at Gallipoli and the anger this awoke. As this petered out the government looked to conscription. The Military Service Act aimed to ensure that everyone young and able enough was signed up to serve King and Country. Young and able was defined as non-Māori men between 20 and 46. It became law on 1 August 1916, just days before Beryl's birth and a month after the start of the Battle of the Somme.

The initial ballot was held on 16 November 1916 in an office building in Wellington. There's grainy cinema footage of the event. Young women in blouses and skirts arrayed along each side of two long tables, under the eye of a magistrate and the government statistician, who rolled two big drums and drew a marble from each. The first marble gave the number of a drawer with 500 cards; the second marble gave the number of the card. It took 20 hours and 15 minutes to draw the 4024 cards. It was repeated almost monthly until August 1918, with just over 138,000 male (non-Māori) New Zealand men conscripted this way.

Men were still volunteering in 1916, and among them was Tracy's little brother Edgar, 5' 5" (1.65m) with blue eyes and still an engineering student when he joined. Edgar served in the New Zealand Engineers and was overseas for two years and 133 days, most of it on the Western Front. I don't know what he did exactly, but I know sappers had some awful jobs: building and maintaining trenches under fire; digging those hellish tunnels of darkness and fear beneath no man's land that were used to mine the Germans. Edgar was discharged in June 1919, at least physically unscathed. He even joined up the second time around: he volunteered, aged 49, and was posted to the Home Guard for the duration.

I knew about Edgar because I found his file. Not only was there no file for Tracy, but I'd never heard any stories of his involvement – and I think I would have if there'd been good ones to tell. If Tracy had avoided service, then how, and what had he been up to? A conscientious objector? I just couldn't imagine him joining poets and communists and the religiously sincere. Owen, perhaps, but not Tracy. I couldn't imagine Tracy in gaol either. There would be a newspaper trail if he had been. Objectors were commonly arrested, their names put in print so the public could help the state in the shaming and their civil rights abrogated for a decade. Not without nervousness, I searched, but

Tracy on one of his climbing trips with Edgar Williams, c. 1917. EDGAR RICHARD WILLIAMS PHOTO, 1/4-120679-F, ALEXANDER TURNBULL LIBRARY, WELLINGTON

I found no evidence of objection or desertion. No military file, not in lists of objectors, not in lists of the convicted.

I decided to try the National Library. Its focus is on nationally important published material – not just old public records that Archives New Zealand keeps. It seemed to be a long shot. I couldn't think of anything of national importance that Tracy could've achieved, but I'd run out of other ideas. To my surprise, I found Tracy in a series of photos, apparently on holiday. He was with a man called Edgar Williams, and it's due to Williams that the library holds the photos. Williams was a mountaineer, a noted photographer and later an engineer and teacher. In his early twenties he was described as 'a gentleman of leisure with a passion for mountain climbing'. It also seems he often had to find friends with cars who could drive him to the more remote ranges and glaciers of the South Island so that he could pursue his passion.

I'm not sure how Williams and Tracy met, but they were two men of similar age (Williams was four years younger), both living in Christchurch. The photos showed them climbing at the top of the Rakaia River and on the Lyell Glacier. Landscape after landscape of scree and ice that could just as well be in the Karakorum as a few hours from Cathedral Square. And it looks as though it was just the two of them, as Tracy is almost always the sole human subject.

They are dressed straight out of the Mallory and Irvine school of fashion: tweed breeches and long socks, sports coats, thick boots. Tracy's rounded shape is distinctive even then, even amid this evidence of exertion. These images did, however, make me revisit my earlier scornful judgments on those photos I'd found of him hunting. Climbing in the Southern Alps in any decade takes endurance and skill. Doing it with no hope of being saved in event of catastrophe takes some courage too – and confidence – as well as a great deal of preparation.

Tracy and Williams are on an adventure. But it is, the records tell me, 1917. The sun is shining in all the photos. My presumption is that it might be near the start of the year too, the end of the summer not the beginning. It's safer to climb then. In the spring and early summer the ice melt makes alpine rivers treacherous. So here is Tracy, sitting on a camp chair by a canvas tent with a giant tin of biscuits by his feet. He's not fighting in Europe, so what was he up to?

One of the benefits of being back in Christchurch was that tracking down such information was meant to be relatively easy, and so I drove one day to the

Edgar Williams and Tracy – seated, by biscuits. EDGAR RICHARD WILLIAMS PHOTO, 1/4-120666-F, ALEXANDER TURNBULL LIBRARY, WELLINGTON

Christchurch branch of New Zealand's national archives, on Peterborough Street. The state doesn't keep many diaries, mementoes or family albums, but it does have an interest in how much you earn and therefore how much tax you might be able to pay. Records for any trading enterprise, ancient or defunct, ended up at Archives, and that's where I thought I'd start.

I knew that Tracy had worked for his father Charles and that the name of the business was C.D. Gough, but nothing came up. I knew from those newspaper ads that it existed and tried to think of how it could be found. It was only by a fluke that I thought about how businesses used to be structured. An incorporated company with limited liability was unusual a century ago. Charles was more likely a sole trader, unincorporated. I tried again, not on the company register but under other businesses, and the file was found. I signed for it and sat flicking through its assorted pages at a white table under fluorescent lights.

After describing himself as salesman at the time of his wedding, Tracy had been promoted the next year and became a manager. By 1918 they had a second shop in Christchurch, in Sydenham. By 1919 he and his father were buying out a rival firm in Ashburton, south of Christchurch. By 1925 Tracy had become a partner and Charles changed the name of the then unincorporated enterprise to C.D. Gough *and Son*. It looked like it worked out well. They had letterhead printed, describing themselves as merchants of

Tracy (far right with pipe) and at least two vicars on a day out.

'boots and grindery' – the latter likely meaning shoemaking equipment, but could also mean they sharpened knives.

Then they did become a company, with Charles contributing most of the capital. Tracy's entrepreneurialism continued to rest on his father's grace. The incorporation, when it came, was handled by the law firm of Dougall & Upham. John Hazlitt Upham's son Charles, who would win two Victoria Crosses in World War II, and Tracy's son Owen were near contemporaries at school. I, in turn, was at school with Charles Upham's grandson. When Upham died the whole school – all 600 and something of us – lined Rolleston Avenue in our dark grey suits and bowed our heads as his catafalque was drawn past on a gun carriage, en route to the military funeral at the cathedral.

· · ·

It was a warm evening years later when I finally worked it out. We'd moved out of Christchurch by then but were back staying at Owen and Avenal's. It was summer and we were visiting to enjoy the garden.

I'd read something about the new resources available across the Christchurch library network. It turned out they had subscription access to all sorts of national and international records, though you could only access them on site. It was a Sunday but the Fendalton branch, just a few minutes away in Jeffreys Road, was still open. I said goodbye to a bewildered family, hopped on a pushbike and pedalled down our quiet road and across the park, green and empty.

They showed me how to use the system and I checked military files again, just to be sure. Nothing. Then I saw that one of the lists they had was of Great War army reservists. These were lettered A to D, denoting number of children. That's where I found him. At the time of that first conscription ballot he was the father of two, by a matter of about eight weeks. As such he fell deep into the reserves list for the second division, class C (two children). In July 1918 he was passed as fit to serve but it appears he was never called. Tracy saw out the war from Fendalton, as was his right, thanks to Beryl and then, it seems, to the good fortune of the conflict's end.

Julia and baby Owen, 1920.

17

Humans become proprietorial quickly, even when it may be unjustified, even when ungrateful. So it was at Owen and Avenal's. The two of us were lucky to be living there but I started to wish we were surrounded by items from our own lives, rather than the earthly remnants of at least four others. I told myself this developing ingratitude wasn't my fault – that it lay with Beryl's possessions, which had tipped the balance. Until their arrival I'd been happy: if not wholly covetous of the life around me, at least interested in what I had found and with no sense that I had any role in changing it. Now it felt suffocating, crowded, ridiculous.

And so from time to time I'd launch loose, brief campaigns to try and bring the house into better order. I started going through wardrobes, piling up clothes to give away: Avenal's fur coats to my sister, Owen's suits to a cousin, ties to my brother. Boxes were dispatched to opportunity shops. I threw away dress patterns, gave away balls of wool. Parsed the box cupboard and jettisoned masses of old suitcases that came from an era before wheels and zips. I threw out magazines, empty boxes, old Christmas cards. With the conquest of even a few square centimetres I could clap the dust off my hands and head downstairs with a smug smile. I told myself I was approaching it all with new energy, but I doubt an independent observer would have agreed.

I tidied Avenal's dresser, putting her hairbrushes and trinkets into a box. I went through the blanket chest and took out the mustiest. I reviewed Owen's remaining socks and handkerchiefs, cataloguing them into those with holes and those without and deciding their fate accordingly – an emperor surveying gladiators. I even declared the longstanding blue bedspread a fire hazard and got rid of it, not without later controversy.

Once I'd done this and left the bed bare, it occurred to me to look underneath it. There, pushed hard against the back wall, was a brown cardboard dress box from Ballantynes. I'd found many others like this. They tended to be filled with old nightgowns or fashions from the 1940s; or just empty, a spare dress box saved up for a rainy day. I lay down on the carpet and stretched out an arm to pull it out. It had no weight, but I flicked the lid back for a look before consigning it to rubbish. Instead of emptiness or lace there were photographs – some loose, some in albums, some crumbling with age, most small, almost all black and white. I'd never seen any of them before. Here was a distraction worth hours. I sat back, leaning against the wardrobes, and pulled the box alongside my outstretched legs.

On top was an album of dark brown card with the name of Owen and Avenal's house on the cover. Inside it seemed to be a record of the place when newly built. The photos were washed sepia by age. The house then was small, low, dark brown, surrounded by a treeless expanse of dun-coloured earth with every human dressed in black. It looked bleak, like some film about the paucity of prospects on the American frontier.

Then, however, I was into photos of people I knew. Owen, aged all of four or five but instantly recognisable, in a long white car, an open-tourer, parked side on to the camera with those high, spoked wheels like a bicycle. I showed it to my brother and he was able to place it as a Fiat Spyder. The photo must have been taken around 1923 or 1924. The shape of the hills in the background indicates it's at Sumner. Owen's all alone in the car and looking straight at the camera. His hair's so blond it's almost white, and he's dressed in white. He almost glows against the rough street, the timber-planked fences. There's Tracy in a pea coat with friends in captain's hats. They're looking jolly on a balcony that could be in Europe. Then some of Owen and his sisters:

Owen on a Sumner street, around 1923.

148

Sumner School, 1920, Alison seated second row, far right, aged six or seven. Note girls with dolls and a teddy, boys with sports equipment.

Owen blond and grinning, sitting on a bench, a backyard fence behind; all three of them in swimming togs in the same place. It's a century ago; these are old people; but childhood is instantly recognisable.

Another loose snapshot showed Owen again, now in his Christ's College blazer and shorts. He's lean and leggy. Fifteen maybe? Slightly older? That'd mean mid-1930s. He and a friend, similarly dressed, stand beside a little yacht on a trailer. The word 'Valada' is on the photo's back in what looks like a pencil wielded by Owen. From an early age he had a form of essential tremor and his hand wobbled as he wrote; the capital 'V' has a serrated look. Steep cliffs rise behind the two boys; it's probably Redcliffs on the way out to Sumner.

As if to prove the guess correct, the next photo showed a primary school class. A girl in the front row holds a slate that tells me, in chalk, that it's 'Sumner 1920'. At the back a boy holds a leather rugby ball under one arm. Several girls have dolls. Sumner School. In the second row, far right, I see a now familiar wide smile and pretty face recognisable from that photo in the ballgown. Alison's more the age I envisaged tragedy hitting when I'd heard she died young. She smiles with her mouth shut, as though she knows something that makes her even happier than she's letting on.

Picnic with *Bell Bird*. Owen is on the rock near the boat, Tracy far right.

Next, an album of a trip Avenal took to Europe with her mother. The first stop's Sydney, a snap of the harbour bridge only partly built, the famous metal arc not yet joined in the centre, which makes it shy of August 1930, when the north and south arch builders met. Colombo next, with the heat coming through the brown and white of the photo; the Suez Canal, all hazy too, and then Europe, France, a photo of Avenal's aunt and mother on the Promenade des Anglais in Nice. It's sunny but they're dressed for a winter funeral, in heavy black and shawls, I think because this is the trip they took after George died.

More photos, one showing Owen and Avenal's house as it must have been when they bought it. It looks more isolated, the garden woollier. The front fence is made of pickets, leaning at irregular angles. Stored with it was a newspaper cutting showing a Lutyens house overlooking the Thames with a bank of Georgian windows. Avenal must have used it as her model for the changes that were made over the years to create the house in which I was now living. She wanted it lighter, more symmetrical.

One photo, mounted on board like a formal school photo, lay in a brown paper sleeve of almost translucent thinness. It was a group of people on a rocky shore. Behind them treed hills rose sharply and a gap in distant cliffs gave onto the wider sea. There is a sailing boat moored to the rocks, a single mast, and *Bell Bird* stencilled on the prow. The water is very still. It could be

150

Owen, Julia, Beryl and Alison on one of Tracy's yachts, *Kereru*.

in the Lake District or Scandinavia or the American woods. But it is a narrow inlet, in the wilderness at the uttermost ends of the earth. Of the eight people in the photo I recognise only two immediately, my grandfather and his father.

The skipper – he must be, the way he lounges on the deck – is mahogany-skinned and singleted. He looks on with a smile and a pipe as three couples sit in a line on a driftwood log, the women clutching straw hats, the men, rifles. They're all smiling. One of the women, I realise on closer inspection, is

Julia. At the far end of the log, away from the boat, sits Tracy, already carrying the weight of an older man. Completing the scene, a small blond boy sits on a rock right at the water's edge, looking directly at the camera. This, again, is Owen, probably anywhere in age from three to six.

But where are Beryl and Alison? If anything, you might be inclined to leave the youngest at home and take the more self-contained children on a sailing trip. Maybe his sisters required more entertainment than Owen, who could be left alone on a shore to play with the stones.

Avenal, aged about 12, near Port Said, Egypt, en route to Europe.

Tracy (with pipe) and nautical friends.

Or maybe hunting wasn't regarded as a girls' day out? But the wives are all there. Possibly Owen's at the younger end of the guessed spectrum; his sisters are in school but he's not. Then it must be a working day? I could imagine the companions being somehow work related. An office day out might be unlikely for the era but I know that in later life many of Tracy's most regular companions were customers or employees.

I could imagine that: an office day out. Tracy walking around the desks, clapping people on the back saying, 'Are you coming?' Choreographed leisure. I start to look closely at the other men. Are they all younger than Tracy? I think they might be.

The photo's been taken from another boat. Maybe Tracy has set up an automatic camera. I can imagine him as an early adopter. For what? To record an expensive day out? The men and women look jovial but they seem to be wearing city clothes, like those photos from the magazine: white shirts, dark trousers, braces and formal shoes, hair slicked back. The women are in light frocks. No animals have succumbed to the rifles on display.

I was getting carried away. It was impossible to be forensic with miniature sepia heads captured so long ago. I slipped *Bell Bird* back into its sleeve and looked at what was next. Lots of loose photos: Tracy racing speedboats (a small silver trophy that lived on a mantelpiece attested to his victories); a cricket match, all whites and straw hats and Tracy standing on the sideline wearing a blazer and panama and looking proprietorial; a gathering in the bush, Owen kneeling in the undergrowth and a grand woman, looking like an elderly Sitwell, with her chin in the air.

A children's grouping outside a timber homestead, Beryl still bright blonde, Alison in a hat, a shaggy dog with paws up for attention. Tracy out with what looks like two vicars and a handful of other male friends. Another car, packed to the gunwales and caught between trees as bare as flagpoles. Another picnic – two or three families, no boat this time but a white bassinet set against the dark bush to hold what I think must be baby Owen.

Then there was a small plastic packet, ziplocked and therefore curated and filed by someone in the last 10 or 15 years. Inside were more snapshots, the smallest so far, likely Box Brownie taken, each no larger than a visiting card. These photos brought me to more familiar territory, though I knew it no better than any other tourist. Mona Vale was immediately recognisable, and so, again, was Owen.

He's out of shorts now and suddenly a young man about town in a grey flannel suit with Oxford bags. His hair is combed just as I remember it. In the first photo he stands by the lily pond. Dark hedges form the background

Tracy and family on a picnic. Beryl is in middle with blonde hair, Alison on the far right. It is probably Owen in the white gown, making this 1920.

and several urns that I recognise from my grandparents' garden are scattered about. There are two girls with Owen and they're all looking into the sun. Behind them is what is now the public carpark. You walk this way to approach the house, which means I can place it in my mind and know that they're therefore facing directly east, with the sun in their eyes; it must be early morning. And despite Owen's suit, the girls are wearing light dresses, it must be summer, or nearly: there's no sign of the dewiness you might get in the early morning in spring or autumn, and the waterlily pads float on the pond, not yet in bloom.

Of the two females, Beryl I identify in an instant, blonde hair, fine face and standing with a black spaniel at her feet – I never knew they had a dog, but the chap here looks very similar to ones in earlier photos. It looks like they may have kept a sequence of spaniels. The other girl is harder to make out but I can see enough to know it's not Avenal. It must be Alison. Three siblings taking the family dog for a walk in the grounds. And now that I have Alison in mind I start to see the similarities with the debutante photo: brown hair falling to the shoulders, straight, not waved or curled like Beryl's. A face with no hard edges, one that I know can house a wide smile. But this must be around 1940 – what age did she live to?

The other shots in the series are mostly landscapes. There's the house from the river, the riverbanks, the different parts of the garden. There are

Alison, Beryl and Owen by the lily pond, Mona Vale, c. 1940.

Alison (left), Beryl (centre) and Owen (seated) playing in the woods, mid-1920s.

newly planted trees staked in dry circles of earth. It's the sort of series you might take soon after moving in; wandering around, capturing all the angles of your new home. Maybe that's why these photos were stored with the ones from Sumner? The old life and then the first look at the new? It was quite a change, reflecting Tracy's escalating fortunes.

• • •

At the company's head office several modern Perspex cases filled the reception area, displaying a potted narrative of Tracy's rise in brochures, photos, souvenirs and other relics.

One of the surprises was that it wasn't just Tracy's enterprise; in fact its initial momentum came from his younger brother, Edgar. He and a friend worked for a business importing electrical goods. Edgar was the chief engineer, his pal Harry Hamer was company secretary. The firm went into liquidation and they bought it out and carried on the business. Tracy came in as an investor. The new firm took their three names while the name of the old company – Carrick Wedderspoon – endured in the telegram address: Cablespoon.

Then, the story goes, one spring evening a few years later, Edgar's friend Harry was at a bridge party in Fendalton. There he heard that a local company which imported American tractors had found itself in bother and needed to offload its business. This wasn't surprising. It was 1932, still the Depression.

Harry telegraphed Edgar, already in the United States researching new stock, and told him to go and look at the tractors and see what they were like. Edgar did so and approved of what he saw. These tractors were technologically innovative: the application of Great War tank tracks to agricultural machinery had hugely improved their versatility on soft ground and overall productivity. There'd been experiments before but it was in the 1920s that the technology took off for non-military use. It had even led to a new word, bulldozer, which entered the language in 1930 – alongside electric blanket and air hostess, as it happened. Edgar and friend decided to take over the local agency.

Running such a business took more capital than dealing in fridges and they turned to Tracy for help. He lent them a further £6000. It was three years after the Wall Street crash, the timing seemed curious to the point of foolhardiness. One historian has called the 1930s the broken decade for New Zealand. Throughout the world it was a time of despair. But in Canterbury the three partners made the business work. In fact the Depression and its policy response seemed to benefit the company and it flourished. To combat the economic despondency the government launched a major public works programme. The goal was both to compensate for the drop in private demand and to soak up unemployed labour. The firm was well placed – selling tractors by now – and benefited accordingly. Tracy would arrange public demonstrations up and down the country like an impresario. He invited civic leaders to come and stare at some barren hillock while his men and machines moved it 100 yards (90m) within the day. Thousands would attend.

Then there was another, related, government campaign to mechanise agriculture. Tracy arranged for his friend, the then minister of works Bob Semple, to drive one of his tractors over a wheelbarrow as they worked on the new airport at Harewood, now Christchurch International.

By now, around 1935, Tracy seems to have decided to get out of boots and focus on bulldozers. His father's firm, of which he appeared to have owned the majority by the time of Charles' death, ceased trading in early 1935 and Tracy wound it up a few years later (there was a closing down sale). About this time the three partners went their separate ways. Edgar took over the electrical import arm, Harry founded a firm that was more akin to an electrical contractor while Tracy stuck with the bulldozers and the original incorporation.

By the time war was looming, the position of what was now Tracy's firm in earth moving, road building – what we today would call infrastructure – was dominant, and it morphed into defence too. By the late 1930s, Tracy's tractors were being fitted with armour plating to create a homemade tank. This was another project of his ministerial friend Semple, of the wheelbarrow. It wasn't pretty and I doubt it would have done well against the Germans but it gained publicity.

Tracy's company started building defences, around the country and in the Southwest Pacific. There had been a burst of airfield development during the 1930s, which grew with the Japanese threat. Sometimes the firm assisted, sometimes just his employees – not many people had experience of handling heavy machinery in those days. In 1941 the Royal New Zealand Air Force formed No. 1 Aerodrome Construction Squadron for this very task and sent it to Singapore and Malaya. The bulldozer that had crushed the wheelbarrow ended up being sunk in the hold of a ship off Singapore.

If Tracy had been comfortable before in Sumner, by now he was successful on a grand scale, and he celebrated accordingly by buying himself a grand new home.

18

I wanted to pinpoint the likely year of those Mona Vale snapshots and so I started by going to the Christchurch City Council to work out precisely when Tracy had acquired the place. I have to admit I found sifting through old handwritten titles, with their copperplate and talk of perches, confusing. This was enhanced by the complexity of the house's ownership, which had been transferred from Tracy privately to the company. From the looks of things he bought it sometime in 1939, though the family may not have moved until 1940. This was later than I'd expected. If it hadn't been for learning about their house in Sumner, I'd have assumed they lived at Mona Vale all of Owen's life. In fact he must've been an adult.

Once it was acquired, Tracy poured money into the place. He hired the country's most famous landscape gardener, Alfred Buxton, to redesign the grounds. He planted thousands of rhododendrons and azaleas. He built a heated in-ground pool – one of the first in the country – in the winter garden. He even bought the neighbouring mansion, the Mill House, giving him a spare home and taking the grounds up to around 16 acres (6.4ha), stretching almost all the way back to Hagley Park. Later he gave the Mill House over for use as the governor-general's Christchurch residence. Mona Vale itself was to be used by King George VI and the Queen on a royal tour that was cancelled by the king's early death in 1952. Tracy retained dozens of gardeners (so the family would say) and there was a service wing that seemed to take up about half the house.

It was also Tracy who installed the lily pond. It's over 30 metres long and Georgian in style and wouldn't have been a fast job. Tracy's speciality was excavation with machines, but this was delicate, shallow, with a lot of expensive landscaping that he'd be careful about. He might have used a tractor of sorts but he would have needed men too. He'd also know not to do earthworks over winter, when heavy rain turns ungrassed land to bog. If he'd bought the house in, say, mid- to late 1939, he might have undertaken the works straight away, in that summer of 1939–40. Maybe the family waited and moved in when the works were done?

That could make sense – the photos are documenting a new house and a facelift, hence the wide shots of lawn, the ambling about the grounds. In the photos it looked warm. I think I'll go with, say, February 1940. This doesn't work with the staked trees, though. You wouldn't plant those over a Canterbury summer. So my second guess is the other end of 1940. The pond was done the previous summer (and hence has lilies by now), the trees planted over autumn and winter. Now the work is complete. That gives me about a year. Owen would have been 20, rising 21, Beryl 24 and Alison maybe as old as 27.

Who took the photos? The shot by the lily pond has a natural feel. The three siblings aren't close together as you would be if posed. The photographer is too far away. It's more as if they have been stopped mid-stroll by someone come through the hedges from the house. Tracy was the one who liked the large gardens, and whose father did too. He was also the sort of person attracted to a gadget like a new camera. But was he the sort of person to take strolls? He went hunting, he went hiking, he raced boats. Did he wander with a camera in hand and photograph bushes and lawns? I struggle to see him doing so. Early morning, Tracy at work? I think it's Julia who has popped around and captured her three children with their dog.

Beryl had a few photos of this world too, in an album with a faux crocodile cover. It had been gathered up with so much else but I'd never examined it properly. I sought it out again now. There were a few photos of Beryl as a girl, all short smocks, long legs, ankle socks and bobbed hair the colour of lightning, like her brother when young. Then, stapled to two inserted pages, were about 10 photos of Mona Vale's interior. There was the hall, the dining room, the drawing room with its cream, almost rococo plasterwork. I see Tracy had an organ too, at the top of the stairs. Proper Dracula. I was surprised at how much of the furniture and art I recognised – chairs, vases, cabinets – until I realised that these pages must have been prepared to show the court what chattels had been acquired while Julia was alive, and so could be claimed after Tracy's death.

It was all empty rooms and close-ups of Chippendale chairs and land-scapes in gilt frames, apart from one photo. A young woman sits in a chair. She's in the room between the drawing room and the dining room, the one that gives out onto the terrace, the one that young people, bounding off the

The organ in the upstairs hall at Mona Vale.

One of four portrait miniatures, this one showing the author's mother, on which Beryl based the outfits for her flower girls, bridesmaids and pages.

The gatehouse of Mona Vale on Fendalton Road. BOB AND NANCY HALL, WIKIMEDIA COMMONS

The author's father (left), mother and the late Jonathan Mane-Wheoki on Vauxhall Bridge one Sunday morning in the early 1970s on their way to St James the Less in Pimlico.

Owen and Avenal in Paris, 1993.

b

Owen on board his yacht *Princess Persephone*, early 1970s.

Avenal and Owen in the drawing room at home, on their silver wedding anniversary.

A painting by Sydney Lough Thompson that hung in Owen and Avenal's house.

Watercolour of the author's mother aged five, by Rudi Gopas.

Owen and the author's mother on the stairs at home.

The author's daughter (and bunny) outside the Beijing tomb of sixteenth-century Jesuit missionary Matteo Ricci.

f

Portrait of Beryl by R.N. Field.

Watercolour of Leeham, Charles Gough's house in Fendalton,
by W. Menzies Gibb, found among Beryl's possessions.

David and Absalom by Pedro de Orrente. WIKIMEDIA COMMONS

Some of the letters
found in Owen's satchel.

stairs and heading as fast as possible for fresh air, would run through. She's side on to the lens, framed by thick curtains that hang in the drawing room doorway. She's lost in concentration, looking through the room to the hall, seemingly unaware of the camera. It's as though she's waiting for someone to come through from the front door. Above her head is a painting I recognised from Beryl's house. To her back are those doors to the terrace. These face east, and even this black and white world is filled with the sense of gold as the morning rays hit her straight shoulder-length hair and create a landscape of light and shadow around her feet. It's Canterbury chiaroscuro. It's Alison again, I'm sure of it.

Three people and a dog going for a walk; quiet rooms full of antiques; reflective guests in armchairs; a large home surrounded by lawns. It's the sort of Christchurch that will always be part imagination and part reality. It might be the Canterbury archetype, for others it might be the caricature. It could be an ornate filtration of English dreams and tastes, transplanted to the southern seas. But it is also one family's actual home and life, and it matched the outline image of Tracy that I'd always carried in my head. Canterbury and Christchurch might have cultivated an aristocratic look – whether faux or not is as much a political as a cultural question – but Tracy seems to have taken it to full flight with all the enthusiasm of the convert.

I began to paint in the background, and for good measure I decided I might as well choose a palette that would add glamour to me by association: Tracy out hunting or reclining on yachts; Tracy in whites watching the cricket; Tracy racing boats. Then I really got carried away. With an eye to my own myths, I told myself he was like a southern Gatsby – that most famous plutocratic pretender of the interwar years. They flourished at the same time, you see, Gatsby and Tracy. Gatsby had a hydroplane; Tracy had a Tiger Moth – there's a photo, leather flying hat, goggles and all. Gatsby had a rich cream car 'swollen here and there in its monstrous length'. Tracy's white Spyder looked just as good.

And the autobiography. Gatsby's improbable version brought Nick Carraway to the brink of laughter. Tracy's genealogical claims were grander but he made them indirectly: not a soliloquy to a friend – I don't think Tracy cared like that – but a family tree on a wall, an engraved crest on the cutlery. Even then, was it serious? It was brother-in-law Wilfrid who did the digging; Tracy might have just enjoyed the look. Gatsby might point to his friend the earl of Doncaster in a photo; Tracy had his hunting and sailing images and his offer of accommodation to regal and vice-regal guests. Gatsby had a medal from Montenegro; Tracy claimed a chest in his hall belonged to Catherine of Aragon. They both liked New York. Gatsby lunched in a cellar on 42nd Street; Tracy would stay in the old Ritz-Carlton on 46th, where Ludwig Bemelmans, writer and illustrator of the *Madeline* books, worked as the maître d'hôtel.

And of course, they had their mansions. Gatsby's was 'a colossal affair … spanking new under a thin beard of raw ivy, and a marble swimming pool and more than forty acres of lawn and gardens'. Gatsby had beach. Tracy had riverfront. Gatsby claimed he had the house so that he could fill it with the 'celebrated people' of the day. Tracy entertained politicians, but they were also likely to have been customers.

Alison at Mona Vale, c. 1940.

Tracy (centre) in a Tiger Moth aircraft.

There's something about the newcomer, wanting to spin modern gold thread into the drapery of the established. They develop worlds based on their own idealised views of society's conventions. They can be obvious as the conspicuous consumers seeking to blend in with the old crowd. It's Toad of Toad Hall and a thousand and one others. It's every character real or literary who has succeeded and then associated assimilation with conquest. Tracy was able to turn himself into a local squire in a way that would have been impossible back in Birmingham, but he maybe wasn't as new as all that. He had the money to put into his brother's firm due to success in his earlier career, which he seemed to owe, at least in part, to his father Charles. Tracy himself might have given his father credit; it might have just been the winnowing of history through family hands that left Tracy's name as the only one to be remembered.

This is not to underestimate Tracy's achievements, in business and in the way he deployed his resources. His wealth and imagination met Christchurch's tastes and created the world of these photos. But I wonder what Christchurch's Tom Buchanans would have thought?

The last photograph in the box under the bed showed seven people standing behind and seated on a sofa. Along the back I recognise everyone now: Beryl, Avenal, Owen and Alison. They are all smiling; again Alison with a partly closed mouth. Does that mean she's happy? She looks more knowing, calm. I'd say secure, or confident, but they both suggest arrogance, which I can't see.

The three older people are sitting. Tracy is in the middle, a woman on either side. One is Julia, his wife. Who's the other one? Everyone is in evening wear. The three young women all wear ballgowns, two dark, Avenal's perhaps cream. Owen and his father are in black tie. Owen looks over-slender for his wingtip collar, and I bet Avenal has tied his bow tie for him.

The formality wasn't unusual for the era, the house or the family. But it felt like a moment, and I tried to think what it might be: Owen and Avenal both young, the other, unknown older woman. I tell myself I know the room as I can recognise the silk damask on the walls. I think of it as a dark mustard gold. I don't know why. Colour photographs from when they lived there don't exist. Someone would have mentioned it once and it has lodged in my brain.

I've looked so closely at this scene, so many times, that other details have emerged. That sofa, the curve of it – I realise it's the one rescued from Beryl's and now standing in the room below me. Beryl herself is a very slight figure here, and angular, quite different to the more roly-poly great-aunt I knew. Alison is a little wider in the shoulders than Beryl but still delicate, and has a rounder face. Beryl's smile is wider than anyone's.

And behind Owen's shoulder, in the top right-hand corner of the photo is the bottom left-hand corner of a painting that I know from his and Avenal's drawing room. It shows the subject's leg only but it is recognisably the nude, the one they'd been able to keep because the engagement party photo showed they owned it before Julia died. This is it. Owen and Avenal's engagement, right at the end of 1940. The family might have only been living there a year but they look at home. The destruction and mayhem of World War II does not seem to intrude into this drawing room in Christchurch.

Knowing the event means that other seated woman must be Edith, Avenal's mother, and as I look at them both, Edith seated in front of Avenal, they begin to resemble one another. Edith looks happy, smiling, her hands in her lap. Avenal's father is long dead, but this could still be why Edith is dressed in black. I look closer and I notice that Beryl is holding Avenal's hand – her best friend is becoming her sister-in-law. Or maybe it's vice versa?

Tracy's expression is more nebulous. He's not smiling but looks as if he might have been. Or as if he's about to say something, or he's chewing. It might even be an 'I don't believe it' smirk. I showed the photo to someone else for a second opinion and she said Tracy looked wry. You couldn't say he looks conventionally happy, and I'm not sure I would have expected him to be.

Six days earlier Owen had turned 21. According to family lore, Tracy

Owen and Avenal's engagement party, New Year's Eve 1940, Mona Vale.
Back, left to right: Beryl, Avenal, Owen and Alison. Seated: Edith, Tracy and Julia.

gave him a present. It was supposedly the retelling of the biblical story of Absalom, the handsome son of King David who rebelled against his father. An odd gift and an odd story, and its shadow makes me look cynically at Tracy's expression. Is he bemused that someone else's occasion is taking the limelight? That may be unfair. He has, after all, agreed to record the moment – perhaps calling a servant through to hold the camera (it's not a professional-looking shot) while seating himself in the middle.

Owen, the youngest, the first to get engaged. His two sisters still unmarried. On some level this marital anomaly supported the sense of enclosure, of difference, about the world this family lived in. Alison and Beryl were attractive, well brought up and well to do. How come both were unmarried? Not that anyone has to marry: just that it was usual, then, for women of their age. It might have been personal preference or, if not preference exactly, then that they had not found the right person. There are all sorts of explanations but it gave me a sense of a cloistering. A family that was its own community living on a property the size of a small village. I have a feeling, unevidenced, of Tracy the late Victorian, the Edwardian, watching the driveway for the approach of young men. Like any father he would have wanted to protect his daughters, but I also don't think he would have been the easiest to win over. By design or by instinct, I believe he kept Alison and Beryl close to him. Mona Vale was his world.

The stranger thing was that, outside the gates, Christchurch was undergoing a surge of modernism. The city's very rigidity was later credited with giving the movement energy, something to rebel against. In September 1940, almost exactly the time I attribute to the lily pond photograph, there was an exhibition of work by the artists' association known as The Group. It was held at the old Canterbury Society of Arts gallery which sat near the Avon on Durham Street, two low Gothic revival buildings in brick, the first designed by Benjamin Mountfort, the same architect responsible for much of my school, the Christchurch Club, many Canterbury churches – much of old Christchurch in fact.

There were around 100 works, almost every one of them by a future giant: Colin McCahon, Toss Woollaston, Rita Cook (later Angus), Leo Bensemann, Evelyn Page, Olivia Spencer-Bower, Louise Henderson; even a couple of works by R.N. Field. These artists presented landscapes and people in ways never attempted before: bold lines, brilliant colours. Romanticism was dead. This was realism heading to the abstract.

Visual artists weren't the only ones at work. Ngaio Marsh was about to start directing plays; there were poets and writers and printers – an all of arts movement in Christchurch. And over in London former Christchurch resident, composer Douglas Lilburn, who studied with Ralph Vaughan Williams, was getting ready to premiere his *Overture: Aotearoa* for a New Zealand Centennial Matinee performance at His Majesty's Theatre. Lilburn's 1939 choral work, *Prodigal Country*, was anything but a panegyric. It set the poetry of Robin Hyde/Iris Wilkinson, Allen Curnow and Walt Whitman to music. One of the lines, from Hyde, is 'Young crude country, hard as unbroken shell.' She rejected pioneer, colonial philistinism, but she also disliked artifice. Owen, Beryl, Alison, standing by the lily pond, encapsulated an almost allegorical Christchurch aesthetic, but there was more going on. As the world Tracy was trying to create was being questioned, torn apart, this family seemed to be going in the other direction. Gone were the bathing costumes and beaches of Sumner; the modern houses and picnics and relaxed, smiling sort of outdoor life. Now it was urns and suits and Tudorbethan and spaniels.

I also liked the stillness. Tracy the extrovert seemed prone to publicity but his home looked private, quiet, self-sufficient, sheltered, not just by wealth and privilege but maybe also by preference. It didn't seem to matter what occurred outside, even war. Or maybe it did matter, and Mona Vale was sanctuary against it.

The house's geography helped. Mona Vale was in the middle of the city but it was a green island with the Avon as its moat. There were gatehouses to keep people out. It was probably Christchurch's best-known but also its most sequestered house. There was room to walk alone in summer with no sounds but cicadas and flowing water. I could imagine the mist lifting off the river in winter and surrounding the house, sound muffled by damask curtains. Inside just the family, Beryl singing opera, Alison reading, Owen pretending to. It was in fact less reminiscent of Gatsby and his open-handed parties than of the Finzi-Continis: solitude, separation, isolation. A family living behind a high wall, a sense of enchantment.

19

As it happened, about the same time that I was looking into Tracy's past, his contemporary legacy – the long arm of the trust structure in which his company was left – was becoming more complicated.

Robert, the trustee, came often to Christchurch. He always had done, to see my uncles and discuss family and business matters. Now that I was living here, I started to be invited to such meetings too. We'd gather in quiet rooms over tea and biscuits. He would place his hands, palms down, on the table and deliver calm, sensible updates.

There were regular concerns, gripes, grumbles. There was always jostling of some sort, but isn't that always the way with families and money? Occasionally a letter would emerge, penned at night by someone furious. This would be followed by phone calls, hurried meetings. More letters, more calls, each one creating its own momentum and adherents before fizzling into abstraction or threats or lamentations; sometimes all three. The causes could be arcane, even to me. Performance was down, someone had been allowed to invest in something they shouldn't have. This plan was going to lead to failure, and so on.

Robert started visiting Christchurch even more often. He was worried, he'd say, things were changing. Using Venn diagrams and dotted lines, he'd try to explain how everything worked: there were the trustees, including him; then there was what they controlled and how they controlled it. The trustees existed because, well, there had been troubles. That was the word he used, the same he'd used with me before, *troubles*. The trustees were there to avoid such unpleasantness. But it couldn't last for ever; it was after all the estate of someone who had died over half a century earlier. And Robert was tired. These lectures disguised as discussions were partly for the benefit of the uninitiated such as me.

Of course, I didn't fully understand the complexity. Maybe I don't still. I understood it was strange that some adults seemed to be paid to oversee other adults. I understood there were two parallel families. But despite Robert's efforts at explanation, it always felt just over the horizon for me. Whatever existed had been there for eternity, and there seemed to be enough of Anthony Powell's Uncle Giles in it all – trustees, grumbling but ultimately a pretty fine life – not to take winds-of-change talk too seriously.

Since arriving home I'd been working remotely for my old employer in China, using the former Fun Room. The desktop was covered with junk, which I hadn't tidied, and so was unusable. Its drawers held old chequebook butts, pencils, hole punches, notepads, promotional pens, boxes of rusted staples and the like. So instead I spread my work things on top of one of the many tall shipping cartons and told myself this was perfectly normal while watching the light soften through the trees in the garden.

The shelves remained lined with ringbinders full of Owen and Avenal's invoices, arranged by year and topic; all in perfect order; all now perfectly redundant. Power bills, a folder's spine told me, from 15 years earlier; gardening receipts from a similar decade. There was art in the purity of this display of domestic administration but even I realised that keeping it intact went beyond sentiment. Periodically I would execute a minor cull to create space for my own files. But this was self-distraction more than anything: the schoolboy tidying his pencil case while the prep was left undone.

For some reason it took me a long time to approach the safe. It sat just inside the door, at ankle level. It had been here my whole life and I must have passed it hundreds of times, yet if I'd been asked to describe this little room, I would've left it out. The safe had the invisibility of the blandly functional. I liked to tell myself that my failure to notice it stemmed from respect: this was Owen and Avenal's locked box. Then I reminded myself that my grandparents were long dead and began to get excited. Did this get checked when they died? When the house was cleared? Something might have been missed; I had to look inside to make sure.

The safe was locked and I had no idea where the key was. I rang my mother, who said the last place it had been stored was on a hook in the far corner of her father's wardrobe upstairs. I was living in an undated time capsule and so when I went upstairs to check, of course the key was still there. I took it back down, slotted it into the lock and the safe door opened.

I had no precise expectations of what might be inside, but I had imagination. A small part of me thought, well, if all the junk was in those

Antique Auction

Over 1100 Rare and Important Items as yet
unequalled in New Zealand

The Collection of the Late MRS TRACY GOUGH

comprising

Porcelain, Paintings, Furniture, Silverware, Jewellery
Rare Books and Maori Artifacts

VENUE: THE HORTICULTURAL HALL
cnr. Cambridge Terrace and Gloucester Street, Christchurch

WEDNESDAY 29th OCTOBER, 1975
THURSDAY 30th OCTOBER, 1975
FRIDAY 31st OCTOBER, 1975
Commencing at 10.00 a.m. each Day

PUBLIC VIEWING TUESDAY 28th OCTOBER, 10 a.m. to 10 p.m.

*PYNE, GOULD, GUINNESS LIMITED
AUCTIONEERS CHRISTCHURCH*   Price $1.50

The sale of Mona Vale's chattels.

folders, the good stuff must be in here. But the opened door revealed no stash of doubloons, no boxes of uncut gems, no canvases torn from frames. It was more paper, arrayed in piles on black velvet shelves. But these documents must at least be interesting and important, I figured, to keep them in a safe. Maybe share certificates, treasure maps, the deeds to an unknown gold mine. What I found were insurance policies, old mortgage instruments, tax records. The degree certificates for my mother and her brothers were there in several large stiffened envelopes. It was all important once, less so now.

On the bottom shelf was yet another old foolscap envelope. I held it upside down and let its contents drop to the floor. Two documents fell out. The larger was made up of the overlong plasticised pages from old photostat machines. When did they get superseded? Late 1960s? It was hard to uncurl and impossible to lay flat. I had to hold it in front of me with two hands, like a herald reading a proclamation in the town square. The first line read, 'In the Estate of Tracy Thomas Gough, Deceased' then beneath it, 'Deed of Family Arrangement'.

This was followed by 32 pages of numbered paragraphs in close-typed, fading courier font. There was the preamble: outlining the development of Tracy's complicated will, then his death and the estate he left. That's what we were dealing with here. The existence of death duties meant every life had to be valued at its end. The deed told me that 'the final balance of the Testator's estate, as assessed for death duties, was £614,651 8s and 10d'. Eight shillings and 10 pence. They were careful with that.

The deed then explained what happened after Tracy died:

AND WHEREAS disputes and doubts have arisen regarding the construction of the said Will and of the Settlement and the rights of the beneficiaries thereunder respectively and inter alia, the particular questions set out in the Schedule hereto have been raised.

AND WHEREAS it is considered preferable to interpret and apply the provisions of the said Will as far as may be legally possible in conjunction with and with the co-operation of the beneficiaries with a view to perserving harmony in the family and promoting its welfare and honour.

I also saw mention of Tracy's second wife. Her name, I learned, was Margaret. She was the mother of Owen's half-brother – of course. I gradually realised I knew her name already: people my grandfather's age at Tracy's company spoke of Peggie; by the front door of the company offices was a brass plaque announcing that a Margaret Gough had opened the building. I think I had let myself place her as a distinguished but distant relative, through age or dignity given the honour of cutting the ribbon. But no, she must've performed the duties as Tracy's widow. The deed was made on 4 October 1962, more than eight years after Tracy died. They'd been working this out for eight years?

Maybe that should have been no surprise, now that I had an idea of the scale. It felt intrusive to be combing over a dead person's finances; more so in fact than rummaging through my dead grandparents' safe or great-aunt's sideboard. But of course I was curious. I wanted to understand what it meant. Inflation adjusting does not work easily over such long periods; what people purchase changes, what people earn for what sort of work changes too. I tried using consumer inflation or house inflation but the answers didn't seem reasonable. In the end I decided to go top down. I checked the national tax statistics for the year Tracy died. From the £600,000-odd, about half went to the Crown in death duties. This sum represented more than 5 percent of the total death duties collected by the government in 1954. When the house was finally broken up it took three days to auction everything that Tracy and Julia had bought together. It was described as the collection of the late Mrs Tracy Gough, but that did not mean Julia.

The other document that had fallen from the envelope was a few pages of cream paper, covered in Avenal's handwriting. The first page was entitled 'Notes taken Sunday Morning' and dated 27 March 1955 – about nine months after Tracy's death. What followed was a list, I guessed, of items they wanted to recover from Mona Vale: mementoes of life there, keepsakes from people there. I empathised with the impulse.

The note was laid out like a lavish inventory: Louis furniture (gilt), Napoleon's dinner set, silver cutlery, Venetian glassware, gold-encrusted champagne glasses, painted vases, Dresden china; 14 or 15 Goldies. Actual inventories had been taken of ornaments: 'Man came down from the North Island & was at Mona Vale 3 weeks, listing all the time.' 'Impression from TT's conversation,' Avenal had written, 'that the furniture and chattels and the house itself were worth about £400,000–£500,000. The china and ornaments and furniture in the music room alone worth around £12,000.'

Along with the twinkle of treasure, the note was also infused with an emotion that surprised me, given my grandmother's hand. The furniture was 'bought before Miss Fife was married'. It was reconditioned 'before Miss Fife moved in'. '"Whitebait" ornament, bought before Miss Fife was married.' 'While 1st Mr & Mrs G were away, Miss Fife kept house.' At point 6, third to last, 'The first Mrs G died of a broken heart.' Then finally 'The First Mrs G. said when Miss Fife was away TTG could not have been a better husband.'

• • •

I wanted to know what had led to this moment. The natural source was Robert, the trustee, but he was trying to retire. His visits, from his point of view, had been in vain. The crumbling was already under way, just within the walls, out of sight, and it would be years until we would see it and understand, by which time it would be too late. Robert had shaken his head and sighed one last time and others, younger, had been found to take his place.

Among these was Godfrey, a friend of mine. He'd been a scholar several years below me at school, gone on to study law, been found to be brilliant and later did a master's at Cambridge. He returned from this, was made a partner at 28 and became an adviser to the bishop of Christchurch. To

Notes taken Sunday Morning   27.3.55

1. Louis furniture (gilt) bought before Miss Fife was married & soon after the family moved to Mona Vale. It was all done up & re-upholstered then. It was all there, freshly re-conditioned at party for politicians (Semple etc.) before Miss Fife moved in.

2. Lists were taken of furniture & ornaments sometime before the 1st Mrs. Gough died. Man came down from North Island & was at Mona Vale 3 weeks listing all the time. He did it for insurance purposes, & he was a man who was well up in valuing antiques. (Dunbar Sloane?)

3. Napoleon's dinner set was stated by Mr. Gough to be worth well over £1000. The figure mentioned was £1500, but it might have been a little exaggerated.

4. Possibility of property in Auckland or Wellington — house where other parts of collection were stored?

5. Confirmation of ① Real silver cutlery which was bought 2nd hand but which matched our family crest. (very valuable)
② gold encrusted champagne glasses.
③ gold encrusted amber glass dinner plates.
④ Hand painted dessert service
⑤ whole cabinet of venetian glassware (in lounge)
⑥ whole cabinet of dresden (& doulton) also in lounge.
⑦ 14 or 15 Goldie pictures. Refer to Mr. Bavistock of Canty. Society of Arts, but would have to be tactful. Suggestion of getting someone known to be _____

First page of notes, from 1955, found in the safe at Owen and Avenal's house.

prepare for his new role, Godfrey had begun delving into the family archives. I arranged to meet him for lunch and see what I could learn. He suggested the Christchurch Club, a timber tribute to Osborne House, once reserved for Canterbury's graziers, now haunted by professionals.

I was a few minutes late and Godfrey, wearing a three-piece suit, was already there, sitting in the orangery.

'You've been hunting skeletons?' he asked as I sat down. 'You must have too much time on your hands.'

'I've been tidying.'

'The whole house? Then you don't have enough time.'

'Just bits and pieces,' I replied, and then I told him about my finds. 'What can you tell me about it? What happened after Tracy's death?'

We paused and gave our orders. It was a quirk in those days that these need bear no resemblance to the menu. The downside was that sometimes what arrived bore no resemblance to your order and monthly bills bore even less resemblance to actual consumption. But everyone seemed to enjoy the mystery. When we'd ordered and wine was on its way, Godfrey thought for a moment more and then began.

'From memory, the deed's reasonably long and detailed. Everyone argued, they reached agreement. The court rubber-stamped it. What else are you interested in?'

'Just the layman's version of what led to it all, why it took so long.'

Godfrey smiled. 'I think you know that already. Tracy married twice. When he died there was a common or garden dispute over the disposition of the assets. Your grandparents and Beryl on one side, Tracy's widow on the other. A wealthy man, two wives. A stepmother, a big house. All that sort of thing.'

'Nothing more to it?'

'I'm sure it was gruesome – these things are. But they're also not uncommon. I mean, it's almost an archetype, isn't it? More Disney than Tolstoy, I'm afraid, in case that was what you were looking for?'

'I don't really have a view, or a goal. It just seems to have taken a long time, and then of course, Margaret's name was never mentioned.'

Godfrey might have shrugged. 'It's bruising. There was a lot to fight over. Even unto the plates and saucers.'

'Yes, I saw that,' I said.

'I thought you said you didn't know much about it?'

'It just seems to have taken an awfully long time to resolve, even if Napoleon's plates were at stake.'

'I take your point. But these things can be very emotional. Money always causes trouble but, adding family … It's combustible. Then or now,' he said. 'And you know lawyers: we're slow but expensive.'

'You don't know any more background?' I asked. 'I have a feeling that if Julia hadn't died, everything might have turned out differently.'

'Of course it would've. That goes without saying. A more usual lens is to think whether her death guaranteed trouble. It didn't have to.'

'I think that's what I mean. Death was one thing and tragic. But not the cause. Well, the cause in one sense but not directly. I'm not making myself very clear.'

'You're not.'

'I mean, what could have made them irreconcilable for so long?'

'I fear,' said Godfrey, 'that you're not so much hunting for skeletons as poking in dead embers hoping for flames.'

'I wouldn't even know where to look for embers. I don't even know when Julia died.'

'Don't you?' Godfrey asked.

'No. Do you?'

'No, but I know Tracy remarried during the war, early forties. It's in one of the docs, referencing his second wife and how long they'd been married.'

'Really? Early forties you reckon?'

Godfrey nodded and the soup arrived. We paused for a moment before I took up the questioning again.

'Tell me about Tracy's will then, from a legal perspective.'

'You would have read most of it in the deed, I think?'

'Yes, but I don't know how to analyse it. What about it stands out to you?'

'It's hard to judge values then by our values now, as you know.'

'Granted,' I said. 'But what does that mean?'

'Just bear it in mind. But saying this, one thing that's struck me as especially tough was the treatment of Beryl. The upshot of the will and everything that followed was the division of the spoils between your grandfather's line and that of his stepbrother. With one small but highly material exception, this was basically fifty–fifty. Half to one son, half to the other. But Tracy had one other surviving child: Beryl. All she got was an annuity.'

'Two hundred pounds a year?'

'Exactly. I mean, nice money, but a modest sort of living even then.'

'Suited to a Christian spinster maybe?' I suggested. 'Or just anti-female?'

'Actually that's a good point. It would've made more sense, by the values of the day, for Beryl to get a modest annuity if she had been married – a pretty supplement to her husband's providing. By the time of the will it would've been clear – or at least widely assumed – that Beryl wouldn't wed.'

'She would've been over thirty?'

'Yes. And as to it being more generally anti-female, remember Tracy's second wife received a lot more: a larger annuity, a gigantic capital payment, the use of Mona Vale and some shares. But not initially.'

'You mean it was personally aimed at Beryl?'

'That might be too subjective, even for me. I'd rather say that on an objective basis, Beryl got the least.'

'It makes more sense, then, that it was Beryl who initially filed the court proceedings.' I'd seen this mentioned in the deed's preamble. 'Though her end result wasn't much different, was it?'

'Oh no, it was. Let me explain a little. The word will is misleading – it's not one document. There's an original will and then three amendments. These amendments are known as codicils. Altogether these make up the will. The deed you saw is essentially the court-approved interpretation of the will, and hence basically became the will from 1962 on.'

'Got it,' I said, 'so clear.'

'Yes, well. Anyway, the last two amendments – codicils – were the ones that specifically left Beryl out. The original will gave nothing to any women – neither his widow nor his surviving daughter. Harsh by today's standards but not uncommon then and, more importantly, fair as between them. The second amendment gave Margaret capital but none to Beryl. The final amendment split Tracy's estate in three: one third for Owen, one for his stepbrother, one third for Margaret. Still nothing for Beryl other than that annuity. This third codicil was what was opposed and ultimately overturned by negotiation – leading to the deed you've seen.'

'I see. Still, it's hard to imagine Beryl as a belligerent.'

'She and Owen would have agreed some strategy for who did what. Or rather, someone would have advised them on this. They had Austen Young, from memory. He was very good. Anyway, some form of strategy is common in litigation. Beryl's formal role may not signify.'

'Out of interest, what was her formal claim?'

'The original claim? I'm not certain,' said Godfrey. 'Oddly, we've previously requested the original file from the courts but it seems to be missing.'

'Missing? Reassuring.'

'Well, it became irrelevant. The parties went into negotiation. It was the negotiation that led to the deed of family arrangement. Only stuff in there has legal standing. Anything else is just positional.'

'Interesting to know what Beryl was claiming, surely?'

'Not really. She would have said that her father hadn't made adequate provision for her – something along those lines.'

'That would have been it?'

'Depends how far the process got before they called a halt. Some of the

Looking up the Avon towards Mona Vale.

participants might have submitted affidavits. They did when the deed was agreed, for instance.'

'Do you have those affidavits?' I asked.

'The ones from 1962? I can probably get them dug out. I'll look into it.'

We had finished eating by now and moved through to have coffee on the green sofas in the anteroom. It looked east over Latimer Square and west into a small courtyard, through which well-lunched older members wobbled to their cars.

'What next, then?' asked Godfrey. 'What are you looking for?'

'Not sure, really. Maybe nothing. Just putting together pieces as I find them. I don't really know what to ask. I'm curious about Julia and Alison, though.'

'Why don't you just talk to the rest of the family?' asked Godfrey.

Yes, why not? I suppose I thought I wouldn't learn anything. Nothing had ever been said. This implied that no one knew or they didn't want to talk about it. Questioning would be either pointless or intrusive.

20

Several months after that lunch, a thick envelope arrived bearing the livery of Godfrey's law firm. Inside was a stack of papers, explained by a covering note from one of his clerks: 'This is the file from 1962 as retrieved via High Court registry from court archives. As a result, it should be the most complete and authoritative version available. It includes the Court's minute as well as the affidavits. We hope it meets your needs.'

There were a couple of hundred pages, all faded as if copies of copies of copies. There were the will and codicils, just as Godfrey had described them. There was the deed of family arrangement itself, which I'd already seen. The first new document was the notice from the court granting probate in respect of Tracy's death and estate. It was neat, innocuous, though it was interesting to see that none of Tracy's children were involved: none named, none participated, nothing about letting them know.

The next document was the minute from the judge, Justice Richmond, recording the approval of that deed of arrangement by the court, or Court, as it's always written, implying the judge is mere channel for the institution's will. Godfrey's characterisation of rubber-stamping may have downplayed it. The minute was six dense pages, outlining Richmond's reasoning for accepting the settlement as presented. 'I am quite satisfied that this is a case in which the paramount interest of all the beneficiaries particularly requires that the publicity and family disharmony likely to result from litigation be avoided.' This appeared to be a clue as to why the court process might have stalled and been replaced by negotiation – a shared fear of publicity.

Richmond continued: 'It is a fortunate feature of the situation that the funds available are of sufficient size to enable adequate provision to be made for all persons interested in the trusts.' This observation seemed correct but was uninformative as to how or why disputes and doubts had arisen. Nor did it illuminate how those played out in the years before the courtroom. 'The present application is made by the trustees, and is strongly recommended to the Court by the trustees and by all counsel.'

Tracy's will had initially specified three trustees, but one, a company executive, had been removed, leaving just two at Tracy's death: his widow, Margaret, and a solicitor named Frank Wilding, younger brother of tennis champ Anthony, who won Wimbledon four times straight before being killed in the Great War. It was to Frank and Margaret that probate had been granted after Tracy's death and now, in support of the 1962 deed of family arrangement, they both provided affidavits, which I now had.

I read Wilding's first. He gave an overview of the events and dates from Tracy's death onwards, including a summary of the allocations as originally outlined. It was a long and dry document, but its factual, almost commercial focus was informative. Wilding disclosed, for instance, that Tracy had created a further trust to hold 20 percent of the company. If he hadn't then presumably his estate would have been worth even more, let alone the chattels that Avenal had documented.

Wilding noted that he would show the judge a true summary of profits from the date of Tracy's death. It wasn't in the bundle I received but I'd found what must have been this exhibit, sitting among the papers at Owen and Avenal's. It showed that by the early 1950s the company was making several hundred thousand pounds a year. Company valuation is an arcane process but to have been able to present it as roughly equivalent to a few years' profits would have taken some intricate footwork. I imagine there were advisers that specialised in this, as there would be today. It seemed that, as Avenal suggested, Tracy may have died wealthier than was formally recorded.

Assuming Wilding can be believed – it was a sworn testimony – Tracy's first stroke took place on 4 February 1949, only about two months before my mother was born. This seems to indicate that he was still in good health when he amended his will. 'From that date until his death,' Wilding confirmed, 'he could not write or speak or conduct any business.' That is how my mother remembers Tracy. Wilding also gave information on the original court action, the file for which was otherwise lost. He mentioned that Beryl filed proceedings on 16 June 1955. That was a year after Tracy's death and just over three months after the date of the chattel list I'd found in the safe. That meeting had probably been a council of war. It was an imagined scene, but it still didn't suit them.

What Wilding went on to say was maybe more interesting – that negotiations between the parties began on 11 November 1957. That means the family was over two years, and maybe longer, officially before the courts under the aegis of Beryl's claim. You'd think there'd be some record.

Then I came to the affidavit of Tracy's widow, formerly Margaret Ann Blair, née Fife. At five pages Margaret's was a sparser document than Wilding's – but then she only needed to provide her impressions, not the legal background. It started: 'I am the widow of the above-named TRACY THOMAS GOUGH who died at Christchurch on the 3rd day of June, 1954 and I am now 56 years of age.' That made her 19 years younger than Tracy. This meant she was only six or seven years older than Alison, the same age difference as between Alison and Owen. An age gap in a second marriage is common enough but the larger revelation came in her second paragraph: 'In April, 1929 I was engaged by the said Tracy Thomas Gough as his private secretary …'

Maybe this shouldn't have come as a surprise, but it did. Tracy married an employee. It is among the most obvious and predictable relationships – which does not make them inherently any better or worse than any other form of connection. But it's such a cliché that I thought I might have heard about it, even if accompanied by a shake of the head or a grimace. I knew nothing, however, and, on reading this, now felt as if I'd just discovered a new planet while looking out the bedroom window.

I have no knowledge, though, of what Tracy thought or felt. Maybe he had long pined for Margaret, thinking his marriage to Julia a mistake. Honour for him thus lay in doing nothing about it until Julia's death freed him. Maybe Tracy was impressed by Margaret's acumen, by her efficiency. She went on to write of her extensive duties during the war. She must have been quite something, travelling round the branches, corralling engineers and salesmen into line.

If I afforded Tracy the benefit of the doubt, which I had no reason to withhold, after Julia's death he could have turned to Margaret as the only other woman with whom he spent significant time. The relationship may have evolved naturally. There's a common amalgam: widowerhood, sympathy, time spent together, probably little time with others, fondness and efficiency on at least one side.

But when a widow or widower chooses to marry someone well known to the family from an alternative, trusted role, it's naïve to think it will go smoothly. In practice the von Trapp children often prefer the untainted baroness to the familiar governess. Owen, Beryl and Alison would have grown up seeing Margaret attend to their father's business affairs. It would have been easy to interpret her reinvention as stepmother as a betrayal, and to project that more onto her than Tracy, as unfair as that might be. I can imagine the sense of discordance, of worlds inverted, and how pure shock might morph into anger and be interpreted as snobbery. *What is she doing here?*

I rang Godfrey immediately.

'Did you read these?' I asked, clutching the papers in my hand. I knew he'd guess what I was talking about.

'Hello there. What do you mean, these?' he replied, coy.

'The court file. That you sent me.'

'I had one of my juniors glance at it.'

'I'm reading it now.'

'Not easy dragging them out of central registry,' Godfrey continued, 'Almost as if they think a sixty-year-old open and shut hearing isn't that important.'

'Yes, yes. I'm very grateful. But I know you haven't read it or you'd have rung me.'

'Why's that?'

'Because you're a gossip.'

'That's slander. I'll have you know that at least once a month I allow myself a few minutes' meditation while not thinking about your family.'

'Ha! Well, what about Margaret, Tracy's second wife.'

'Yes?'

'You'll never guess what I've found about her.'

'Tell me?'

'She worked for him. She was his secretary from 1929.'

'You're right,' Godfrey said, 'I would've rung you. But you're not about to moralise, are you?'

'It's just ... I mean, marrying your secretary?'

'You are moralising. It may not be original but doesn't mean it's sinful. He was widowed, after all.'

'No wonder there was such a stoush after Tracy died. They would have been horrified.'

'Snobs.'

'Oh, come on. You know what I mean. This sort of thing never goes down well. Just being realistic. Not just Owen and Beryl. Many, many children would respond similarly.'

'Doesn't make it any more justified. It may have been the romance of both their lives.'

'Maybe.'

'Look,' said Godfrey, 'Everyone's entitled to a happy life. So she landed Tracy. He was a big boy. He could make decisions.'

'I agree – but I still doubt it would have been openly welcomed. I don't think it would have made it easier once Tracy died, let's put it that way.'

'Granted.'

'You know I never saw a photo of Tracy in my grandparents' house?'

'Look, I'd love to talk interiors with you but I have to bang my head against the wall for half an hour, so if you wouldn't mind …'

'Okay, very funny. I think it's significant, that's all.'

'People are entitled to be happy, even if it doesn't suit some others, especially those whose business it isn't. Like you, for instance.'

'We'll talk about this some more,' I said.

'I'm so looking forward to it.' And he rang off.

His advice was wise: I didn't have a right to judge, but I still felt such a relationship was predictable, in a way that Tracy generally wasn't. He was the centre of attention, the originator. This hewed unconventionally close to convention. It was explicable, but I could also see such a relationship alienating most bereaved children – not just the Owens and Beryls of the world.

Would Margaret have cared? It's always hurtful not to be wanted, but if you're a woman in the 1930s working in a large industrial concern, then you have talent and spirit. I knew Beryl and Owen were both soft, gentle, forgiving, calm, loyal, faithful, sensitive; and I extend their characteristics to Alison for want of any knowledge of her. But Beryl was a little scattered, though sharp of mind beneath it, and Owen was wise and practical but not an intellectual. They weren't the sort of people to put themselves forward. Their peers would probably not have judged them to be ambitious. I could imagine these characteristics colliding awkwardly with someone who had carved their own life and their own success. Margaret might well have thought them all spoiled, entitled and ineffectual, even complacent.

Was it a case of wicked stepmother, or was she really the plucky hard-working Cinderella, ignored by the spoilt sisters? Maybe it was somewhere in between, as it most often is. It seemed only fair to find out more about Margaret, to see the narrative from her side.

I knew Margaret was Scots. She was born in July 1905. She would have been 24 when she first got the job with Tracy. By the standards of the day, she married later than usual. Her wedding to Tracy was her first and she was 37. That itself should attest to her genuineness: she had eyes for no other.

The marriage certificate I sent away for confirmed that Margaret had been born in Glasgow. Margaret's mother was Sarah-Ann and her father was John. But her father's surname was Kane, while her mother had three surnames, at different times. She is listed as Blair at birth and then as 'Fife, formerly Kane'. The most plausible explanation is that Margaret's poor father, John, died young and that Sarah-Ann remarried. Margaret may even have been young enough that it made sense for her to take her stepfather's surname. If it was thus, it was a sad story that told of a tough life, no matter what their economic circumstances.

Emigration might have provided escape from the prospects of Glasgow, as it had done for Charles from Birmingham. I tried checking passenger lists of arrivals but never found her. The only ones I discovered were much later, when Margaret was travelling to the United States with Tracy, first in the late 1930s as his secretary, and in the 1940s as his wife.

At the end of her paragraph nine Margaret recorded: 'I became married to the said Tracy Thomas Gough on June 17th, 1942.' The wedding date was only 18 months after the last photo I had of Julia, at Owen's engagement. That wasn't a problem on its own, but when, then, did Julia die? A year of widow or widowerhood was both social norm and accepted minimum and, frankly, was a longer time proportionately then, when life expectancy was about 61 for men and 65 for women.

I was discussing all this recently with a priest friend. He has stopped sending cards to widows and widowers on the first anniversary of their bereavement because he's found that so many are by then part of a couple. Ever compassionate, he explains it thus: a quick second marriage is not a betrayal of, but a tribute to, the first. The bereaved was so happily married that he or she tries to find the same again as soon as possible. It was common that this might be a friend of the deceased or, historically, even a sibling. Almost all widows or widowers are sad and lonely. Their life can never be remotely the same, while even their children may eventually return to their own lives, or embark on new ones: as Owen was doing.

The rest of Margaret's testimony was devoted to her career in Tracy's service: appointed office manager in 1936, general manager in 1938 and so on. This history was delineated to show that she contributed to Tracy's material success, and that of his company, as much as anyone. Fair enough, everyone had to argue their own corner.

Margaret probably didn't need the war to advance her, but it might have helped all the same. Male mobilisation provided unexpected working

Owen (left with arms crossed) in the Royal New Zealand Air Force during World War II, likely at Wigram Air Base, c. 1943.

opportunities for women. Margaret, already in place and on the up, seems to have accelerated her career. Enlistment might have removed people above her but it also gave her a greater challenge to meet and by which to prove herself. It sounds as if she did so. And unlike many women, who lost their work when the war ended, Margaret's position was secure before the conflict was over: 'On March 27th 1945, I was appointed Managing Director and Secretary.'

That date was a Tuesday, as it happened. The Red Army was preparing to besiege Berlin, the Americans were in Germany and Churchill had briefly crossed the Rhine. International papers were carrying headlines like: 'This is the Collapse', 'British Armour Racing Through Open Country', 'Disintegration Follows the Great Collapse', 'Allied Armies Pour Through Smashed Line'. In short, the end of the war was seen as close to inevitable. Owen, I know, was in the air force. The chances for his demobilisation and return to civilian life, to his father's company (his previous employment), are as high as they've ever been. But now when he leaves he will find that his father's secretary is not only his stepmother but also his boss. Maybe it's just coincidence and it just happens to be near the end of the war. But I would say that any acceleration in Margaret's career could be taken poorly by any serving son. Maybe Owen didn't take it personally. Maybe he did.

· · ·

Owen's affidavit was the last document in the pack and he began with a lost family:

> I, OWEN TRACY GOUGH, of the City of Christchurch make oath and swear as follows:
>
> THAT I am the only son of the first marriage of Tracy Thomas Gough of Christchurch (hereinafter referred to as 'the deceased') who died at Christchurch on the 3rd day of June, 1954,
>
> THAT the deceased was twice married, my mother, Julia Daisy Hill Gough, having predeceased him.
>
> THAT there were three children of the marriage of the deceased and my mother, namely Alison Mavis Gough, Beryl Daisy Gough and me, this deponent.
>
> THAT my elder sister, Alison Mavis Gough, never married, and also died prior to the deceased, without leaving any dependants.

It was all not much more than I already knew, other than for Alison. I suppose it was implicit that she'd died before my mother was born in 1949, but I hadn't known. Now it was at least certain that Alison was dead by June 1954.

Owen went on to cover his own life: birth at Sumner, Christ's College, joining his father's business: he worked there for almost six years before the air force. Then Owen came to Tracy's second marriage: 'my father, the deceased, married Margaret Ann Blair Fife, then a spinster, who had been employed by him in a secretarial and then a managerial capacity for many years … There is one child of that marriage, namely Blair Tracy Gough, who was born on the 5th day of August, 1946.' Owen, or his lawyer, wanted to make it clear that Tracy married his employee. He considered it significant. He felt, I reckon, angry about it and that it would reflect poorly on Margaret's claims. Owen would, however, perhaps have been upset about Tracy remarrying anyone.

After stating that he served in the RNZAF until 5 September 1945, Owen noted that 'upon my discharge my father re-employed me as a member of the company and I was posted to the workshops in Sydenham in the said city of Christchurch'. Owen's wartime service meant he was short of commercial experience and so arguably was not qualified to take on a more senior role when he returned to his father's firm. When he did go back, after three years in the air force, it had been Margaret's company for about five months.

Owen joined as a mechanic. He wrote: 'the company owns a demonstration farm, Matata, situated in the north of the country.' A demonstration farm was almost exactly that: somewhere prospective customers could come and watch how the machines worked. They needed space and distance so the machines could rumble about. Matatā is still just a little seaside settlement, not far from Whakatāne.

Owen continued: 'In the month of February 1946 I was sent to this farm with my wife and baby and we lived in a caravan.' I remembered hearing of this episode from my mother. Avenal had once told her that soon after they were married they lived in a caravan surrounded by nothing but mud. I think they were there for 18 months. It seemed an unusual way to welcome Owen back. He was de-mobbed less than five months before he was sent off to the middle of nowhere. The first child Owen refers to, my oldest uncle, would have been 18 months old. And this little family arrived at the caravan just as summer was finishing. No wonder Avenal recalled mud. In winter it would have been everywhere; they would have been sloshing through it to an unplumbed caravan while Tracy and his second wife lived at Mona Vale. It felt like nothing less than banishment. Owen hadn't taken the hint about rejoining the company on the lowest rung; now he was sent to its remotest outpost.

I found it interesting that Margaret didn't mention the birth of her son; only Owen did. This child was born about six months after Owen's move. I was feeling rather sorry for Owen by now and so wondered if this, too, was significant. At that time pregnancy was commonly diagnosed via what was called 'physician observation'. This meant the doctor blending a visual inspection with knowledge of any menstrual changes and nausea and other common signs. It was neither accurate nor efficient and it meant pregnancies were confirmed much later than they are today: the standard was at about the three-month mark. That would have been exactly the time Owen was posted to the wilderness. Anything in it? I'll never know. But bearing a child is the sure-fire way to secure a throne, and remove any requirement to treat with their previous heir presumptive. Occam's razor would say it was just coincidence, nothing sinister. Tracy himself might have initiated the move to Matatā – toughen you up, Owen.

The thought of Owen in his little Christchurch flat – it's mentioned elsewhere in the document as his and Avenal's first marital home – and then in the caravan made me feel guilty about living in his house, sitting in his library, driving his car. It also made me think of how I saw him, how

I represented him, including in the eulogy: the suits, the hats, the sailing, the serenity. That serenity might not have come without significant effort, without management of his memories and his emotions. The novelist Amor Towles makes the point that to have, then lose, leaves people much wiser about the world and its vanities in a way not shared by the newly or solely successful. I suppose it's learning what we now call resilience. This is what Owen had, and it manifested itself as a well-mannered equanimity in all situations.

21

After a year and a half of working from home, I decided I needed a change. I was into my thirties and didn't think I could carry on standing by an upside-down box, just talking to myself and a computer. I got a more conventional job at an office in town, more finance stuff. Then a few of us set up our own firm together. We were four: William, Alan, Sally and me, working out how to run our own business for the first time and telling people they should take our advice. I'd just got married, too, to the girl who'd arrived in Beijing. I was growing up, but we stayed at Owen and Avenal's: the two of us and Daphne, the dog.

My colleagues and I had set up shop in the cheapest space we could find, a pair of tiny panelled rooms, three floors up a stone tower in the Arts Centre, which had once been the old university. My mother had attended lectures here before the whole place decamped to the suburbs. Lord Rutherford had studied below us and his old rooms were now a museum. Opposite these was a café that sold excellent sausage rolls. At the far corner of the old campus the former student union – where they'd run a recruiting station in World War II – was now a bar.

What could be better than a stone tower, even if we ruined it by working there? Its size meant we paid per year what most people did per month. Our fridge, kettle and server sat above one another, vying for limited power sockets. There was no heating but there were high ceilings and sun poured in through Gothic windows. To the north, Christchurch's ornamental tram chimed on its loop of what approximated the old town. Below us was a small lawn outside the Court Theatre. Over the road, to the west, were the Canterbury Museum, the Botanic Gardens and, further along, the lantern of the Christ's College dining hall, peering above its finials.

Occasionally I'd cycle in – down Glandovey Road as far as the train tracks, then south on the bike path that ran beside them. I'd cross Fendalton

Road and then on my left the high brick wall of Mona Vale began. I'd ride alongside the grounds to the back gate and turn off towards Hagley Park. Then it was almost total quiet: trees, golf course, river, shallow Lake Victoria – a giant bathtub really, built for model boats. Before passing through the Mickle Gates onto Rolleston Avenue, I'd glide past the back of my old boarding house looking out over the Avon and Hagley Park. Its front was stone and Gothic, but here, at the rear of the building, it was faded brick and Georgian, with one of the finest views in Christchurch.

From the edge of the park it was a short distance to the office. I'd go past my old school's front gates, the same view of the quadrangle that I'd snatched from the back of Owen's car, past the museum and into Worcester Boulevard, the long street that looked straight down to the cathedral.

The first earthquake, the September one in 2010, came early on a Saturday morning in the dark. The noise, as almost everybody remarked later, was like a freight train at close quarters. Every item in the house moved. Glass trembled against glass, tables slid, pictures shuddered on walls, even clothes rustled their compliance with tectonics. I think the very weatherboards clattered.

I woke, turned to my startled wife – southern England is not prone to quakes – and said, 'We're best off in bed.' It was the first thing that came to mind. It proved incorrect, but we were lucky. Once the shaking stopped, I stepped into the upstairs hall. The chandelier was swinging through almost 180 degrees, one second pointing at Avenal's portrait, the next at Owen's. It was a violent, tinkling pendulum calling time.

The drama woke the day. As the light arrived, the city and surrounding countryside found widespread destruction. The impact seemed most acute on Canterbury's older institutions: stone churches, brick homesteads. Many of these were damaged beyond repair. The epicentre was west of the city in the farming hinterland, where the fault had ripped open paddocks, moved fences and bent train tracks.

But, remarkably, neither in the city nor the country was there loss of life. For this, at least, people counted their blessings, and as this information spread so too did the sense of a close call, bordering on a miracle. Everyone had been awake since the shake and friends arrived early, driving by to swap experiences. I donned a fez and cooked breakfast on a barbecue. Then I called other friends – everyone might be shaken but they could recount their stories jovially, self-deprecatingly almost. Most of our friends, younger, childless then, were groggy from the night before. One of the few with children had crawled under his daughter's cot, not knowing what was going on but trying to respond to his wife's shouted order to 'go to the children's room'. Many of them had damage to attend to, but they all knew it was better than it might have been.

At our home the casualties were decorative and insubstantial only, or so we thought until a few days later when a friend and I climbed onto the roof to seek the source of some rubble that had fallen to earth. Up there, the two of us still swaying with the aftershocks, I saw that our three-bay chimney, about 1.5 metres wide and 2 metres high, had snapped off and landed flat above our bed. We'd been saved by Owen's sense of make do. He'd never removed old roofs – just laid new ones on top. There were sarking boards, corrugated iron and then tin tiles on top. The three layers sandwiched together were strong enough to hold several tonnes of Canterbury brick.

It was different five months later. September hadn't been a close call, it had been a mighty warning shot. The February quake didn't happen at night. It erupted in the middle of a weekday. Like a lot of people, I was at work.

On that day, 22 February 2011, it was just William and me in the office. Alan was out of town for a meeting and Sally had popped out to the shops. It was warm in our small office. Our high windows were open and several floors below us we could hear a primary school group discussing a series of statues that lined the road and the tram clattering past.

The first jolt was sharp, out of nowhere. Often you can hear an earthquake roll in; there's a second to brace as you wonder if it's a large truck or a train before you realise that the land itself is trembling. We didn't get that on 22 February. Just a shock. Then a pause of a second or two and then a massive tumble of falling and shaking that pulled the room apart.

William claims I pushed him out of the way in the race to the doorframe. I say that, being younger and a quicker thinker and mover I got there first and that he then grabbed me, one hand either side of my waist, as he struggled to stand upright and we briefly became a two-person conga line: me holding onto the door jamb, William holding onto me. I remember thinking that we must look silly, amidst noise and mayhem, two grown men dancing badly in a doorway.

The shaking stopped. A stone pillar had collapsed and fallen through the window above my desk. Our room was full of dust held aloft in the light. It was immensely quiet. No more voices reached us from the ground.

'That felt deadly,' said William.

'We've got to get out of here.' Perhaps we both said this. We all knew about aftershocks. All of Christchurch knew about aftershocks, which could finish buildings off and make bad decisions final ones. We knew we were three floors up in a room made of brick and stone, but it's a measure of how uncritically we'd assessed September that we'd never even thought of moving somewhere safer.

The narrow corridor to the stairs was blocked by a large wire sculpture that had fallen from its plinth and we pulled and tossed it out of the way. We'd never liked it. Then we could go as fast as possible, bolting round corners, swinging open doors, flying downstairs.

That front quad, itself dangerous enough, felt like a wide open space of safety, but no sooner had we emerged onto it than William started worrying about work.

'We need to go back and get our stuff,' he said.

'You know that sentence is the start of a story that never has a good ending, right?' I said.

'It will make our lives a lot easier.'

'It's a stupid thing to do.' We both knew it was stupid.

'We'll be quick,' he said.

And so we turned around and went straight back in. Vaulting two, three steps at a time as the dust and plaster fell, we reached our office and grabbed what we could, filled our satchels and ran back down. We were silly, and very lucky.

And the aftershocks kept coming.

'What now?' I asked.

'We wait until we can get out, and we get out.'

All around us the stone buildings started to crumble, exposing us to falling masonry. The easiest escape route was under a buckling archway. We could see the Botanic Gardens and safety on the other side but chunks of limestone kept dropping from it. Every other route took us deeper into the complex or back inside.

The ground kept wobbling and at times it was hard to keep our balance. I became mesmerised by the Great Hall. With each new rumble it expanded like a bellows, then contracted. Each judder made it inflate fractionally more than the last time so that it must soon burst and rain rock and rubble over all of us. But I kept watching, standing still, satchel over my shoulder. I doubt it is a sight I will ever see again – inhale, exhale, inhale, exhale – a giant stone building breathing in tune with the flexing land. Beside me William was worried about getting to his family. I had fewer concerns, with no children then and my wife out of town. As the moments passed and the violence of the aftershocks subsided, the hall finally settled and was still, out of breath.

In the quad near us was a large touring party of retired Americans in polo shorts and white baseball caps who had tumbled out of the café and in between shakes were trying to navigate that archway to freedom. They would gather, gaze upwards, wait for a gap in the trembling and then run through in ones and twos. It was almost as mesmerising as watching the Great Hall. They all got through safely. They must have been terrified. Older and less mobile, they were more vulnerable than me.

Despite the crumbling, William decided he needed to go now too. It had only been five or maybe 10 minutes since the first quake, but we knew the traffic was going to jam and his family would be worried, knowing the sort of building he worked in. He shot off, heading out the back towards his car, and I was on my own. The arch looked stable and the gaps between shakes was moving from seconds to minutes so I went through and crossed Rolleston Avenue to the gardens.

There were hundreds of people there already and more pouring in. Everyone was quiet, just walking in slowly or standing in small groups talking in hushed voices. I saw two convivial barristers I knew who shared chambers. One was in a black fedora. But since they seemed to be consoling other colleagues, I kept my distance.

I managed, finally, to reach my wife, who had been in a meeting out of town. She figured I was just calling to chat, and she'd ring me back later. It took multiple calls for her to guess it might be important.

'There's been an earthquake,' I said.

'Another one? How's it all?' She was smiling, I could tell. She was having a nice time. The news wasn't out yet, and September had shown us destruction without bloodshed.

'No. A big one. It's bad.'

'Where are you?'

'Gardens,' I said.

'What are you doing?'

'Still working it out. I dunno. Go home, I guess.'

'What do you want me to do?'

'You stay there. I'll let you know how things go. I should be able to ring more easily from the landline at home.'

'You be safe.'

After this the phone lines began to clog, my battery started to die. I couldn't contact anyone. I couldn't go to work. I didn't have a car. I realised that I had nothing to do but walk home, but I still put it off for a while, almost like I didn't want to leave the scene of the enormity but also, frankly, a little lazy about walking.

After a time I left the gardens by the way I'd entered, out the main gates next to the museum. William Rolleston had fallen backwards off his pedestal, as if a bickering fellow politician had given him a blow to his chest. He was heavy – marble – and the force had embedded him into the pavement, decapitating him in the process. Later someone took the head for safekeeping. I saw a photo: written in marker on Rolleston's neck, alongside a phone number, was the note, 'My head is at Christ's College.' I know, old boy, I know.

On that day I couldn't have told you if the statue was Rolleston or FitzGerald or some other worthy, but I stood near its diagonal body and looked straight down Worcester Boulevard. The view should have ended at the cathedral's door but instead there was a dust cloud. You couldn't see anything of the city. In the foreground, people in dark suits walked towards me and the safety of the gardens' open space. Like those behind me already there, they were all quiet, their pace slow. Some were covered in dust and silt.

Then a young woman ran up to me through the crowds, eyes red and cheeks damp. She was my colleague Alan's youngest sister, Melanie.

'Where's Alan? Is he okay?' she asked.

'He's not at work today. He's at a meeting in Auckland.'

'Oh, I was worried. I couldn't get hold of him.'

'He's maybe still on the plane even,' I said, 'that's probably why.'

'Oh, that's great,' she said and, seeming a lot happier, she left to make her own way home. I think she was heading across the park too.

I carried on walking down the boulevard, but only as far as our office, looking across at it from the other side of the road. There was no crushed school group beneath our windows. They must have moved so fast. A miracle, as the stone gable above our office had fallen off and landed where they'd been standing. It had exposed the Court Theatre's costume store and I looked up and saw colourful gowns and cloaks fluttering on racks above the broken windows of our office, like the last banners of a ruined castle.

I retraced my steps to Rolleston Avenue. Usually quiet, the road was filled with the cars of people anxious to get home or to schools. I wasn't going to achieve anything standing there so I set off to walk home.

I passed Christ's College first. The dust of more smashed limestone was spread around the quad and on the slanting roofs slate avalanches had exposed thick, chocolate-coloured rafters. I paused for moments only. The place had obviously already been evacuated – it was empty of humans, which gave the sense that this damage had been done slyly, while no one was looking. I read later that several old boys went that day to see how the school had fared. One was a 93-year-old, who cycled over from his retirement home on Park Terrace to check. You would think that such a large collection of old stone buildings would collapse and people would need help, but the main danger had come from a falling angel. One of the corbels holding a hammerbeam in the dining hall had been dislodged and had flown to the ground, his fall only broken by the stone book he held permanently open across his chest.

I carried on down the road and was soon back at Hagley Park. By the entrance some enormous trees – cedars or macrocarpas maybe – had been ripped from the ground and lay on their sides. There were now two wide riverbanks, and the Avon itself, between me and the traffic, which I could see was heavy and halting, but the noise was dulled by distance and by weeping willows in leaf. There was no one else around and it was peaceful and I stood there a moment looking at these trees, torn from clay craters and lying with their roots exposed in giant knotted circles.

For some reason, instead of cutting straight across the park – the shortest way home – I followed the path around the edge that follows the Avon's course. It's the way we'd always had to run at school. The river was normally shallow and clear, the bottom weeds always visible, but that afternoon it was brown and swollen.

It's about a kilometre from where I entered to the north edge of the park, and the whole way I can't remember seeing anyone. At the Harper Avenue corner I rejoined the rest of the world for a minute, waiting to cross. Here it seemed like any other day, the traffic thick but moving and no other obvious changes. Then I was over the other side of the road and into the heavily oaked outcrop of park known as Little Hagley. In spring it's carpeted with daffodils and bluebells. My mother once told me they were first planted when she was a girl. At Helmores Lane I turned over the bridge – later deemed unsafe and closed – and into Merivale. From here I carried on along familiar streets. I was only steps from town but it was almost as quiet as the park, quieter than usual in fact.

It took me about an hour to get home. Finally rounding the gates onto the driveway, I could hear the alarm blaring but otherwise all looked normal. Only Daphne, our dog, was out of place. She'd curled up on herself in the middle of the front lawn, about the spot where Marcus sat for Avenal in the photo I had found.

I felt guilty that I hadn't thought of her till now. Earthquakes made her bolt. She seemed to think the land was only trembling precisely where she was, and so if she moved elsewhere she'd be better off. She'd been petrified enough to vault the fence that confined her to the back garden. This was otherwise impossible: she weighed nearly 70 kilos and was as limber as pig iron. In performing this feat, she had somehow avoided being flattened by the rear chimney that collapsed onto the laurel bower right where she would have leapt.

She'd obviously been thinking of me, which made me feel guiltier, and came to lean against my leg – you had to hold your balance with her weight resting below your centre of gravity – and ask for a rub. As I told her everything was fine I realised that, in the rush, I'd left my house keys at the office. So Daphne and I stood there side by side, like Marcus and Avenal, looking at the house while the alarm blared and wondering what to do next.

Together we walked closer and I planted my face against the windows to see inside. All the paintings were on angles or on the floor. The dining room was carpeted with the sharp remnants of the china from which my grandparents and I ate roasts, while all their crystal had been reduced to sparkly dust, like very expensive glitter. But one of the dining room windows had popped open and when a friend happened to pass by soon after, doing the rounds on a pushbike to see if everyone was okay, I levered him through and he opened the front door before continuing on his way. I was grateful.

I kept Daphne outside and walked around. The kitchen was the worst. Every cupboard was open and crockery, glass, food, oils and aromatic sauces (soy, oyster, fish) were joined in unholy alliance on the floor. In the drawing room there had been mass casualties among the Meissen figurines. The library chimney had compound fractured. Bricks were appearing through the wall and had collected in a heap in the grate. I didn't want to think what that indicated. Books were everywhere.

Some internal walls were slumping, the lath and plaster drooping within them and collecting as paunches above the skirting boards. The stairway was covered in dust released by cracks in the walls and ceilings. My grandparents' portraits were still hanging perfectly straight, looking at one another with their usual calm amusement. The saddest was the clock. It had lunged forward, smashed into the bannister and then onto the floor, where it lay in pieces.

Beryl's black slate clock fared worse. It had jumped off its shelf and exploded into an unrepairable, unrecoverable number of pieces. I kept it for years before realising there was no saving it and tossing it away. My mother reproached me for it though, and later I ended up searching for and finding a similar replacement second hand – it just wasn't Beryl's.

Upstairs a chimney was leaning into a bedroom, held in place only by wallpaper. My grandmother's dresser, heavy wood, had been flipped up in the air and spun some distance, smashing its mirror. This pattern was repeated all over the house with glass panes cracked where the pressure of compacting doorways found a weakness. Doors themselves were popped or shunted open, not to be shut again for many years. At the bottom of the garden the Wendy house was shorn in two, the roof clipped from the walls but still sitting in place.

Once I'd looked all over the house, my first actual action, shameless materialist that I am, was to take Owen's old car out of the cracked and tumbling garage and, sacrilege, put it on the lawn. Someone must have swung the satellites our way that day: for years afterwards the aerial image for the house showed the car on the lawn, ready to be packed up, ready to flee. Yet apart from this when I looked out the window, nothing was changed.

It was one of the numerous small oddities that my father was down for work, a day-long conference. A further oddity was that I hadn't really thought about it until he got through on the landline shortly after I arrived home. He'd been at lunch near the airport and they'd all ducked under tables, he said, and they were now heading back into town to Lancaster Park, where the conference was being held. It sounded as if it would just carry on. This seemed to become a theme: there'd been a shock but just a few kilometres from the city centre people had no idea of the severity. I knew other visitors that day who'd been at the university. After their event broke up they walked down Riccarton Road and across the park into town, only there to learn of the destruction.

'I don't think you should go back there,' I said to Dad, 'the town's been totalled.'

'They think it's okay. Apparently we're going to drive around the edges.'

This is what they tried, not very successfully, to do. They met chaotic traffic and damaged streets. By the time they reached the venue it had already been cordoned off and so they headed back to the airport. We spoke again.

'I might have to stay the night,' he said. 'Can you come and collect me?'

'I don't think you want to stay here. It's a complete mess. I don't even know if the water is on.'

Owen and Avenal's house after the 2011 earthquake. The rear chimney is missing, boarded up. Robin Hood Oak's lower branches are in the top right-hand corner.

'Well, there might be the chance of a flight.'

'If there is, I think you should take it.'

'I'd still like to see the house.'

I drove out and collected him. This might've been around four o'clock. By now news was creeping out about the liquefaction that was swamping east Christchurch, of the army asserting themselves at major intersections, of the scale of the destruction. It was known by then that whole buildings in the city centre had collapsed. Families were said to be already leaving town, driving north, south, west, anywhere to get away.

I brought Dad back to the house and through the front door. As soon as he entered he realised but took a few seconds to absorb it all.

'Mummy will be very sad,' he said.

Just on dusk I dropped him back with the conference, which was having some luck arranging movement back to Wellington. As I left him there, he in the carpark, me on the move, his expression was the same one I've seen when I've been heading somewhere unusual, possibly unsafe, on holiday.

'Where are you going to stay?' he asked.

'A friend's invited me to his parents' place in North Canterbury.' That friend had also popped by briefly with his wife, also doing the rounds to check on people. They could, they said, because their house was newer, less

Christchurch Cathedral following the February 2011 earthquake. FLIKR WIKI

wobbly, and they didn't have any damage themselves. They helped me to sweep up some crystal before they headed to the country.

'I can take Daphne,' I continued to Dad. 'I'll drive up there later this evening. Hopefully the traffic will have calmed down by then.'

Then it was proper twilight: still, peaceful, no wind. If I hadn't known that hundreds, maybe thousands of people were leaving town, would I have sensed it? It seemed quieter than usual, even on these usually calm suburban roads. Only a few kilometres away, back the way I'd walked, all was chaos. My experience had been acute but I'd been fortunate and the worst was over. For so many others it had been deadly and for their families the worst was just beginning.

I waited until after nine to leave Christchurch and spent the time tidying. The earthquake had made a lot of decisions for me, and the house would eventually look very different, but that afternoon it felt I was like fighting back an avalanche with a teaspoon. Sometimes the landline would ring, people looking for friends because other lines were jammed. I took messages and said I'd try to pass them on.

As the night came in the tidying felt lonely and pointless, given the scale of the work needed. I loaded Daphne into the back of the car and left. My friend's parents' house was in the countryside about 45 minutes north of Christchurch, surrounded by immaculate gardens. All their plumbing worked. They hadn't felt much at all, they said. I only stayed a night, though. The earthquake had bent many doors and windows at our house and rendered them unshuttable so I didn't want to leave the place unattended for long. I was also worried about what Daphne's ablutions would do to my friends' emerald lawns. So I had a good night's sleep, woke with the dog and left early, still trying to work out what to do, and not looking forward to what lay within the house or within the city.

22

In the months and years that followed you heard many people say out loud, 'I'm glad they didn't live to see this.' *They* were people already gone, people who had perhaps lived their whole lives in Christchurch, so much of which was now disappearing in this disaster and its aftermath. We were glad our grandparents or parents or elderly friends weren't around. But how lucky we were to have the luxury of such reflections. To be still there ourselves.

Old brick houses disintegrated. Timber, more common for our houses, fared better. The city's tallest building was displaced by half a metre and dropped at one corner by more. Worst of all, of course, were the collapsed high-rises, the fires, the falling, crushing rubble, the scores of people trapped. Within a fortnight the prime minster was saying at least 10,000 houses would require demolition. The cathedral was left a spireless ruin. The original buildings of St George's Hospital, where my mother and all her brothers were born, had to be demolished. At the Arts Centre they took the stone turrets off and placed them on the street. The low-rise unreinforced masonry commercial buildings with Italianate airs that made up large parts of the centre of town disappeared en masse.

The first few days after the earthquake I tried to neaten the house and make good. Builders used a broom handle to snap off the remains of the rear chimney. It came away in one piece. Nothing had held it in place. They patched the gash with ply, then put bracing through the hallway and around the remaining internal chimney, the one that poked into a bedroom. After the builders left, I felt the house must be safer, but it looked much worse. I could step through the front door and hang my coat from the bare timber posts holding up the ceiling. Similar measures were multiplied a thousand-fold throughout the city.

While the builders propped, I tidied, trying to put aside the daze of the day itself. I started in the kitchen, mopping up gelatinous gloop with wads of newspaper. In the dining room I tossed the sharp triangles of crockery into a box to go to the tip. I kept a few small pieces: of a bunny bowl from childhood, of a fine white plate. Years later I took them back to a curio shop near where I used to live in Beijing and they made them into shard boxes – bits of china set into lacquer or silver. They'd mastered the art during the Cultural Revolution when Red Guards smashed old vases and bowls and families scrabbled to salvage physical memories.

In the library I picked up lines of books, a hand on each end as if holding a concertina, and stuffed them back whence they fell. I tried to right the pictures and ignored the bricks gathered in the hearth. The last of Tracy's Goldies from Mona Vale was still on a wall. I covered it in bubble wrap and gave it to a friend who'd secured a ticket on a flight out. He took it in his hand luggage and said he felt like a Frenchman fleeing the Directoire. Another friend drove down from Auckland in his lorry-sized car to help. We loaded the boot with other pictures, stacked flat, one on top of the other, with blankets in between. Then he took them north, flowing with the streams of traffic which left the city every day that first week.

That left everything else broken, dusty, irreparable. I gave up on salvage and resigned myself to disposal: furniture, lamps, broken books (how?), broken frames, broken glass, figurines smashed to smithereens. The past is hidden in some material object, wrote Proust. I had always agreed with this, and liked to think this view was more than just camouflage for hoarding.

But now the weight of retention was too great. The only way to think of it all was as meaningless detritus. Anything else created too much sadness and heightened the sense of loss rather than compensating for it. And anyway, among the wreckage of a city and of lives, thoughts of what possessions to keep felt tawdry; an undeserved privilege. Everyone was sweeping treasures into trash cans while mere kilometres away, hundreds of people were trying to pull bodies from buildings or resuscitate them, or make a bridge or a road safe, or remove rising filth from living rooms and driveways. I lost objects. A hundred and eighty-five families, it later emerged, lost something infinitely more precious; 115 died in one single terrible building.

There were orders to stay away from the centre of town. They set up a red zone and entry was banned. There was a curfew. The defence force conducted its largest home operation and armoured vehicles appeared at major intersections to deal with the curious or the amateur helpful. Overseas police and search and rescue workers were flown in. A national emergency was declared for only the second time in Canterbury's history; the first time was the previous September. The sewerage was assumed to be damaged city-wide. Lucky it was summer and gardens sufficed.

In the absence of wives and families who left town to escape the continuously trembling earth, what formed among my friends was a bachelor colony as we grouped together in fives and sixes at a few houses deemed the least affected. The previous year's earthquake had been more widespread. This one was concentrated in the central city and the eastern suburbs, which were hit hard. There the liquefaction was worst, the land becoming slushier, houses slumping, water levels rising, roads and pipes unworkable. Portaloos were delivered by the hundreds.

The western side of the city escaped lightly. On some streets near us almost nothing had changed, unless you looked closely at the houses and could see a tell-tale missing chimney or bolted gates. I returned to work within a day or two, sitting on my friend's sofa, a computer on my lap. The first food outlet to reopen, which we heard of via friends, was a takeaway pizza shop on Harewood Road. Pizza began to form a large part of our diet.

The exodus – and the damage – meant the roads were now empty. The town was deeply wounded but the emptiness made it eerie, like New York in August, like someone in shock who has sat down to process. The evenings were still long and warm, there was nowhere else to go and in the suburbs of the north the closest we got to the chaos and the destruction was the sound of a helicopter skating low against the blue as it sent us pictures to watch on our television sets.

Into the surrealism came odd snippets beamed from beyond barriers only kilometres away. On the TV news one day the reporter, live to camera, said they'd just driven through an intersection where an obviously drunk man, wearing a Michael Jackson wig and eating an ice cream, was directing traffic with a magic wand. It worked. Then they cut to a singlet-clad young man with a thin moustache. He recounted how his shop had collapsed, then pointed down the block. The camera followed. He explained in a deadpan voice that his brother-in-law's premises had suffered the same fate. He'd been a fortune teller, we were told, but he hadn't seen this coming. Two or three nights later we watched live as a floodlit excavator ripped through the roof of the Christchurch Club, looking for someone apparently, though that quickly turned out to have been a rumour. There was a lot of rumour in those days.

The aftershocks kept coming. Over 360 that first week, I read. We weren't counting, but you got used to them. It was easier to be confident in a wooden house surrounded by garden and knowing that no one you knew was in danger. The rescue operation in the centre of town worked around the clock for that first week, gradually revealing the scale of the human loss. Then the search was recategorised as recovery, and the funerals began.

In the end, we left Christchurch too. Our move had been planned before the earthquake struck. My wife had found a new job in Wellington. She was due to start soon. We'd been on the lookout for a house there for ages and had found one two weeks earlier. It was low and made of timber, with rooms that didn't make sense and doors wherever you didn't need them. It had a tin roof and a garden straight out of Canterbury: hydrangeas, rhododendrons, a spreading magnolia by a green gate like the one left open for guests to the garden party in one of the paintings at Owen and Avenal's. The tenders were due 23 hours after the earthquake. It would have been hard to carry on living in Owen and Avenal's house even if we'd wanted to, with its chimneys peering into rooms and its drains flooding, but it also felt ridiculous to seek out another earthquake zone. Yet we did, and moved in on April Fool's Day.

• • •

Initially I returned to Christchurch each week. I'd go to work and stay in Owen and Avenal's ruined house, like Lampedusa in Palermo was how I tried to cheer myself. Office space was impossible to find and my colleagues and I ended up in an internal windowless room in a paint shop, among factories, opposite a skateboarding park. Still, we were better off than many. Only the living can complain.

This was the routine: arrive, taxi to house, meet the loss adjuster, discuss progress (nil), point things out, get quotes, discuss more issues; cross town in Owen's old car and try and concentrate amid the fumes, then back to the house, broken, lonely, to stay the night; potter on my own in the dimness and continue the tidy-up, a shard at a time.

And throwing things out – box after box, skip after skip. The hardest was that dresser of Avenal's. Smashed, too hard to repair. My efforts only ever felt like tinkering in a house not just crowded but smashed up too. The place would have to be completely pulled apart to be put back together again, and when the time came for repair there was so much that would need to be cleared. Even if I was just killing time between contractors, throwing more out would help.

In this way I came upon an old leather satchel. It had always been there, on the floor in the same small bedroom. I'd even touched it once, to move it to one side to clear space for a friend to come to stay. But like the safe in the study, it formed part of the landscape and I thought nothing more of it. Now that landscape had been changed and everything stood out, everything was reviewable. The satchel's leather was so dry and worn it flaked to the touch and looked as though it would disintegrate in a stiff breeze. I assumed it contained the usual ensemble of invoices, statements and other now pointless paper, but I'd learnt some caution. As I picked it up and looked at it more closely than I'd ever done before, I noticed Owen's initials, 'OTG', embossed in fading gold on the flap. Did he drop it in here the day he retired, never to look at it again?

The straps were rigid with age but I managed to open it without snapping them. Inside I found receipts for school fees, a motoring magazine and several old bills. All as expected. There was also a small paper bag, the sort you'd put sandwiches in. It was bulky and I opened it expecting more receipts. Instead it was a bundle of old letters in small envelopes, covered in flowing script. The postmarks were blurred, but I could make out that they all seemed to be from the 1930s and 1940s. Almost all were addressed to Owen, and from the handwriting I could tell they were mostly from his sister Beryl, with Avenal a close second.

I paused. How much time needs to pass to elevate nosiness to research? The archaeologist doesn't worry about poking his nose into a pharaoh's bedroom but it's more sensitive when the timescale is less epochal. Reading someone's letters without permission on the day they arrive? That's espionage. Reading them 70 years later? That, I decided, is history.

The paper was wafer-thin, folded into tiny squares to fit. The writing was in pencil or frail pen, which was fading or smudged and hard to read. I started with the ones I thought were from Avenal. They seemed to cover the reinitiation of her friendship with Owen. Her family had moved away from Christchurch and she now wrote to Owen at his home in Sumner. These were all dated the mid- to late 1930s. They hadn't made it to Mona Vale yet. It wasn't clear how Avenal and Owen met again, nor how long they had been out of contact, but it seemed to be recent. Avenal says how nice it is to be in touch once more. The tone soon grows warmer, even if this is diffused through the formality of letters that are both detailed and well structured.

I could guess at Owen's comments through Avenal's responses. She dismisses his self-deprecating bear-of-little-brain routine, which I have no doubt Owen felt was valid in comparison with the scholarly Avenal. She did this while also correcting his spelling and grammar. Owen was never that articulate with pen or voice and the few letters that survive from him to Avenal seem to labour this point, or else slip into the predictability of narrating the day's events, meteorological observations and the like. They're typical creations of a shy young man to a girl he rather likes.

The letters showed me that Owen and Avenal met from time to time, Avenal travelling south or Owen north. There is the anticipation, the countdown, a gap; then the moroseness of being apart again, the pain of goodbye. Then it's clear that they're engaged, and that the engagement is secret. Avenal talks of her embarrassment at saying goodbye to Owen at a dock or railway station and wishing 'everyone knew'. Judging by the dates, it looks as if they kept it to themselves for up to a year. Maybe this accounts for Tracy's unusual look in that engagement photo at Mona Vale: he suspected something was up and had now found he was right.

There was correspondence from Owen's mother and father too. The sole letter from Tracy was sent mid-May 1941 and postmarked Cairns. He tells his son about the Great Barrier Reef and then notes, pointedly, that he has only heard 'from Mummy'. He says he'll be home around 9 or 10 June. I knew by now that Tracy remarried in June 1942. If Julia was still alive in May 1941, then the intermarital recess was shorter than I'd expected.

Julia appears too, writing to Owen. The first is 28 February 1939: 'My word I got quite a shock when I received your letter this morning. It's nearly three weeks since you left for the [West] Coast.' Julia talks about the weather, mentions how Owen must enjoy the 'outdoors life' and that she, Alison, Beryl and others are off to the pictures soon. She also remarks, after saying what Tracy is up to, 'I do hope that deal for Fendalton does not come off (but I am afraid it will).' This would have been Mona Vale. I'd never heard of Julia's views on it all. I suspect she was comfortable where she was and thought the whole thing a little over the top.

The next extant letter from Julia is dated 4 April 1939 and she is still writing from Sumner. 'How are you old chap?' she begins, 'We have decided to go out to the Selwyn for Easter' – this is the Selwyn Huts where Owen and Avenal first met. 'The weather is just glorious and hope it continues so.' Avenal will stay with them down there too, and Beryl is excited. Perhaps the reintroduction of Owen and Avenal came via the mothers? I know they remained friends. Perhaps Avenal came to stay at Julia's invitation, with her son in mind?

The letter is mostly news and updates, chatter. But at the end Alison makes an entrance too, the first reference I've seen to her in writing other than the record of her death. Julia says: 'Alison is much better but the doctors say it is not her heart but her nerves. She will have to go for a trip. I think I have told you all the news for the present so with best love from all, from Mummy.' Owen must have had some form of update in between these letters, some report of an illness for Alison. In what I could read, however, there was nothing specific. The mention of nerves though? From P.G. Wodehouse, if nowhere else, I knew that a nerve specialist was an old-fashioned term for a doctor who dealt in psychological issues.

Alison appeared in person in the next two letters, both written to Owen and the only two I ever found from her. Here was her handwriting, and her voice. Her first was of 25 February 1937, addressed to Owen at the Central Hotel, Nelson. He is on his first work trip away, aged 17; she is replying to his letter. She has been studying bookkeeping and shorthand and is getting a lot of help from a friend of Owen's called Gordon. 'We got to know each other more than we have ever done before. I agree with you, he is a jolly nice boy.' But, she goes on, 'my word Owen, we miss you.'

Beryl has been modernising the house – this must be in Sumner – and the sisters have been out for a canter at New Brighton. Grandma would like a letter to herself. Is he getting enough fruit? Has he been to see the bishop of Nelson yet? The implication is he's a family friend. Avenal and her mother have been visiting but got away all right; and so on. 'Beryl is still getting all the opportunities she can to drive. The car is still whole though she gave a cow the feel of it on the hindquarters the other day.' Nothing changes. Alison finishes with a request for another letter. She seems amusing and dry.

The second letter from Alison was dated 14 May 1941, almost exactly the date Tracy wrote to Owen from Cairns. Owen is away again, on the remote West Coast at Franz Josef Glacier. It's unclear whether he's holidaying or there for work. I assume the latter, since his father knows the address.

Alison writes from Mona Vale now. The deal for Fendalton has come off, the move has happened. The tone is genial, but the older sister gleams through as she encourages Owen to write to their father. But had *she* done so? A typical line of Alison's: 'the gardeners have been working and are continuing to make the place look nice. Mummy has been lying on the seat out in the garden, enjoying the fresh air and sunshine.' I could pinpoint almost exactly where Alison must have written this: either the drawing room or the smaller room that connected to the dining room, where she'd been sitting in that photo of Beryl's. They're the only rooms where someone would sit and write and also face the garden. I think I can guess at which window Alison sat, the one with a view of lawns sloping to riverbank, the Avon, a few trees at the edge. Under one of these trees, near the Winter Garden, is where I think Julia's bench would have been, facing the north and the sun, from where she could watch the line of the shallow river's flow until it reaches Fendalton Road, leaves the grounds, joins the rest of the world.

It must have been a fine day to be outside, even though it was late autumn. Those big trees would have been looking bare. The gardeners would have been raking leaves into piles. It was 'fine, mostly cloudy' in Christchurch that day, with a maximum temperature of 13° Celsius. But why, then, comment on your mother being in the garden? Maybe there's nothing to it, maybe it's a throwaway line. The family letters are full of talk of weather and being outside. It's just that I know Julia died. I knew she was dead by the time Tracy remarried in June 1942, and 14 May 1941 is getting close, especially given there is no obvious mention of Julia being ill. The letter also told me that Alison, too, was still alive. Whatever might have been ailing her in 1939 has passed. As at the middle of May, 1941, there seemed to be nothing wrong. A family enjoying a Christchurch garden. Yet by June 1942 all has changed. Owen is getting ready for the air force and Tracy is married to Margaret.

• • •

The letters I found from Beryl were also from 1941, both addressed to Owen at Mona Vale. Beryl was away at Mrs Southgate's riding school in North Canterbury. The first letter is just dated 'Monday the 1st'. I can tell the year from the postmark but the rest of the date is obscured. In 1941, Monday was the first of the month in September and December. September was the more likely: Beryl thanks Owen for the gift of gumboots. 'They certainly are needed up here.' Her birthday was in August and Beryl was never the sort to open Christmas presents early; I'm the same.

The letter is chatty and light. It sounds like Beryl. Looking at the collection before me I can see she wrote to Owen often, so the quotidian would play a big part. But after the opening pleasantries Beryl writes, 'Please forgive this note Owen, but I want you to know that I am thinking about you for our family does seem so small.' Someone has gone, as I was working out they must, soon. It's not clear who or how, until the next paragraph: 'Have you had any news of Alison up to date? I would be so pleased if you could drop me a line to let me know.' It must be Julia then, she has died sometime between mid-May and 1 September 1941. But nothing in the letter gives a clue as to what has happened.

The next letter was just two days later – 'Forgive pencil + writing' it says in the top corner – and it confirmed Julia's death. 'It seems so strange not having Mummy to write to, Owen, which makes your letters all the dearer to me. How I wish Mummy could have had this holiday up here, she always loved the beautiful. You know Owen, when I think of Mummy I instinctively think of beauty, for she was beautiful herself.'

It would have been worse for Owen with Beryl away. Perhaps she left for a break, to get away from the sadness? Alison was away too. It was only eight months since Julia had sat in front of Owen in the drawing room, smiling at his engagement to Avenal. It was only three and a half months since Alison had watched her mother enjoying the sunshine on a bench in the garden; and only about eight months until Tracy remarries.

Owen is 21 but his mother is suddenly dead at Mona Vale. Et in arcadia ego.

Beryl continues: 'I quite understand your feelings about what you said Mummy had foretold, but Owen, deep down I feel that no good can come from having resentment towards anyone. We family must not judge. If anything would bring back Mummy, I should leave no stone unturned. I feel that Daddy has in the past been most unhappy and if we can give him happiness at all we should do so.'

Owen and the word resentment are unnatural companions. Beryl's gentle implication is that he's angry. About his mother's death? That would be natural. But what had Julia said? What had she prophesied? It's such a cryptic few lines but the mention of 'Daddy' and giving him happiness? Had Tracy already mentioned the idea of remarriage to his children? This is what the tone and substance of Beryl's letter implies, supported by what I know happened. It's been a maximum of three and a half months since Julia's death. If Tracy is already contemplating remarriage then anyone, even someone as gentle and loyal as Owen, would be resentful.

208

23

The rest of Beryl's letters were short and engaging and the roughly chronological order in which they'd been stored helped to pull me through at speed. They took me into 1942. Beryl is at Mona Vale but Owen is once more away, in Wellington for the hernia surgery he needed to get into the air force. Avenal lived in the capital and Owen went to recuperate with her and her mother (and also with some friends), after the operation. I strongly suspect Owen had it in Wellington for this opportunity.

Beryl wrote daily, sometimes twice a day, morning and evening post, her feelings for her younger brother sharpened by the loss of their mother. Each letter was just a note of a page or two in sloppy handwriting: 'I'm writing this in the post office', or 'do forgive the scrappiness, I've just borrowed a pencil', and then saying, 'Well, shall this time say good bye until tomorrow.' Owen was not equal to such a flood and Beryl often ended, 'Do let me have a reply Owen.'

Beryl regularly wishes him well for his convalescence and just as regularly asks after Avenal, passes on regards, wonders how long until he's up and about. Overeas the air battle raged over Europe. Singapore fell, Rommel was rolling across North Africa, the Japanese flattened Mandalay and were landing in New Guinea and the Solomons. MacArthur had evacuated from the Philippines. Malta was under siege and Darwin had already been bombed. The chaos of the wider world intrudes only once, however, in a letter of Beryl's of 22 April 1942, when she writes: 'I say that's a bit of a hardship about having to wait for the bath and they must be hardening you up for life in Egypt by the sound of things. Wouldn't Mummy have found it a hardship, it made me think of her.' Owen, with the RNZAF, would not have been sent to Egypt, but that wasn't the sort of detail Beryl would retain and North Africa would have been much in the news.

The same letter implies there might have been some cooling in whatever resentment Owen had been carrying in September 1941. 'Daddy,' Beryl writes, 'was so pleased to hear from you and you should have seen how he chuckled over your letter.' Beryl misses Owen: 'You know old chap, you will be able to come back to Mona Vale while you are resting and waiting to get into the air force. It will be marvellous to have you back home again. She continues: 'By the way old chap, how are you off for finances? Your old sister is head of the exchequer so let her give a helping hand.'

I doubt Beryl's writing style is to everyone's taste, but it is to mine. It is of its period and her upbringing. I like the old chap and jolly hockey sticks approach. Still, it can't disguise that putting Beryl in charge of finances was a surprising choice. With Julia dead, in a traditional household such as theirs this job would have fallen to Alison, even had Beryl been famously good with money, which, as far as I could see, had never been the case. Alison was the eldest and the one studying bookkeeping, whereas Beryl never struck me as being numerically precise. As ever, I probably don't give her enough credit – she would have needed to budget carefully when older as she gave most of her money away.

The next day's letter from Beryl, on 23 April 1942, included a mention of Alison: 'This afternoon – Thursday – Grandma and I shall go to see Alison. She is looking very much fitter. Owen in fact I am most hopeful for her in many ways, lately.' I guess that explained the finances, but where was Alison? Not so far away that Beryl could not visit easily. She might be in a house on her own or perhaps doing war work, but the use of the word 'fitter' implies something to do with illness and recovery. Is there any sort of link with 1939? Or it might be unconnected and more innocuous – a sprained ankle perhaps, caught tripping over the spaniel? Whatever the explanation, it meant that Beryl was at home without either brother or sister, trying to keep things going in the shadow of her mother's death. There is a letter from the next day, after the visit: 'You will be pleased to hear, Owen, that Alison was looking so much better when we went to see her yesterday. I am convinced now that every day is making a difference to Alison and she just lapped up news of you old chap.' It definitely sounds recuperative, but also serious. 'Every day' implies a string of days ahead and behind.

There were four more letters from Beryl after this. The first, also written from Mona Vale, was dated 27 April 1942, a Monday. It was a typical specimen, giving a rundown of the last day or so's engagements: people for dinner, a twenty-first birthday party, meeting a woman called Nola who was a refugee from Vienna and was now teaching French at Medbury prep school.

There was encouragement for Owen to write to Tracy again. 'As far as I know,' Beryl concluded, 'it is pretty definite that I shall be coming to see you this weekend. Joves! Won't it be good to see you!' Then there is a letter from 13 May 1942: 'Owen you know you have promised to come back to Mona Vale after your holiday. You have no idea how bucked up I am at the feeling of seeing you again.'

The next letter, on 20 May, indicates that Tracy has recently been through Wellington and seen Owen. Beryl has been helping in the wards at the Public Hospital. 'My goodness Owen it makes me realise what a lot I have to be thankful for when I see just how ill some of the poor patients are.' It seems Owen has announced that he and Avenal have firm wedding plans: 'Yes I'm afraid it has come to me as a surprise that it is going to be so soon … I should be delighted to come up, wild horses couldn't keep me away.' But Owen's is not the only wedding mentioned. Near the end Beryl says: 'Owen you did know that Daddy is being married on the 14th June. I will write again as soon as possible. You have given me much to think about.'

The last letter was dated 25 May, five days later – maybe Beryl has been to Wellington to see him. Owen and Avenal have been engaged for at least 18 months officially, and probably longer unofficially. It's clear from the letter that the news is out that Owen wishes to marry on 12 June 1942. Beryl is writing to beg him to change the date as it is not yet public. This letter is utterly different: thoughtful, serious, didactic. Beryl isn't asking Owen to reconsider his date so that she can make it to his wedding, but rather so that Owen can attend Tracy's. It's not a matter of choice, rather an absolute requirement of filial piety. Beryl adds that she's depressed by circumstances, that she feels like the family is on a precipice, and she says: 'Owen dear, if you do not approve of Daddy's marrying Miss Fife better to write to tell him, but that does not alter the fact that you have made, unfortunately, arrangements to be married on a day which makes it impossible for Daddy and probably myself to attend.'

It was so unlike the Beryl I knew, so unlike the Beryl of the other letters, that if I hadn't been holding her handwriting in front of me, I'd not have believed it was her. Nor could I find it easy to think of Owen as the sort of person to engage in a form of standoff, to need to be talked back by his older sister. But talked back he was. I knew from the affidavits that Tracy married in June, and I knew from their golden anniversary party, held in my first year of boarding school, that Owen and Avenal married closer to Christmas – mid-November in fact.

I looked at the May letters closely. On the 20th Beryl is confirming she will attend; by the 25th she is begging Owen to change. In the former letter she also writes: 'Daddy has not yet arrived home but I am expecting him tomorrow. I see that there is a letter to him from you.' Maybe it's not pure piety driving Beryl but a sense of fairness: Beryl knew of Tracy's date before Owen published his own. I believe Beryl's letter to Owen was the first Owen had heard of the proposed date for Margaret and Tracy's wedding. And I think it crossed with the letter waiting for Tracy on the hall table at Mona Vale, and that this letter contained the news of Owen's proposed date. I could imagine a formal communication to his father as the first step and, knowing Owen, I doubt he wrote more than two letters inside a week. And then this crossing of plans, if that's what it was, ends in an unfortunate standoff that Beryl tries to mediate. Or I am underestimating Owen? He knew Tracy's date and his own announcement was an attempt to stop it. That didn't feel like Owen though.

I don't know if Owen attended his father's wedding, but I have a photo of Owen and Avenal's wedding party emerging from St Peter's in Wellington. They're all standing on the church steps. Owen is in uniform, as is Avenal's brother, who gave her away. Beryl is a bridesmaid along with Avenal's niece. It's a small group, but then again, wartime weddings were modest and Owen had only been serving for a few months: I doubt he qualified for much leave or could afford a large event.

• • •

The final three letters I came to in the satchel all involved Margaret, Tracy's employee and bride-to-be. The first – maybe a draft, hence its presence in the satchel – was from Avenal, dated 8 January 1942:

Dear Miss Fife,

I am sorry that in our hurry this evening you turned your back on what was meant as a helping hand. In a desperate attempt to set right anything I had said amiss, I asked you to forget what I had mentioned. Now I realize how futile it is to ask anyone to forget such a thing, and indeed I should like you to remember that before I left for the North Island, I really tried to set right something which will bring unhappiness to you and others.

I remain,

Yours respectfully,

Avenal Holcombe

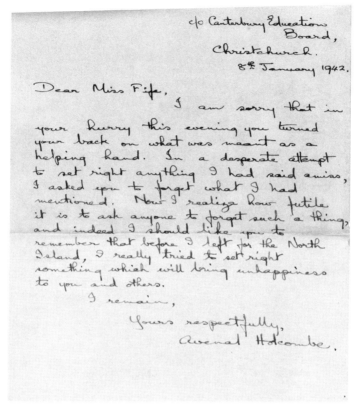

c/o Canterbury Education
Board,
Christchurch.
8th January 1942.

Dear Miss Fife,

I am sorry that in your hurry this evening you turned your back on what was meant as a helping hand. In a desperate attempt to set right anything I had said amiss, I asked you to forget what I had mentioned. Now I realize how futile it is to ask anyone to forget such a thing, and indeed I should like you to remember that before I left for the North Island, I really tried to set right something which will bring unhappiness to you and others.

I remain,

Yours respectfully,
Avenal Holcombe.

Avenal's draft letter to Margaret Fife, January 1942.

This would have been the family's first Christmas and New Year without Julia. As could have been expected, it seems to have gone badly wrong. Only months since Julia's death, Dad's brought along his new girlfriend, who happens to be his younger executive, a business-like Scot planted in the Mona Vale drawing room. Beryl's September 1941 letter – where she talks about Owen's resentment and wanting to make Daddy happy – indicates that Tracy has from at least that date had marriage on the cards. Avenal and Owen, if not the even more saintly Beryl, would've headed into Christmas with a sense of dread, but leaving aside the personalities, the scene is gruesome enough.

I'd characterise Beryl and Owen as meek, but that didn't mean they couldn't experience raw emotions, or get angry. Avenal, however, was not mild or retiring, and she was intelligent enough to take on anything or anyone. She was polite but firm. In a Christian sense she was righteous, though not self-righteous. She was loyal, too. I could imagine her standing

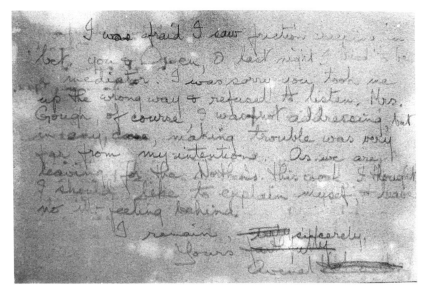

Reverse of Avenal's draft letter.

up for Owen and Beryl – in a lamingtons and arsenic kind of way – if she felt it was necessary.

But turning this letter over I see that maybe I am wrong and am again underestimating some of the characters in this tale that I claim to know the best. On the back of the letter is another draft, this time in pencil and hard to make out as the paper has become sort of tea-stained with age: 'I was afraid I saw friction creeping in bet[ween] you & Owen & last night I tried to be a mediator. I was sorry you took me up the wrong way & refused to listen. Mrs Gough, of course, I was not addressing, but in any case making trouble was far from my intention …'

I can see why Avenal redrafted. This has a saltier (from a distance, amusingly so) tone that I doubt would have been seen as a genuine apology. Mrs Gough – i.e. Julia – was clearly a very sensitive topic in the house.

Margaret's response was not here – perhaps Avenal's draft was never sent – but from the next letter it doesn't look as though relations have improved. On 7 March 1942, from Mona Vale, Owen wrote his proposed stepmother a valediction:

This is a most difficult letter to write, and I do so want you to understand me, and remember I do wish you the best in life to come. I have felt during the last few days that you really do wish to help me, and I feel you are always going to be a real friend to me in the future. I am pleased you will be my Dad's partner in the future, as I know only too well what a difference it is to have a real one who will always stay with you, through thick and thin, as I have found in Avenal.

I now feel that I will no longer be required at Mona Vale as you will always be able to look after Beryl and Alison in the future, like my mother did.

Peggie I am going away to Wellington where I can be near Avenal, and when I say that, I am sure you will understand how much she can help me to keep going. I am going away for two reasons, one is I feel I must be near Avenal, and the other is because I am afraid I rub my Dad up the wrong way.

To him I am afraid I am a complete failure, and I know he is disappointed in me, although I have really tried to do as he has wished. I am afraid neither you or anybody else can change his mind about me. I have just unfortunately always done the wrong thing in his eyes. I feel I have caused such a lot of trouble when I have never meant it in the past, and so I am determined not to do so in the future.

To the outsider I always appear to have everything and also not a care in the world and it will always be like that to everyone. But I have had rather an unfortunate and sad life. One of the biggest knocks was when I thought that my Dad had lost interest in me. I want you to explain, and I know you can that I have always appreciated all he has done for me, and that perhaps the fault has been in me, that things have not gone as they should have.

I realise the big step I am taking, moving out into the world on my own and I am prepared for it to be really tough. I have only £100 in the bank and the few clothes and trunk in my bedroom, but I am going to try and make a go of life with it.

Now I do want you to please understand that my going away is only being done as I feel it will be for the best for all, myself included. You saw only too well that evening when you had to help me, that my Dad was quite convinced that I was all wrong and so I feel I will never get any further with him …

I would just like to wish you the best of luck, and I am sure you can make my Dad as happy as my Mother did. She was the loveliest person in the world to me.

Well I will say cheerio here, and let's hope the next twelve months brings us luck.

Owen

'To an outsider I always appear to have everything and also not a care in the world.' That's an accurate assessment of how I always saw Owen – dapper, smiling, relaxed, comfortable. To then read that he felt he'd had an unfortunate and sad life is shocking. It might also sound self-indulgent.

It's shocking because Owen never spoke like this. He never spoke of himself, let alone with sadness. He never grew angry, despite elaborate provocations from grandchildren. I never heard him complain, never heard or saw from him anything remotely resembling self-pity. He never asked for anything more than the butter to be passed. He never showed any emotion other than the sunny ones, for fear, I think, of making someone else feel awkward. And he was writing from Mona Vale, not from a dosshouse. On the face of it, life had not been hard – or at least it wasn't until he lost his beloved mother.

But Owen must have been so sad when he wrote this. He wasn't much more than a boy, and his heart had been broken by the death of his mother: 'She was the loveliest person in the world to me.'

I found Owen's presentation of his relationship with his father unsurprising. Not that I had any evidence of how they got along, just pale impressions, many filtered through family: the tale of Absalom; Owen's relatively low self-confidence that came across in letters to Avenal; knowing that Owen had never been a hunting, shooting type; the pleas to Owen to write to his father (though he wasn't a great correspondent at the best of times). It felt close to textbook: an ambitious, successful, full-throttle father and a mild, pensive, kindly son. Owen was the younger brother of two mothering, artistic sisters; the son of a gentle, musical mother. What I can't tell is how different it might have been had Julia lived.

Owen had never said anything to me about his father and how they'd got along and nor had anyone else. And why would they? Tracy was a name, a letterhead, almost a legend – and some possessions. But I'd begun to realise that this silence could be a commentary of its own. Tracy was something of a buccaneer, he had a swagger, he had a habit of doing what he liked. I could imagine him being frustrated by Owen, perhaps by his lack of drive. For his part, Owen perhaps felt betrayed by his father's early remarriage, as well as disliked for his relative lack of commercial acumen.

This was it then, the Fall. This letter of Owen's marked his self-expulsion from Paradise, or at least his retreat. But I think he would say it happened a year earlier. In fact I suspect if you'd asked Owen at the time he'd have said he had no choice. December 1940 and he is in black tie with his fiancée, parents and sisters, smiling into the camera in the Mona Vale drawing room. Fourteen months later his dead mother is about to be replaced and he leaves Mona Vale never to return. In so doing he cedes the field to Margaret as the new chatelaine.

Is a battle analogy justified? Owen has after all confided in Margaret. He has thanked her and invested her with the care of his sisters. He had impeccable manners though. He may not be a letter writer and he might have come close to friction at Christmas, but he would know how to withdraw elegantly.

Leaving was probably the easiest, if not the only option for him. It's telling that the letter wasn't to his father: despite it all he found Margaret easier to write to, or he blamed his father more. I couldn't quite bring myself to accept that Owen's polite and modest farewell was a product of genuine fondness for Margaret.

I know I shouldn't consider Owen's view in early 1942 through the lens of the disputes that followed Tracy's death, and I am trying not to. But even so, if there is warmth I think it is a tribute to Owen's good nature more than anything else. If he'd been comfortable with the marriage and therefore with Margaret, he would've stayed. Could he have been comfortable? It seems hard. A quiet, loving son of 22 had just lost his mother. So he walked, Beryl stayed. But the important thing is that they both kept going, Owen without a hair out of place and a smile on his lips, helping, chuckling. Beryl with never a complaint, wishing only the best for people and thanking God daily for His mercies.

There was one more letter, small, tightly folded, same packet. It was a reply from Margaret. It was almost as if she could hear me speculating and came to intervene. Here was her voice, direct, not muffled by legalese. It was dated a month later. Her tone is ostensibly generous, the gracious victor. Margaret compliments Owen on his desire to do something for the war effort. Her letter welcomes him to come home anytime – but this also underscores that it is her invitation to extend. I can't imagine Owen enjoyed this. Margaret does not, however, ask Owen to reconsider. I'm not sure if that's significant, but she concludes with two comments that surely are. First: 'Well my dear must off – I've got a big family to write to these days.' Second: 'Dad joins with me in sending his love.'

24

Progress on the repairs to Owen and Avenal's house first stalled then evaporated altogether. This was true for thousands across the city, as insurance turned out to be just a right to join a disputatious queue. I had the luxury of not living within the ruin and so the frequency of my visits to Christchurch declined. As time passed, earthquake damage metastasised into dilapidation. After a year, two years, three years, there seemed little reason to keep trying.

Paint peeled in flakes revealing rotting boards. The roof patches we'd put where the chimney fell blew away in a storm. The front porch was crooked. Each stay there'd be more plaster dust, flowing like sand from cracks in walls and ceilings. The kitchen retained the aroma of smashed sauces. Falling bricks had damaged the balcony and water stained the walls and ceiling of the drawing room below, blackening into mould. Curtain rails drooped from atrophied plaster. The drains still worked irregularly, as did the waterpipes. The guttering dropped from two sides of the house and, being copper and soft, flopped across balcony railings like giant deflated inner tubes. Ants invaded. The heating stopped.

The house sat alone. The windows were always dark when I arrived and each time through the door was more depressing than the last. If staying the night, I'd seek dinner from friends or have takeaways on my own in the kitchen (only one light working), then to bed, wake up in the cold and head to the airport in the darkness, sneaking away from this tumbledown wreck. I didn't only visit in winter, but that's how it feels from this distance.

The climax of Shirley Jackson's novel, *We Have Always Lived in the Castle*, is the night the local townsfolk help to destroy the beautiful home of the two Blackwood girls. When the girls return from their hiding place after witnessing the rampage they move 'very slowly toward the house, trying to understand its ugliness, ruin and shame'. They walk around, inspecting the damage. They see their mother's torn curtains, the broken furniture, the smashed glass. They know that belongings can be sacred, that a beloved's history can generate love and memory via a vase or a desk. The girls remain there, alone in one corner of the house while the rest of it decays around them. They board up doors and windows and vines encase the burnt roof. Over time bold sightseers start to creep up the drive for a look: '"It used to be a lovely old house, I hear," said the woman sitting on our grass … "Now it looks like a tomb," the other woman said.'

At Owen and Avenal's I became resigned to the disintegration. I spotted a giant weed growing in the laundry, popping its head up between the washing machine and the tub. I left it there; it had made more of a success of the circumstances than I had. One time I arrived to find a soccer ball on the front lawn. One of the neighbours told me the children were too scared to come and retrieve it.

The Blackwood sisters take one unbroken Dresden figurine they find in the garden, 'setting it in its place, below the portrait of our mother and for one quick minute the great shadowy room came back together again, as it should be …' All our figurines were broken, though, as I would be reminded when catching a glimpse of a tiny porcelain hand hidden in a dark corner. And creeping weather-tightness issues meant it was sensible to remove the last pictures, even the portraits of Owen and Avenal. A van arrived. The bare minimum remained.

I finally got around to doing something about the smashed longcase clock. I called Holliday & Sons, one of the city's oldest antiques firms and the only ones who could repair both the woodwork and the mechanism. The wait, they told me, was four years. They were as good as their word; four years to the day I rang them and they came and collected it.

Rose Macaulay would tell you there is pleasure in ruins, and generally I'd agree, but the charm is dulled when the ruins have been created before your eyes and remain full of living memories that seem to bleed through the cracks. It would have been easier if the house had gone altogether, been preserved intact as a memory. I'd tease my mother that the bulldozers were ready and new plans drawn up. She'd say, 'Oh no', and we'd both hope I was joking. I knew, of course, that the house wasn't mine to abandon. Even if it had been, I doubt I would have followed through. I'd just grumble to myself and fly down for another meeting.

One night after what felt like my thousandth visit, I was back in Wellington trailing a cloud of dudgeon behind me. My wife, fed up with my griping, spelled it out to me. It's not about the house, she said. The house

Portrait of the author's mother aged 17, by R.N. Field.

is pointless. It's about your mother's childhood and happy memories of her parents. It's about putting a figurine back in place. Not for your mother directly, but helping her do it for Owen and Avenal.

I guess I knew this but my sympathy had become buried under layers of dust and the sense of sadness the house now exuded. This atmosphere meant that, on my visits, I began to spend more time in the garden. I took to walking around, filling bags with the acorns that carpeted the grass beneath Robin Hood Oak. These shiny little mobile memorials that I could take with me. I'd always think I had enough and then I'd crunch onto some more, all smooth and each with the potential to grow into a giant. What a waste to leave them, to be broken by boots or mown down as saplings. I would reach down and grab another handful of the silkiest and drop them into my bag too. I could spend an hour breaking my back this way, almost without noticing, and I was sometimes caught, suddenly, realising that the taxi was at the door.

I'd take the acorns home in my satchel and put a few into old pots. You don't dig them in but place them on top of the soil, as you never know which end is going to want to head down and which will wish to reach up. The acorns that didn't make it into pots I might spread as living souvenirs around my garden, a handful here, a handful there, leaving growth to the chances of nature.

Some I'd give to my mother who reminded me that she used to do the same about 25 years ago. I'd forgotten. She'd gathered up acorns and taken them to a small patch of remote, sloping land she bought north of Wellington. She planted 2000 oaks altogether. It had been years since I'd visited and I kept meaning to drive up with her one day and walk the hills and gullies, inspecting these descendants and perhaps adding a few more by my own hand.

We weren't the only ones with this habit. A friend of my mother's called in unexpectedly one day and dropped off a small bag. It contained a handful of acorns. She had been at a family reunion in the Far North and collected these from underneath the oak in the family churchyard. This oak had been planted by Bishop Selwyn from acorns he had collected while leaning against a tree, waiting for a meeting at Windsor Castle. Another friend, unconnected, dropped in an envelope of acorns from old trees on their farm in the Wairarapa. I took the stories as encouragement and validation.

But it was fruit, not nuts, that I was supposed to collect, fruit from the orchard. My mother always asked for pears from that drooping giant by the pool. I thought them hard and tart but she liked them. I took the odd bag back with me, fearing the waste otherwise, but they were heavy, and hard to explain in a briefcase. Acorns were more portable, less likely to leak, and if everything else was wiped away they might sprout into something grand, living mementoes of a broken world. My mother might feel consoled too.

• • •

A little over two years after the February earthquake we gathered one evening at a bistro in Wellington. It's in an old wooden building with a turret of its own but surrounded by concrete towers. There's a small brass-topped bar with a mirror beside it. The ceiling's low and the tables are close together, but carpet and tablecloths and decades of good behaviour mean that the noise has a softness that matches the lighting.

There were four of us: my mother and father, my wife and me. We were there to celebrate my mother's birthday. We sat in a miniature circle, almost elbow to elbow, knee to knee. We said happy birthday quietly. We ordered. We handed over a present. Then, not long after everything was settled, I told my parents that we were expecting our first child. If all went well the baby, gender unknown, would arrive in December.

The news was premature, only four weeks old; and it was not meant to be our celebration. But I wanted to tell my mother about it that evening for the same reason we were celebrating her birthday a day early. First thing the next morning she had to report to the hospital. She'd been to see a doctor a few weeks ago. They had found something. There were shadows. Within moments, it seemed, she was diagnosed with ovarian cancer, stage 3C. This meant it had spread, in her case to the lymph nodes. It was the last stage before 4, which is generally terminal and for which treatment is palliative.

She was lucky: she was allowed surgery to see if there was a chance of removal and survival. The surgeons didn't know what they might find, or might be able to remove. They didn't know if other organs would be damaged or how well it might go. They didn't know how long it would take. They told her to be there at 7am. She wasn't looking forward to it. She didn't like mornings at the best of times.

A few days earlier, between the diagnosis and this appointment that could be either macabre or miraculous, she and I had gone to see her lawyer. She was issuing me a power of attorney to deal with business matters while she was incapacitated.

'It's very limited in scope,' Michael, the lawyer, said. He was a family friend and I think was trying to reassure rather than warn me, 'just to have responsibility in relation to anything that comes up with the family business, and just while she is in hospital and recovering.'

'Happy to be in charge,' I said, or something along those lines.

Michael slid two copies across the table and I had a brief read. I signed both. Michael told me to keep my copy safe, and I nodded. I thought of storing it with my other important documents, but I had no idea where they were.

At dinner we ate and talked. As we had hoped, my mother was happy with our news. I was happy she was happy.

'What will Daphne think about this?' my mother asked. Daphne had a head the size of a bowling ball and made the glasses tinkle when she snored. She wasn't the sort of beast people might naturally trust with a newborn.

'We think she'll be good with children. She's loyal, and gentle.'

My mother agreed. 'After all, Nana in the film of Peter Pan is a St Bernard.'

'Reliable evidence.'

The next morning we were all up before dawn. We met at the surgical reception desk where my mother checked in, trundling a bag behind her with luggage labels flapping off it. The bag was due in Christchurch a year ago.

We sat and waited. There were grey chairs and no windows. I was hungry. She wasn't allowed to eat. We waited. The surgeon appeared. It was early. She would have just arrived, too. She was French, energetic, friendly, young. She smiled. My mother was to go with her. There was a pair of frosted glass doors a few metres away. They would go through here.

How do you say goodbye when you don't know if you'll see someone again? I think we all just hugged her and said we'd see her soon. The surgeon held the door. My mother stepped through, pulling the bag behind her. At the threshold she turned and waved and smiled: the boarding call, off through security, passengers only. Bon voyage. One more wave, a blown kiss? Happy birthday. She was gone. The doors were opaque. That was it.

That left three of us standing there, like the pillars of a temple whose roof has been shorn away. Still but pointless, waiting for the erosion to take hold. Silent too, for a moment, and then my wife and I left for work. Even if they could do nothing, it would still be several hours. My father stayed.

Four hours was meant to be about average in theatre, they said. Much shorter would mean there was no hope. They would have opened her up, seen it was pointless, put her back together and sent her to recovery with best wishes. If it was much longer, there might be complications.

Four hours would be about 12.30. Hope became a parabola centred on lunchtime. The morning needed to go swiftly but of course it dribbled and every long minute gave a chance of bad news. When 12.30 finally arrived it brought nothing with it. On the other side, time now needed to be held back but it slipped like sand, each perfidious minute disappearing before I could clutch it back.

One thirty. Two o'clock. Two thirty. Now what? You just have no idea. My father was at the hospital, sitting and waiting. I imagined him alone with his own thoughts in a grey chair. Married 38 years. I didn't think he needed my yapping. If there was news, I would be told. If it was bad, I would be told.

Three o'clock. Three thirty. It was hard to do anything but watch the minutes. The parallel with the school day. Waiting for Mum. When would I last have done that? Thirty years ago? But she's the one behind the gates now.

It was eight hours before my father rang: she's out of theatre, he said, she's all right. She's in recovery. Recovery is off limits. It's where the newly harmed and the newly saved sleep off the narcotics and stop bleeding before they're moved to wards. I knew nothing more than that she'd survived; nor did he.

She'd be in recovery for at least two hours. The working day had finished before it started but only now I left my desk and made my way back to the hospital to wait. The hospital was already in bed. Reception was unlit and unmanned. Visiting had ended hours earlier. It was quiet, as it had been at 7am. What events and tragedies and miracles must happen here every day. I sat in the fluorescent light of the waiting room and thought about reading. I ate a sandwich. My father was there too.

Between 8pm and 8.30 there was the commotion of an occupied gurney arriving. I didn't see her as she came past, I didn't see her face. Just the bustle of pale blue polyester as a small crowd pushed her towards a smaller room. My father and I emerged from the brightness of the waiting room into the dim ward. We followed the orderly trail to a door opposite the nurses' station. The surgeon was there and she spoke to us.

'We managed to get everything we could see. She's very, very lucky. But she's lost a lot of blood. We'll be monitoring her blood pressure. You can go in and see her.'

She was propped up, her hair matted back against her forehead. She looked as if she'd been drained, which in a way she had been. Her face looked bloodless, yet she was propped up as if for breakfast in bed. She hadn't been allowed to drink anything the night before. She was so thirsty, she said, but you had to lean forward to hear her croak this out. We passed her a cup and she took a sip of pale juice through a straw.

Smiling. You look great, we say. You're very lucky.

But I was thinking, You're so small, like a child. I could pick you up with one arm and hold you. But it would do nothing. I could do nothing.

My father sat on one side of the bed, I sat on the other. Then I stood and arranged her possessions, unpacking the few clothes from her little blue rolling case into the two or three drawers available. She was fortunate to have her own room. It had a window even. Nurses came in and out. We're watching her blood pressure, they said.

We sat there. She drifted in, and out, and in. So pale. Wrists of rice paper. Eyes open, smile. Eyes shut. Nurses kept entering and checking machines, machines tied to her, tied into her. They did it without a murmur and we waited. Eyes open, but so tired. Are you okay? Smile. Eyes shut. Eyes open. Are you okay? I'm very cold. Pull the blanket right up around her neck, outlining her chin. Now she's a face only. Like in an open casket. Or like a Klimt, that's a nicer thought.

A nurse came in again. They were all polite, friendly. She looked at a machine, eye-height for her, and frowned.

'Her blood pressure's dropping,' she muttered and I moved so that she could get past me. Then someone else came in. I stood in the corridor, near the door. There was a flurry as cornflower-blue uniforms flowed silently past.

'We're calling the par-nurse,' someone said.

What was that? Like a para-nurse? Paramilitary, paralegal. A sort of nurse?

'The par-nurse will be here shortly. We're trying to stabilise her. She's lost a lot of blood.' I tried to stay out of the way while staying close. A young woman arrived. Her tunic was darker than those of the other nurses, navy. She had short dark hair. She seemed to be carrying a toolbox.

I moved a little further away from the door, ending up beside the nurses' station; the citadel of authority guarded by a chest-high enceinte. All around signs, posters and messages were pinned to boards – where to get advice, what not to eat, who to call. There was one poster with bold red lettering on white, 'PAR Nurse', it said, and gave a phone number. Written underneath was an explanation for people like me, 'Patient at Risk'. I see.

Then I noticed my father wasn't nearby. There were few places he could have gone. I wandered down the corridor and back into the gloaming around reception. It took a second for my eyes to adjust and I saw him sitting alone in a chair, his legs stretched out, his head angled to one side, resting on his hand. His eyes were open.

I turned back to the corridor, into the light, and walked back to her room and the quiet commotion. I kept my head down, though, eyes focused on my shoes. Look at the shoes. I never polish them. Too lazy. What else don't I do that I should?

I peered into my mother's room again from the corridor. They'd hooked her up to more lines. The nurse in navy was in there with a couple of the others. They were pouring proteins into her. Transparent proteins from a plastic bag from America were stopping her blood pressure dropping any further. It took some time.

I was there for three more hours before the nurses said they thought my mother was stable once more. The navy nurse left. We could go home and rest. She was sound asleep, had been for some time, drained into unconsciousness. They promised us that if anything happened they would let us know. I gave them my number too, in case they couldn't reach my father.

I drove home. It was a cold night. April. The same month we'd come back to Christchurch six years earlier. Onset of autumn and what feels like a purer blackness at night. At home I sat on my own in the bathroom with the door shut, trying to be quiet but distracted beyond reason by thoughts of what, any moment now, life had a chance of becoming. Then I got undressed and washed.

When I came out I saw I'd missed a telephone call. There was no number but no one else was going to ring at one in the morning. Dad must be fast asleep. I found the hospital's number and called straight back but there was no telephonist on duty and I didn't know the right extension. I pulled some clothes on, a thick jersey against the cold, and headed back to the car. I drove as quickly as I could on the dark and empty streets, thoughts of what might await me blotching my vision.

I parked and had trouble finding my way in. In the dead of night they lock almost all the doors and I had to enter via the emergency department. Still not knowing what was going on, I found an internal phone and dialled her ward. Someone answered.

'We couldn't keep her blood pressure up. She moved to intensive care about half an hour ago.'

Where is it?

'Third floor, up the stairs.'

Intensive care does not have fixed visiting hours. It's also higher security. People wounded on both sides of the law might be inside. There are heavy doors and entry is by intercom and monitored.

I was let in. The lights were low and it was almost silent, just whirrs and beeps. There were long lines of beds and machines, separated by curtains. At the foot of every bed sat a nurse on a stool, watching each patient constantly. There were a lot of people in there and much movement but the quiet made it feel still.

My mother was about six beds up from the door, pale, frail, propped and asleep. Patients are always propped up to keep the lungs safe; they're very vulnerable in the sick. There was a chair near the nurse and after a whispered introduction – everyone whispered – I pulled it over and sat by the bed. It didn't take my mother long to open her eyes, I think her sleep was very shallow. She looked at me.

'Oh, you've come?' she said.

'I thought I would, yes. You can't just go running off on us round the hospital.'

She shut her eyes and smiled. It was a few moments before she opened them again.

'It must be very late?' Her voice was faint. It sounded as though she still hadn't had enough to drink.

'I didn't have much on.'

She slept for longer now, and when she spoke next she might almost have been narrating a dream. 'I feel like I'm standing on the edge of a cliff.' I didn't know – don't know – if she was saying it to me or to herself. I don't know if she even remembered. She kept her eyes shut as she said it, so I didn't need to try and hide anything.

I stayed there for an hour and a half while my mother slept, wandering through a maze I built in my mind, with every turn ending in awfulness. I was doing nothing more than indulging myself, not helping her. She seemed properly asleep now, regular breathing. The nurse smiled and said she was stable and so I left with a promise, again, that they would call me if anything changed.

There's no day in ICU. The only light is a sort of phosphorescence from the machines that makes the sheets and sick faces glow. Everyone in there tiptoeing past death's door and hoping not to get caught.

The next few days were as precarious as that first night. Gradually, though, they were able to reduce the volume of stuff being pumped into her from those transparent bags. Her blood pressure could stay at normal levels with less support. We came and went all day, every day. In the waiting area outside a woman was told that her husband had a brain aneurysm and would die soon. There were children in there too. We were the fortunate.

After 10 days my mother was moved back to the women's ward. The reduced tension made this now seem like pretend-hospital, a rest cure. If you were here you weren't sick, not really, not like the poor people in the half-world of ICU.

She still was sick, though. Still frail and pale, still struggling to talk or stay awake. She began to be allowed a meal on a tray but I would try to bring her yoghurt and fruit from the café on the ground floor where I'd get myself the same breakfast each day, followed a few hours later by the same lunch. She could sip drinks more frequently and word by word her voice recovered, alongside her consciousness.

As soon as she could stand and move, we took her home. It would be more restful there, less movement. She needed to recover properly so that the sequel, six months of chemotherapy, could start. We bought big bright cushions to help her sit up in bed and tried to sterilise the house. Infection was a threat. At home she could smile more. The district nurse visited daily to change dressings and take tests. After a month my father took her out for a coffee, and we photographed her as she left in the car, back in the world once more.

25

A few weeks into my mother's convalescence, papers arrived for her announcing that the convoluted structures created by Tracy's death were to be put before the courts for wind up. These structures had existed for my mother's entire life. Their impending removal reinforced the overwhelming sense of disintegration: the city's destruction by the earthquake; people scattered; the landmarks gone; the house in ruins; the clock smashed. Now sickness and more finality.

The removal of the trusts was going to require an application to the High Court – akin to Owen in the 1960s. It was as Robert had long foretold and it promised to be complex and contentious: where would rights devolve, who would now do what. When I'd accompanied my mother to see Michael, we thought something like this might happen. We just hadn't thought it would happen so soon, nor that the surgery would leave my mother so weak. Anyone who wanted to have their say on the matter would need to submit their own evidence. I'd already been wandering at leisure among the hedgerows of family history. Given my mother's indisposition, the easiest thing was for me to carry on and write it up as well as I could.

The way I broke it down in my head was this: the complexity of Tracy's arrangements came from a dispute. The dispute came from a complex will. The complexity came from having two families. This meant that at its core, in an historical if not a legal sense, was the transition from one family to another. The perfect, lavish life Tracy had created for his wife and children had been shattered when he became a widower. That was a sad fact. It was also a fact that he'd remarried. This shaped the family's future. And it seemed to come down to one 12-month period: 14 May 1941, the last mention of Julia, to 17 June 1942, the date of Tracy's marriage to Margaret. Between these two Julia had died, Owen had left and Alison, it seemed, had vanished.

Mothers, then. That's where I was, that's where I started.

Julia would have been in her early fifties when she died: not unheard of, but still premature. I wasn't sure where or how to find out more, or if there was anything more to find out. I'd come to the end of all the stories that Owen and Avenal's house seemed willing to discharge. But I remembered my mother mentioning where both Julia and Alison had ended up: with my grandparents in the family grave. My trips to Christchurch were already morbid, staying in a decaying, greying house. A drive to a cemetery would at least be consistent. So one day on a visit I got into Owen's car, laborious to restart again, and headed back to take a look. I should have gone long before this.

The east of Christchurch – Bromley, Linwood, Avonside, out towards Burwood and the beach – was one of the areas hardest hit by the earthquakes. Roads and bridges were buckled and the heavy old car would alternately waft and lurch, float and thump through it all. The damage was everywhere. Empty sections where churches had been. Long grass. Much more plywood, still more abandoned houses.

A brick mansion over this way was one of my favourite buildings in the city. It was as close to genuine Regency architecture as we had in the country and its long garden façade ran parallel to the road. You glimpsed it as you drove past. That was old Christchurch in many ways, a touch of beauty at the end of a straggling garden. This house had been semi-abandoned and in need of restoration for several years before the earthquakes. I held my breath as I turned the corner, away from the run of the Avon, but I knew the answer and the empty garden and unobstructed view confirmed it.

Wide, tree-lined Linwood Avenue ushered me the final distance to the cemetery gates and once there I could navigate to the family plot. I remembered from Owen's burial: it was at the far end of the central drive, with a sole tree nearby. I parked, got out and looked at the tombstone. Family surname across the top as I remembered. Below was a new slab of marble. It had been arranged by my mother and her siblings once Owen's burial had completed the plot. From the bottom were Avenal, Owen and Beryl, the three newest, and above them two other names:

In Loving Memory of
Julia Daisy Hill Gough
20 September 1887 – 30 May 1941
Beloved Wife of Tracy Thomas Gough

Alison Mavis Gough
28 March 1913 – 3 June 1942

I don't know if you have ever stood on a quiet bit of seashore, on a still night, and out of nowhere a boat has appeared? Maybe it's a fishing trawler back from the day's work, or a pleasure craft running late. Around you is blackness, ahead of you is liquid blackness, quiet lapping reminding you that the texture changes from hard to soft by your feet. In this blackness there's just the thud of engines and a single spotlight, scanning the water for the mooring or the jetty.

But it doesn't feel like this. It feels as though that light is picking you out and you know that behind it is a bulky machine that you can't see. The night is calm and the noise carries well, louder as it comes near, and still you can only see the light and hear the noise. This is how I felt seeing these names and dates. I'd picked the boat out from the shore, or it had me. Not only Julia dead, as I knew, but Alison too, within a year.

I didn't have the chronology to hand as I looked at the grave. I didn't have it memorised then, as I do now. It took me a long time to go back through letters and documents to patch it all together: Julia dead at the end of May; Tracy contemplating remarriage by September; his secretary in place as hostess by Christmas; by the following March Owen has left home; by May the next year Beryl says they're on a precipice. Less than a month later Alison is dead too. It was disintegration. Was it destruction?

I realised now why those letters lived together in that satchel; why they even survived: they were the last ones Owen had from his mother and sister. They covered the year from mid-1941 to mid-1942, the saddest of his life.

On 14 May 1941, according to Alison's letter, Julia was fine and sitting in the garden. Alison hadn't mentioned her mother having any illness, but perhaps it was already well known that Julia was fragile: hence the otherwise mundane reportage. I could relate. When my mother first left the house after her operation and weeks of convalescence, I told everyone. I wouldn't have mentioned a trip to the shops if she'd been fine. But there was no real anxiety in Alison's letter, or in any of the others around this time, and both Owen and Tracy were away. I can't imagine they would both have left if Julia was seriously unwell. Finally, Julia, by Tracy's own report, was even writing to Tracy.

The balance of evidence is that, as late as 14 May 1941, everything was all right. Julia may have been fragile but she was all right. Yet she was dead 16 days later. It might have been accident, haemorrhage, stroke or a heart attack, or some condition that rapidly, unexpectedly, worsened. I feel that given the timings, the circumstances, Julia's death, when it came, must have been a shock to everyone.

On the day Julia died, Friday 30 May 1941, Beryl was to perform in a 'grand demonstration concert' by the winners of the recent Christchurch Competitions. To my mind this shows that life was relatively normal until near the end. Beryl would never have committed to be away from her sick mother. Her song was to be the 'Indian Bell Song' from the opera *Lakmé*. The libretto is rather mournful: where will the young girl go?

What about Tracy and Owen? Owen, for instance, would have needed a day at least to get back to Christchurch. Unless it was an accident or a heart attack, he should have been able to see his mother before she died. I hoped he had; I thought he had. If Owen hadn't been present there would surely be some written evidence, and I think this would most likely have been kept with the letters I'd found. I think Julia might have declined in a way that gave some notice, that Owen came home and was there for the end.

I was less sure about Tracy's presence. His letter to Owen indicated he expected to return home around 9 or 10 June. Let's say Julia collapsed the day after Alison's letter and a cable was sent to Tracy: that would have been 15 May and Tracy would have been in Sydney.

Julia's grave at Bromley Cemetery, Christchurch, shared now by Alison, Beryl, Owen and Avenal.

In those days the top trans-Tasman liner was the *Awatea*. It made 23 knots and its record crossing was 56 hours. Say three days Sydney to Wellington and then, with a good connection, an overnight ferry to Lyttelton. Tracy might have arrived in Christchurch by the 19th or 20th. But a telegram any later than 24 May and he would have struggled.

I tried to use passenger and immigration records to check whether he'd returned in time. I found several trips of Tracy's: 1934 to San Francisco, and again in 1939 when, on the way home, Tracy ran off the ship to post a letter to Beryl from Pago Pago: she'd just become a finalist for the Melba opera prize and had told him, by 'radiogram'; 1937 to Sydney just with Julia. I even found Tracy travelling first class to Sydney in 1925. It supported my revised image of him as possessor of inherited or at least established affluence pre-dating Mona Vale … But I didn't find Tracy coming home in mid-1941. This doesn't mean he didn't, but there remains a chance that Julia died without her husband.

Is that how Tracy would have wanted it? I was suspicious not because he remarried – that much is common – but because he mooted it so soon after Julia's death, and because it was to a long-term employee. Did Tracy thus leave knowing Julia was sick and hoping to avoid the end? This implies a callousness that is hard to attribute to anyone, let alone kin, let alone a husband, even a distracted one. He and Julia were still writing to each other. There was some relationship there.

• • •

Death is private but becomes less so after 50 years. At that date the curtain is drawn back and anyone can order a copy of a death certificate. I did so for both Julia and Alison. It seemed a sensible next step. I should have thought of it before.

Julia's arrived first. It was a tiny slip of copperplate writing, photocopied onto an A4 page surrounded by white space. It told me she was 54 and that her place of death was 62 Fendalton Road, the address of Mona Vale. And in the cause of death column? Three explanations are listed, each one begetting their own sequence of speculations: coma, 12 hours; acute mania, 14 days; diabetes.

I'd heard of Julia's diabetes, but not that it had killed her. It seemed an extreme end. Mania is still used as a psychiatric term, albeit with a stricter definition than in the 1940s. It's sometimes seen as the opposite of depression, a sort of euphoria and heightened energy level and sense of self. Commonly it's a syndrome of bipolar disorder, formerly known as manic depression. But I think here it's more likely to have been a portmanteau, in the way hysteria once was for women. Either way, it means that Julia would have been regarded as mentally ill for the last two weeks of her life. That time period also meant this alleged mania started only two days after Alison's letter. Was it brought on by the diabetes? How? And how did it move to coma? There were no further clues on the certificate and no record of any further inquiry.

The certificate itself had been signed by one R.F. Bakewell, and registered by the undertaker. I discovered that Robert Bakewell had practised in Sumner. Presumably he'd been the family's doctor when they lived there and so was the natural contact. It was a long way to come for a new patient otherwise.

The death certificate also told me that Julia was buried two days later, the first into the family grave at Bromley. The service was Anglican and taken by Canon Frederick Redgrave, the vicar of St Barnabas, just along Fendalton Road from the Mona Vale gatehouse, about equidistant between Mona Vale and Owen and Avenal's home. It's also where my parents were married. I don't know who attended the funeral but the mention of 14 days made me update my thoughts on Owen and Tracy's presence. There should have been enough time to call them home. Though oddly, Julia's death notice in the *Press* said 'suddenly'.

I'd learnt from Godfrey that wills, like deaths, became part of the public record and so I searched out Julia's. Tracy had filed for probate as her executor. Using the standard wording of the era he swore 'That the said Julia Daisy Hill Gough died at Christchurch on or about the 30th day of May 1941, as I am able to depose, having seen her dead body after death.' Julia's estate came to about £2000, which she left to her children, with a life interest in favour of Tracy. It was a traditional disposition and with it I seemed to reach the end of Julia's story: descendant of Pilgrims, born in a colony, farmer's daughter, married a salesman, died manic in a mansion. My thoughts turned back to the eight words of medical explanation. I showed the certificate to a friend, a pathologist called Frank, and asked him what it might mean.

'I'm not sure how much I can help,' he started. 'I'm more of a cancer guy.'

'Pathology is the study of disease, right? You'll be fine. I'm sure you know more than me.'

'You're asking for a diagnosis after 70 years when you've literally given me three lines?'

Julia in the garden at Sumner, 1920s.

'Think of it as a medical crossword.'

'What can you tell me about her, then?' he asked, 'Was she fit? Overweight?'

'I don't know about fitness or general health. I'd say she may have been a little overweight but not extreme.'

'All her life?'

'No. I've just been looking at photos. I think she just put on a little weight later in life. Fairly common, no?'

'Any idea how long she had diabetes?' he asked.

'All I heard was that she had it. I don't really know. What could have made it more acute?' I asked. 'Can you get a coma from it?'

'I can only do this on the basis of some big assumptions.'

'Yes. Appreciated.'

'In the simplest terms,' Frank said, 'diabetes can lead to a coma. You can induce a diabetic coma from too much insulin or not enough. Severe hypoglycaemia can come from too large a dose of insulin and can lead to coma.'

'Like an overdose?'

'Any large dose.'

'And insulin was being used then?'

'Pretty sure. I think it became commonly available for medical use in the early 1920s. It was commercial by the 1930s. It should've been available here. It's not my field, mind.'

'Noted. And not taking insulin could be just as bad?'

'Yup. You get what's called hyperosmolar hyperglycaemic syndrome, or HHS. It's more common for Type 2.'

'That's the sort of diabetes you contract later in life?'

'More commonly – but even that's a gross generalisation.'

'But you think she was Type 1?'

'I really can't say, but if she was, there's also diabetic ketoacidosis and coma. More common for Type 1. It's caused by too much sugar – so not enough insulin. You can fall into a coma and die if you miss your injections. Was she a drinker?'

'No, I don't think so.'

'Okay, well, notwithstanding what type she was, and on the limited information you have – and reminding you this is not my area – we can say that she might have had access to insulin and that too much or too little of it might have led to coma. Helpful, isn't it?'

'Either way something she might control?' I asked.

'If the assumption on insulin is correct, yes.'

'The two weeks of mania?' I said.

'They used to think the link was direct – between psychosis and diabetes. Even into the nineteenth century.'

'Has medicine moved on from then?'

'You'd hope so. Diabetes can cause a lot of other issues: stroke, heart attack, hypertension. I don't know enough about the treatment but I'd guess that not following a course of medication could lead to delirium and confusion in the later stages. That could present itself as psychosis. Diabetes mellitus could certainly cause all of these symptoms and death. And marked hypo- or hyperglycaemia would impair the workings of the mind.'

'Sorry, mellitus?'

'Sweetened with honey. Sorry a technical term. Just diabetes for you.'

'Thanks. So this hypothesis might work: she stopped medicating, deteriorated, became delirious and then died.'

'Yes, that could fit the extremely limited data we have. Taking too much insulin might have done the same. We're just speculating. The medical detective in me would ask: why would it happen then? What changed? Was it a hot summer and she got dehydrated in addition to missing or underdosing her insulin?'

'It was late autumn, almost winter, so I doubt it.'

'The thing with insulin is that it may be unpleasant to administer but patients don't generally feel better when they stop taking it, unlike some antipsychotic medications. So it's not something you'd stop taking for that reason. So why stop? What else do you know? How were things at home?'

How were things at home?

'I'm still trying to find out,' I said.

26

And thus Alison.

Alison of the ballgown and the long gloves. Alison by the lily pond. Alison of the wide, pretty smile and the spectral presence. Alison the debutante. Alison of the letters, watching her mother, teasing her sister. Alison who died a year almost to the day after her mother.

She died young, but no one had said how, no one had ever really talked of her, as though she may have just been forgotten. If it had been cancer, wouldn't someone have said? An accident? Possibly. Though you'd think if there had been some dramatic car crash or drowning, that the story would have filtered through.

Some other chronic illness? There were nerves in 1939, and she was away from home in early 1942. But Beryl's letter to Owen of 27 April 1942, which was only a month from Alison's death, was full of inconsequential news and chatter. There was nothing about Alison, nothing at all. Then three letters in May 1942 – again none mentioning Alison. The last one was the 25th. That was only about a week before Alison died. Beryl mentions a precipice – but she is talking, I believe, about the schism between Owen and Tracy.

As with Julia, the circumstantial evidence implied something sudden. One sudden death is happenstance, but two – mother and daughter – is calamity. It might also be alarming and more than faintly Gothic. What would the neighbours have said, in chatty, fluttery Christchurch?

Alison's death certificate, like Julia's, was just a narrow strip of writing. A life recorded in 22 words and two signatures. It told me that Alison had died from 'myocardial failure due to exhaustion of acute confusion'. It took little effort to translate that into English – it meant effectively a heart attack, heart failure. She was 29.

But this wasn't as odd as what another column told me. It listed the place of death. I was expecting Mona Vale, 62 Fendalton Road, like her mother.

It wasn't. Nor was it Christchurch Hospital, or St George's, or a doctor's surgery. Alison died at Sunnyside Mental Hospital. *Sunnyside.*

The name is pure Orwell, and infamous enough to have its own place in Christchurch's schoolyard canon: 'He belongs in Sunnyside,' 'They look like they've escaped from Sunnyside.' And so on. Sunnyside's reputation was more than matched by its look: a great château-like structure, all towers and gables, mansarded roofs and heavy doors. What would you call it? Sanatorium Gothic? It may not surprise you to know that it was mostly designed by the ubiquitous, and talented, Mountfort.

Canterbury was relatively progressive on mental health. Sure, the first few years anyone designated as loony was locked in Lyttelton Gaol, but this was commonplace worldwide. Canterbury opened its first specialist asylum, Sunnyside, in 1863, only 13 years after European settlers were living in flax shacks by the Avon, 10 years before the university was founded and a year even before the foundation stone of the cathedral was laid. In this, Canterbury followed the gradual reform in England, which passed the Lunacy Act in 1845, the better to protect the mentally ill, though admittedly from a miserable starting point. The key campaigner in this area was Lord Shaftesbury, one of the Canterbury Association's members.

Sunnyside was purpose-built from the 1860s to the 1890s. In old photos it looks moody and, to modern tastes (even mine), a little sinister, but its appearance reflected the fashion of the day. Asylums had previously been about incarceration but attitudes now considered the patients' wellbeing. Reflecting this, Mountfort, under the guidance of the health authorities, made a conscious effort to emulate a large and grand country house. There were big windows, French doors and expansive grounds. Patients could wander at will – so they said – and were not just held in cells, as had previously been standard. And you could maybe convince yourself that it resembled Biltmore, or somewhere in Normandy. The name itself was part of this more enlightened approach, an attempt to remove the stigma of madness and institutionalisation (though the word lunatic remained in the name until the turn of the century).

Despite these aspirations, Sunnyside still became a byword for almost mediaeval treatment and mysterious goings on. In February 1928, for example, *Truth*, the country's main, indeed probably its only tabloid newspaper, ran a prominent article under the multiple headlines:

The Darker Side of Life in Sunnyside Asylum
Serious Charges
Patients' Relatives Complain of Violent Treatment by Attendants

Truth was not often accused of reliability, but the stories were representative of many other articles across numerous publications over decades. Sunnyside management would be called upon to answer claims, but only ever responded that they were precluded due to privacy concerns, regaining some sympathy in the process.

In 1946 a small pamphlet entitled *Misery Mansion: Grim tales of New Zealand asylums* was self-published by Arthur Sainsbury, a campaigner for mental health reform. The book claimed to present 30 tales of 'suffering and ill-treatment that the public would not condone'. The minister of health decided he needed to defend the accusations, which he did vigorously in Parliament. Sainsbury of course responded and the spat was in and out of the newspapers over a period of months. The pamphlet went on to four editions,

Sunnyside Asylum, Canterbury.
Completed 1892.

Sunnyside in the late nineteenth century, soon after it was built.
1/2-002755-F, ALEXANDER TURNBULL LIBRARY, WELLINGTON

each one with a few more pages than the last, and gave Sainsbury the platform to point out to a wider audience that he drew on the government's own statistics.

Sunnyside, with 1400 inmates at the end of 1941, was one of the largest of the country's eight psychiatric hospitals. There were then over 8000 psychiatric patients nationwide, with over 1200 admissions during the year. The odds weren't good for them. That year there were 557 deaths as opposed to 313 discharged as recovered. Admittedly some deaths were due to cancer, some to old age and a few even died on absences but still, the mental health system was not somewhere you wanted to be. In fact the 1940s and 1950s may have been the nadir of Sunnyside's malevolent fame. It was a period made most notorious by the writer Janet Frame who, in her memoir *An Angel at My Table*, described the 'new electric treatment' she was given after admitting herself as a voluntary boarder in 1948: 'I could not remember. I was terrified. I behaved as others around me behaved … I felt utterly alone … As in other mental hospitals, you were locked up, you did as you were told to or else, and that was that.'

Why then was Alison there? The mention of her nerves was two years earlier. That 1939 letter also referred to her heart, but if Alison had been having heart problems severe enough to cause myocardial failure, shouldn't she have been in an ordinary hospital? The death certificate gave as little insight as Julia's, but it did mention a 'Coroner's Verdict'. That meant there was an inquiry, and therefore that there should be a report.

I went back to Archives New Zealand, who were able to confirm that yes, they did hold a coronial inquiry file in relation to her death, but it was classified in perpetuity. I explained the family connection and was granted access to a buff folder containing a pile of papers with the royal coat of arms on the front. Honi soit qui mal y pense.

'An inquisition taken for our Sovereign Lord the King at the Sunnyside Mental Hospital … The said Coroner having inquired, for our Lord the King, when, where and by what means Alison Mavis Gough came to her death, doth find that Alison Mavis Gough died at Christchurch on the 3rd day of June 1942 and that the cause of death was Myocardial Failure of Acute confusion.'

The coroner, Ernest Charles Levvey, relied upon a sworn deposition from H. Hunter (this may have been a mistake, as in other files he's referred as James Dewar Hunter), the Sunnyside superintendent, which was included in the file. He went into more detail idiosyncratically capitalised:

The body viewed by the Coroner is that of Alison Mavis Gough, whom I knew when Alive. She was committed at CHRISTCHURCH and admitted to Sunnyside Mental Hospital, Christchurch on the 27th May, 1941. She was then suffering from SCHIZOPHRENIA and was in FAIR BODILY HEALTH. She has been confined to bed since 28th of May 1942 on account of ACUTE CONFUSION and died on 3rd June 1942 at 12 noon, in the presence of Nurse M.E. Wylie and relatives. The relatives were advised of her illness and have been notified of her death. The cause of death was MYOCARDIAL FAILURE DUE TO EXHAUSTION OF ACUTE CONFUSION.

Though much of the wording resembled that on the death certificate, there were three important pieces of new information here, all more or less shocking: first, that Alison had been in fair bodily health (making a heart attack less explicable); second, that she'd been in Sunnyside for an entire year; third, that she was alleged to be suffering from schizophrenia. Schizophrenia is serious. If the diagnosis was accurate, then 'nerves' was an equally serious form of understatement. It wasn't clear to me how schizophrenia led to 'acute confusion', which in turn led to heart failure and death. How could you die of 'confusion' in a mental hospital? What was confusion? Alison spent her last five days in bed. You couldn't die from that. Lying in bed doesn't give you heart failure and as far as I know, being bipolar doesn't either, not at the age of 29. None of this made sense, other than in the context of the contemporary mental health system. Alison was on long odds as soon as she stepped inside on 27 May 1941.

It wasn't just that Alison had been at Sunnyside for a year by the time she died, but that she had been admitted only 13 days after penning a chatty letter to her brother and only three days before her mother died. I couldn't believe Alison would have willingly left Julia's side when she was in a coma. The circumstances of Alison's admission felt as murky as those of her death.

I had other questions too. Hunter reported that Alison died with relatives present. Who were they? Why, then, the need to record that – presumably other – relatives were advised of Alison's illness 'and have been notified of her death'? There were a few ways of interpreting this slightly convoluted statement. Possibly the relatives were there and then were also formally notified, in line with some formal procedure. Alternative theories of mine were that the illness immediately preceding Alison's death was new – the family had to be told of it. Another was that the relatives with Alison as she died may not have been those formally registered as next of kin.

If this were the case, who might have sat with Alison in her final moments? Julia was already dead. Owen was in Wellington recovering from his operation – when Beryl wrote to Owen on 27 April he was still in hospital. Maybe Alison deteriorated from the 28th, hence her confinement to bed, and hence why no news in Beryl's 25 May letter.

If Beryl cabled on, say, the 29th, the day after Alison was put to bed, Owen, still recuperating, might have made it home the next day or the one after. I like to think he got there but I can't be sure. As to Tracy, my theories pulled me in opposite directions: he was there and then formally notified; or he wasn't there and had to be.

Was Tracy definitely in Christchurch at the time? Perhaps he was too busy arranging his second wedding to make it out to Sunnyside? That sounds spiteful. If I make an effort to be more benevolent, I'd say that Alison's death was so sudden it took Tracy by surprise. She might have been chronically ill but not terminal. This fits with the paucity of reference in Beryl's letter, but doesn't sit well with the advice of Alison's illness and her confinement to bed.

• • •

If there is any benefit from dying within an institution it is this: the record seam is richer than for those who die in their own beds. Bureaucracies cannot help but record themselves. Alison was in hospital. There must be a patient file.

Any private health matter is sensitive. You can't just call up someone's medical records the way you can a death certificate. On top of this there are extra precautions for the records of Sunnyside and of other so-called asylums, which are kept not within the health system but stored centrally, at Archives. And they're not just classified, like the coronial report, but subject to a form of super-injunction. All you can see are the categories of record that exist: admission book entry, individual file, register of deaths and so on. These are arranged in multi-decade snatches and alongside the record of every period is a red line that indicates restricted access – the 'sealed in perpetuity' rider that was becoming familiar. There is no detail available beyond the red line, other than with the authority of the contemporary legatees of the old mental hospitals, known as district health boards.

Accordingly, I wrote to the general counsel for Canterbury's board, explaining that I was investigating a great-aunt's death. I gave her name, that she had no children and that I was the direct descendant of her brother; that

I knew nothing but her date and place of death and wanted to understand more. Within a few weeks I heard back: they'd granted me permission to see Alison's full record, thus giving me my only confirmation that such a record existed. I went to the headquarters of Archives New Zealand in Wellington and asked to see everything they had. They searched under Alison's name, but found nothing.

I said, 'It must be here – I know she died there. I've seen her death certificate. The letter implies there's a file.'

The research assistant at the computer thought for a few moments and then tried some misspellings. After several attempts she found Alison's records, under 'Gouch'. I thanked her. Sometimes it takes luck and experience, not just pieces of paper. I put in an order for what had been found, and a few days later it had made its way out of the basement and I was sent a full copy, about 30 pages, mostly in tight, tiny cursive script.

The file began on the day of Alison's admission, 27 May, four days before the official start of winter, but the old weather reports say it was fine and bright. A nor'wester had helped to bring the temperature up to 18 degrees, more like spring than late autumn. I knew Canterbury days like this. The mornings and evenings are freezing but the days are bright blue and you can sit outside for lunch.

Were the gardeners still at work as they had been a fortnight ago? Had the leaves been cleared? I suspect everything would have been tucked in already for the long cold months ahead. Inside the house there would have been the wing full of servants; Julia, upstairs, dying in her bedroom as Tracy was to do, Beryl and Alison both by her side. Are they nursing her? Or maybe there is professional help for this?

Alison's letter to Owen on 14 May 1941 was lucid, amusing and sensible. She might, of course, have written the letter and then had a period of psychosis an hour later, say, or a week. But there was nothing to suggest it; the letter was perfectly clear and calm – no febrile stream of consciousness, no wild accusations. Yet she was an inmate 12 days later. Why, how? A return of whatever happened in '39?

I have no medical knowledge. I also realise that you can never really know what anyone is thinking. But in this case I don't feel extensive psychiatric expertise is necessary, just some humanity: Julia worsens, the coma begins, death is near. Anyone watching a mother die would be affected but in this case, Alison breaks down and has to be removed.

Really no one but Tracy could have arranged this: neither Beryl nor Owen would have had the authority, and Owen might not have even been there. The more relevant question is whether either of them could have prevented it, or whether they agreed with what occurred. I have two daughters now. The elder is so close to her mother that their partings are hard to watch. I could imagine her being distraught, hysterical if something dreadful were to happen along the lines of what Julia experienced. To the point that I would send her away to be incarcerated? I don't think so. While her mother was on her deathbed? I would say definitely not. But then, I have the luxury of living in a time with more medical options. Tracy may have wished for another way; he had just arrived back from Australia to find his wife near death and his eldest daughter disintegrating. Tracy might have been blasé; he might have wanted Alison's drama out of the house so he could concentrate on Julia; he might have been warm but practical and seen Sunnyside as his best bet. No matter: Julia loses her eldest daughter for her final days. Once Julia dies it is just Beryl and Tracy in the big, lonely house.

• • •

There were two ways to get into Sunnyside: as a voluntary boarder or by court order.

Alison's file recorded that 1941 was not her first stay; she had entered before, in 1939. Julia had mentioned the nerves and said that Alison 'will have to go away for a trip'. I thought Julia had meant taking the waters or some other equally genteel restorative activity. It seems that what she really meant was an institution. The four-month gap from letter to Alison's arrival on 6 August implied that it took some time to talk Alison into the idea of entering Sunnyside as a voluntary boarder. This was one of the innovations of the Mental Defectives Act 1911 – the concept of voluntary boarders was seen as stigma-reducing.

As the government yearbook for the time states: 'Persons labouring under mental defect, but capable of understanding the meaning of the procedure, may seek admission to a mental hospital as voluntary boarders.' Alison was one of 175 female voluntary boarder arrivals in 1939, about equivalent to the total female voluntary boarder population in the mental health system, possibly indicating an annual turnover around 100 percent.

Alison was given a single room and assessed the day after her arrival.

She is suffering from primary dementia. She is conscious and has full apprehension of her surroundings. She realises her position here and is fully oriented to time and place. She currently recognises people who are about her.

She can understand anything said to her and has good association of ideas. Her powers of reasoning appear adequate. She has a good memory for all periods … She has had a good education. She has auditory hallucinations and will sit with her head on one side, listening intently.

Questioned about the voices she says that she hears people say, 'You are mad,' and at times hears the command 'Go.'

She also has illusions. She hears the voice of a woman who is talking in the next room and she maintains the woman is talking about her. From these delusions she is developing disorders, that are faint and fleeting, of a persecutory type, that she is unwanted …

It went on for another few paragraphs, but you get the idea.

If this had been the first thing I read about Alison, I would have thought her a little mad too. But I already knew the timeline of the following two years and a little about the pressure the family must have come under and I find it hard to assess her health other than in this context.

Like others dismissed as mad, it seemed as if Alison was just seeing the future, or narrating her fears. Was the woman in the next room even a fiction? Was there someone there, talking to Tracy maybe, whispering in his study, saying Alison is unwanted, that she must 'go'? It seems to me it is easy to develop a sense of persecution, of being unwanted, when you've ended up in an institution.

Alison is described as being in good physical health and with good teeth and a good education. They also record a laparotomy scar – from a surgical incision into the abdomen. The record doesn't state what this might have been for, but it was most likely from an appendectomy. Tracy provided some background too. He notes that she has been treated by Doctors Baxter and Bakewell and that they have used paraldehyde, 'considerably' it seems to say. There is a reference that implies there has been a nurse at home (which is still Sumner at this point). It suggests that efforts were made to treat her before resorting to Sunnyside.

Where the form asks whether the patient has any obvious cause for anxiety or grief, Tracy writes: 'Disappointed over non-appointment to a position at school.' Alison is 26, she has been doing book-keeping. Maybe she applied for a teaching role? It sounded from Beryl, after all, that Tracy didn't want his daughters at his company – they had to stay home. Margaret was not subject to the same compunction.

I carried on reading.

Alison is calmer a few days after arriving. She seems almost to be treating it like a holiday. Possibly the significance of her situation hasn't sunk in. Three days further on she is being described as childish and fatuous. By 20 August she is laughing 'foolishly' but is bright and cheerful and doing needlework. This cheerfulness lasts a couple of weeks and on 6 September Alison is telling the staff that she is in perfect health. It doesn't seem to help. The next entry is a full month later. She is no longer so elated and has a 'feeling of frustration'. I'm no doctor, but this doesn't seem like an improbable trajectory.

A further month passes before anyone bothers to record how she's faring. It's now 6 November 1939 and she's 'much improved, is quiet and well behaved'. She is released three days later. It feels as though she's had to learn the right way to behave to get out. The final note, on 9 November, says simply, 'Discharged recovered.' Good news but still, three months on the inside. She even missed the outbreak of World War II.

• • •

In 1941 it didn't take four months to get Alison to Sunnyside and she did not go voluntarily. She was sectioned: 'Alison Gough, spinster, of Mona Vale, Fendalton, committed under Section 8 of the Mental Defectives Act'. She was 'Suffering from delusions and … violent and restless in her actions.' I noted, however, that although the coroner had said she had arrived suffering from schizophrenia, there was no mention of this in the admission notes.

Mona Vale to Sunnyside. It sounded like a line on a model train set.

Only the Supreme Court had the power to section someone and it required an application supported by the evidence of two doctors who had conducted examinations. For Alison, the first was Robert Bakewell who, later that week, would make his second appearance in this family story when he certified Julia's death. Bakewell was recorded as Alison's usual physician and was mentioned in the 1939 file. He examined Alison on 27 May 1941, the day of her committal, at 37 Head Street, Sumner. It's a private house now but presumably was then his surgery, since he gave another address in Sumner as his residence.

Bakewell certified that Alison was very violent, 'smashing anything that came within her reach; shouting and laughing and calling out to the spirits and never still except when under a sedative and suffering from various delusions'. He mentioned that in 1939 Alison had 'a similar attack that lasted for 3–4 weeks' and that in the previous week she'd begun showing such symptoms again. He didn't specify what comprised the delusions. A sense of persecution maybe? That someone is trying to get rid of her? In which case, the events that followed seemed to prove her right.

And only a week of illness? The 1939 episode might have predisposed those around Alison to judge – and condemn – quickly. But the reported briefness at least aligned with the earlier evidence: Alison was fine around mid-May but according to Bakewell deteriorated around the 20th. That was three or four days after the start of what Julia's death certificate described as her acute mania. Julia's collapse I am sure precipitated Alison's.

But Bakewll put the cause down to heredity. He injected Alison with morphine. He also wrote that Nurse Webb of Redcliffs 'informed me today that she had found the patient very violent all night and during the morning'. This implies that Bakewell examined Alison in the afternoon and that Nurse Webb was in residence at Mona Vale. She may have been present for Julia, not Alison.

After Bakewell, Alison was taken to Harley Chambers, overlooking the Avon on the corner of Cambridge Terrace and Worcester Street, across from the timbered Canterbury Club and not far from that marble statue of Scott. I knew the Harley building well. I used to walk past it each time I got a lunch leave into town from school, wandering up to Whitcoulls to browse the books and maybe get a non-dining hall sandwich. The Harley's a ruin now, courtesy of the earthquakes and the complexity of repairing old masonry buildings. It's covered in graffiti and, where it's not boarded up, the windows are broken.

It was once a lovely building, though, and in 1941 housed the medical chambers of a Dr Hector Quentin-Baxter. This I think must be the same 'Baxter' as mentioned in 1939 by Tracy. He was a leading neurologist and now provided the secondary supporting examination for Alison's committal. Quentin-Baxter's description of Alison was simple: 'maniacal'. He must have seen her three days earlier too as he noted that 'on 24.5.41 she was in a state of sub-acute mania. She spoke in a loud voice and expressed ideas of self-condemnation and speaks in an immodest way about her past. She attempted to hold me by force. She required close supervision.'

Quentin-Baxter just puts a line through the next section where asked to list 'the following facts concerning the said person, indicating mental defect, have been communicated to me'. Further down, where he is asked to

Harley Buildings, Christchurch, before the earthquake. CREATIVE COMMONS

state 'the factors which have caused the mental defect of the said person', he agrees with Bakewell and writes 'Heredity'. He finishes by saying she needs constant supervision and sedation. 'I further certify,' he added by hand to the form, 'the matter is urgent.' This also echoed Bakewell, whose wording was 'I further certify the matter is one of urgency.'

Alison was living at Mona Vale and so she must have been driven to Sumner from Fendalton for the first inspection by Bakewell, and then to Harley Chambers. If Bakewell's claim that Alison held him by force on the 24th is correct then I can't imagine that this shuffling back and forth across town occurred without struggle. It looks as though it took them all day to complete the committal requirements: Mona Vale, Sumner, back to town, out along Lincoln Road to Sunnyside. Alison was not admitted until 5pm. The admission record noted that, upon arrival, she had 'bruising on torso and arms'.

• • •

The formal applicant to the court for the sectioning was neither doctor, but Tracy. This at least confirmed to me that he was back from Australia and was at Mona Vale for his wife's illness and death. He must have got the news efficiently and travelled swiftly.

In the application to the court, Tracy wrote that Alison was mentally defective on the grounds of 'suffering from delusions and was violent and restless in her actions'. It's a standard form and confirms that Alison had had just one prior event of this nature, that Dr Bakewell was her usual 'medical attendant' and that the drug paraldehyde had been used. The question 'To what causes do you attribute patient's insanity?' is left unanswered. Elsewhere one of the questions asked whether the patient was originally dull or clever. Tracy wrote 'ordinary'.

At the bottom of the form Tracy added an extra handwritten note: all notices regarding Alison were to go to him, at his work address, 'marked personal'. In effect that meant everything about Alison would be accessible via his office.

The court approved Tracy's application, but not until the day after Alison's admission. This was legal in an emergency only, which would be specified by the certifying medical practitioners, hence the statements of urgency. A magistrate then had to be provided with all the required information within 24 hours. I guess Alison might have deteriorated, otherwise they seem to be saying that she's been sick for a week yet it's so urgent we can't get clearance in advance.

In Alison's case the magistrate signed off the next day by repeating the standard formula: 'Now therefore I do hereby order that the said patient continue to be detained in the said institution in accordance with the Mental Defectives Act 1911.' And that was it: Alison was sectioned.

27

I can't know how Tracy felt as Alison left, but if he cared for both her and Julia – or even either – then sending his daughter away was a feat of self-discipline. Facing tragedy with your wife, you'd normally want your children by your side. The reproductions can become more of a comfort as the original slips away.

Alison was 28 years old – her birthday was 28 March – when she was admitted to Sunnyside. The admission form described her as 'a young woman in poor physical health, with no communicable diseases'. She has deteriorated since she was discharged in good order in late 1939. I suppose you would when under the stress caused by her mother's health.

The Sunnyside file continued: 'She is confused, unable to give an account of herself and does not appear to realise where she is but she is able to recognise certain people about her. She is aurally hallucinated by the voice of God and has delusions that she is the wife of Christ. Her conversation is rambling and incoherent ...'

Julia was suffering from 'acute mania' for the two weeks before she died, from roughly the same time Bakewell mentions for the start of Alison's illness: the week leading up to 27 May. It looks as though the two women collapsed alongside each another.

In the Sunnyside admissions book, in the remarks column for Alison, the diagnosis initially written was paraphrenia – a sort of lighter version of psychosis that may not include hallucinations (a key feature of schizophrenia). At some point that has been crossed out and 'heredity' inserted, as per the diagnoses of both Bakewell and Quentin-Baxter. In 1941, 'heredity' accounted for 119 of the 1242 national admissions to asylums.

Tracy supported this with one further piece of information in his court application for Alison's committal. In answer to the question whether any relative had been of unsound mind, Tracy wrote: 'mother's sister in Sunnyside'.

It seemed there was another mystery aunt and another gap I didn't even know about.

I had no other option than to ask my mother about it. I didn't even have a name.

'Have you heard of this?' I asked her one day, 'Julia's sister? She went to Sunnyside?'

'Oh yes, that's Great-Auntie Vida,' she said, 'She had a goitre operation that went wrong. She was never the same apparently. It sounded very sad.'

The explanation had the feel of family folklore but, after double-checking, it seemed plausible. Goitre was a problem before the discovery of the uses of iodine, and it seems the operation to resolve it, though common, had risks. Goitre is an enlargement of the thyroid gland that can be caused by too little iodine, amongst other things. But if a goitre needs to be removed – for instance if it begins to block the airways – and too much thyroid is removed in the operation, it can cause hypothyroidism. This means the body can't produce enough thyroid hormone, which means it can't regulate its metabolism. This can have physical effects including weight gain, puffiness around the face, muscle weakness and aches, swelling in joints, heavier or disturbed menstruation, thinning hair, a slowed heart rate and so on.

Thyroid deficiency has also been associated with psychological deterioration including forgetfulness, fatigue, mental slowness, inattention and depression. One journal told me that 'at times, the psychiatric presentation may be so striking that patients are first diagnosed with a primary psychiatric disturbance rather than hypothyroidism'.

• • •

Veda (later known as Vida) Florence Hill Philpott was Julia Daisy's younger sister by six years, born in 1893. By now I knew the drill. I redrafted my letter to the Canterbury District Health Board and was grateful that I was again given approval to see a long-dead relative's file. While I was waiting for this to be processed, I cast around for other records. I found a probate application for Julia and Vida's father, Noah. He had died intestate and Vida's brother had sought a grant of administration. By coincidence, this application was made in September 1941, and Vida was ruled out as a potential executor because she was at Sunnyside. It seems highly likely that she was there as her sister lay dying in her mansion and as her niece was committed.

There were more medical-related records I was able to find too, less sensitive than those of the mental health system. If a child over a certain number of weeks dies stillborn it is recorded officially as a birth and a death. Vida had a stillborn child in 1927, when she was 34. She wasn't married. I found no other records of children. The gender of the dead child was not recorded.

Then I got Vida's Sunnyside file, so large that it came in nine different bundles. She had been in Sunnyside first in 1925. Her notes from then recorded 'a well-nourished [I thought of a slowing metabolism] woman in good bodily health'. She was recorded as 9 stone 13 ounces (63 kilograms) and 5 foot 5 inches (1.65 metres). It also noted 'old operation scar (collar incision) for exophthalmic goitre'. It seemed like there was something in the family story. I had to look up exophthalmic – it means protruding eyes. This along with goitre indicates that she had Graves disease, an auto-immune disorder. Among other symptoms it creates a build-up of tissue behind the eyes, making them bulge. Graves also causes hyperthyroidism – too much thyroid. Vida had a goitre removal operation. There is no way to know for certain if this operation took too much thyroid and pushed her to hypothyroidism with its consequent psychological presentations, but the rest of her 1925 notes were telling.

Mental condition: 'she has a dead feeling. There is a lack of energy and concentration, and from being an energetic woman she has developed into a listless, uninterested person, content to lie idly in bed. Her brain "feels dead".' The quotation marks are verbatim from the notes and so, one assumes, from Vida. Also noted was that 'she has not menstruated for three months'. Vida was 33 on admission.

I ran my theory past my friend Frank and he said it was entirely plausible. Such an operation now would be followed by medication to keep Vida in balance, but that wouldn't have been the case in 1925. He also confirmed that even now thyroid disorders can easily be misdiagnosed as psychiatric ones, most particularly depression. Vida's mental health then was an accident of auto-immune followed by difficult surgery. It was merely a sad coincidence with Alison. To cite Vida as evidence of congenital madness was therefore misleading – but possibly no one would have known this at the time, if even now it can be confused.

I'm not sure when Vida was first released from Sunnyside. I can see that her notes go up to June 1925. The only comment is that she worked in the laundry 'in a mechanical fashion'. It's a scene, to me, of Dickensian misery, but she is 'always willing to help' and by late June is being described as 'clean and tidy [this seems to have meant in the personal hygiene sense], converses with others and is progressing satisfactorily'.

The rest of the page is blank, and there is no record of discharge, as you'd expect to see recorded if she had indeed been let out. There is, however, a record of Vida being admitted as a voluntary boarder in June 1928. This could imply just a change of status but I'm inclined to think she was released, as her 1928 application gives her address as her father's home in the Christchurch suburb of Shirley, not Sunnyside itself. This was confirmed by the admission notes in 1928: 'She was a voluntary boarder in Sunnyside three years ago for a period of two months.' This means she was outside Sunnyside for her pregnancy and the birth.

Vida remained a so-called voluntary boarder for nine years, but at the end she was not released. On 18 August 1937 she, too, was sectioned because 'She has demented considerably since her admission and is now far withdrawn from reality.' This was allowed. The Act specified that 'If a voluntary boarder should after admission show mental defect sufficiently pronounced and sustained to render it improper to classify him any longer as such, application for a reception order is made to a Magistrate.' The two doctors mentioned in the paperwork were Beale and Hartnell. Beale had worked at Sunnyside from 1916 to 1925.

Vida's career in Sunnyside thenceforth was uneventful. It seems that this poor woman might have been turned into an automaton by a surgical accident. The only change came when, in August 1942, she was moved to Seaview, another asylum that sounded like a Torquay guesthouse, in the small West Coast town of Hokitika, beside the pounding waves of the Tasman Sea. From the town's high street you can see all the way to Aoraki/Mt Cook. Today Hokitika is over three hours' drive from Christchurch, via Arthur's Pass and the Otira Gorge.

Why move her away from where she'd lived since birth? Why place her on the remote West Coast? In Vida's patient file – hundreds and hundreds of pages recording daily or weekly progress or regress – there was no fanfare, no recorded medical rationale for the move. No recorded administrative reason either. No correspondence. Just a single line: 'Transferred to Hokitika.'

Beryl was listed as Vida's next and only kin and hence her main guardian. Vida's move did explain why Beryl owned a house on the West Coast at Punakaiki, which otherwise seemed too remote and rustic for her usual tastes. Beryl must have bought it to have somewhere to stay on her visits to Vida. Punakaiki village, about an hour's drive up the winding coast road from

Beryl's companion Ella (left) with Vida, c. 1960s.

Hokitika, is perched on a rocky corner of coastline near the mouth of the Pororari River. Vida's file included copies of regularly sent notes, from various hospital superintendents, thanking Beryl for gifts or biscuits.

Beryl travelled to the West Coast at least twice a year to visit Vida, once in the summer, once in the winter. She would take Vida out for several days in a row, normally in the afternoons. This made me smile at the memory of Beryl not being so good at mornings. My mother remembers going on a family holiday in the 1960s, staying at Beryl's cottage. With Beryl, they took Vida out for a picnic. Apparently Vida was amazed to learn she had all these relatives and was deliriously happy to be on an outing.

Vida died in 1974. We found her grave in the Hokitika Cemetery on a family visit to the West Coast in 1995. On it was a small vase of flowers, in which my mother also saw Beryl's touch.

I looked at the file closely to understand why Vida might have been moved. In February 1942 Hunter at Sunnyside was writing to Noah Philpott: 'I have to report that your daughter's bodily health is causing some anxiety. She has become much weaker generally and it would be advisable to visit her in the next few days.' I know these sorts of communications: come home, there's not much time.

A picnic with Vida (far left) and Alison, Beryl and Owen, c. 1925.

There is extensive correspondence between Beryl and Seaview in Hokitika from at least January 1943. The Public Trust was paying Beryl the 'comforts allowance' for Vida, with which to buy her essentials. I've no idea of the capital source for this – whether it was welfare or Vida's own capital, though the latter seems unlikely. Her listed profession was 'domestic'. The fact it was paid to Beryl seems to have been opposed – convention was to pay it direct to the mental hospital in question it seems. To me it shows how close they were. These notes from Beryl continue right through the 1940s, 1950s, 1960s and 1970s: asking about Vida's welfare, enclosing goodies for her such as stockings, requesting leave. The tone was reminiscent of boarding school.

There's the transfer notice, which says nothing, just 'I order the transfer' and the locations and date. The only connection I could find was that Dr Raymond Bellringer, the superintendent at the hospital at Hokitika, was mentioned by Beale and Hartnell, the two doctors certifying Vida in 1937. Both made reference to the views of 'Dr Bellringer of the Mental Hospital', by which they meant Sunnyside, where he worked until 1941. By the time Vida was moved, he was the superintendent of Seaview. This probably wasn't unusual, since it would have been a small community of mental health experts, but it was the only link I could discover. If there was a capacity issue at Sunnyside maybe this link would argue for Vida's move to Seaview rather than the mental hospital in, say, Dunedin.

• • •

The first notes in Alison's 1941 file weren't made until four days after her admission. She 'rushed away from her room, evaded the nurses' and punched through a window, badly cutting her arm, including the arteries. Obviously she was being held in close confinement, not allowed to wander the building and gardens at will.

Two days later she is recorded as being noisy, banging the walls. On 10 June, the next entry, she's found trying to tear off the bandages and pull out the stitches. She's stopped but succeeds three days later and has to have the wound redressed. By 17 June, four days after the stitches incident, Alison is clear and talking well but frequently mentions 'certain' (unnamed) people she doesn't like. This is a theme throughout her file – she can talk about almost anything in a perfectly sensible way, except particular people she doesn't like and thinks are out to do her harm.

A month after admission, on 27 June, Alison is 'very restless' and noisy. She 'mistakes the identity of people and thinks that people are going to do her an injury. Can usually be made to be quiet and then talks reasonably about almost anything. Her mother died just after Alison was admitted, she is not to be told yet.' Alison sounds calmer but I am not surprised to read that the sense of persecution endures. She has been locked up against her will, she is sick, she is paranoid.

A whole month goes by before the next visit and doctor's notes on 27 July: Alison is restless and violent towards the nurses; she has lost weight. What would she have been doing? Just sitting in her room, or was she able to stroll outside? Having seen Vida's file, I knew they could record outings and visitors. Alison's file had no record of outings or visits. It might be an omission; it might have been lost over the years. I hope so. I hate to think of anyone being stuck behind any set of gates with no way out, and no one to visit.

Another whole month until the next notes in Alison's file, on 27 August 1941: 'She normally talks fairly reasonably but after a while becomes confused and loses the train of thought. At times is noisy and wanders aimlessly about the ward shouting "that bloody woman" and accusing people of breaking up her home.' This was the most detail so far. I had only one idea of who she meant by 'that bloody woman' and I was getting a fair idea of where, on the spectrum of blame or victimhood, Alison felt her father belonged.

The overwhelming majority of schizophrenia cases have delusions of persecution, but what if the persecution wasn't a delusion? Alison's home was indeed broken up. Her mother did die. Her father did marry that bloody woman. Her family was never the same. She might not have been personally persecuted but what she told the doctors did indeed come to pass.

Another month passes. 'She is emotional, weeps and becomes wildly angry with some outside people, blaming them for her mother's death.' This is the first indication that she's been told. It's also about the time Beryl was writing to Owen to exclaim how hopeful she was about Alison. Did someone – Beryl herself? – visit Alison and think she looked well? If so, then the records must have become incomplete with time as there is no mention in the file. Alison has, however, lost more weight, and doctors describe her as often walking aimlessly about. It feels as though Julia's death has broken her.

By 27 October Alison is quiet and does not mix well with patients. 'She is a little depressed.' An understatement, surely. Then: 'Blames her father for the death of her mother.' After another month there's no real improvement, but then a comment that implies further deterioration: 'she has very poor powers of conversation'.

Three whole months pass until further notes are made. There is no page missing. The notes are all on one cramped page, written by hand and just a few words per entry. Nothing for three months. It's February 1942 and Alison is rambling, emotionally unstable. Maybe she's just no longer troubling the staff but the blankness is stark against the earlier details of violence and struggle. She has, perhaps, accepted her situation.

Still no visitors are listed. I like to think that Avenal, Owen and Beryl came to visit her for Christmas. Beryl had once written that she'd been to see Alison and she was looking fitter. That was April 1942.

On 2 March 1942 they took Alison's blood pressure. Nothing else, nothing else to note. On 10 April 1942 she was very emotional, unsettled and worried. By now Owen has permanently left Mona Vale too and poor Beryl alone is left, writing to her beloved younger brother twice a day. Who else did she have? As an unemployed single woman, where could she have gone? 'You know old chap, you will be able to come back to Mona Vale while you are resting … It will be marvellous to have you back home again.' It wasn't a suggestion, it was a plea.

The next item in the file was Alison's medicine records. She was given morphine at 10.45pm on the day of her arrival; Bakewell had already administered some that afternoon, when he inspected her. That same day she was also started on paraldehyde, a depressant and an anti-convulsant. Her

The family on holiday: Alison (centre in hat) aged about 10, with Owen and Beryl to the left of her.

first dose was administered at 11.30pm. It had been a long day and, surely, one of horrors for her. To have been given morphine twice and then a further sedative – it makes me think she's trying to fight back.

The paraldehyde – which she has apparently been given before, according to Tracy in his sectioning application – was to be a five-day course but it kept getting repeated: 'after meals and two tablets during night'. It was stopped for a day on 13 June 1941, a fortnight or so after admission, but then begun again the next day. Dosages were increased on 1 July and again on 1 August. This continued, on and off, until 1 November. The paraldehyde began again on 22 May 1942. That seems a large gap.

Alison's notes record her deterioration and that seemed to lead to the reintroduction of the drugs. What I can't help but realise is that she's approaching the one-year anniversary of her mother's death and her own confinement. At 7.45pm on 22 May 1942 she was given paraldehyde again. Around four hours later she was given morphine. She was given paraldehyde again one and a half hours later, now 1am on the 23rd.

Alison was given paraldehyde the next day, and the next. On 26 May she was given more morphine. On 27 May she was confused, excited, incoherent. She was given paraldehyde again on the 28th. After two days off, the regime changed. The doctors recorded 'marked signs of exhaustion'. It was as if they

Alison's medicine record from Sunnyside. Note the last dose: she was dead within 10 minutes.

then reversed the regime. They started to give her cardiazol, which was, is, a convulsant, not an anti-convulsant like her earlier drugs.

The use of cardiazol was consistent with contemporaneous thinking about how to treat psychosis. To shake it out of you. It was a form of drug shock therapy but it could lead to uncontrolled seizures. Alison was given more of this medication at 5pm on 1 June 1942, and more the next morning at 3am. The next day she received a dose of morphine at 11.50am. That was her last medication. The final entry for 3 June 1942 said, 'Died 12:00.' It was the first anniversary of the day her mother was buried.

The coroner had said that Alison died in the 'presence of relatives'. I had that one note to Noah Philpott when Sunnyside was worried about Vida. Might they have sent something to Tracy? Nothing in the file, but then it seems incomplete, notably so for visitors. Could it have been Vida who was there? That would make sense of the formal communication to the others, but it doesn't feel conventional and I've no idea if it would have been allowed: bureaucracy might oversee a high death rate but it's still a bureaucracy and rules are rules. But if a young woman was dying and there was no one else about, might they ask the aunt to come? I don't know, but from the fact they kept dosing Alison I have to hope the staff didn't think they would kill her. Alison died within 10 minutes of her final morphine. That was not long enough to get from Tracy's office on Oxford Terrace to Sunnyside.

Then on 18 August 1942, having been in Sunnyside for almost 20 years without an apparent problem, Vida was moved over the Southern Alps to Hokitika. Possibly overcrowding? The numbers of inmates at Sunnyside was around 40 higher at the end of 1942, but that's only about a 2.8 percent increase and nationwide, inmate figures were down. It may have been enough to move long-term residents over the hill and far away. But in the file there is no record of any correspondence. Maybe they wouldn't keep a copy of their outward letters, but there are no letters of opposition or acknowledgement in return either.

• • •

I asked for and was sent the relevant page of the register of deaths at Sunnyside. All the other names had been redacted but you could see the ages and causes of deaths. There were 11 deaths on the page, which covered only three weeks. Nearly all of them were recorded as having myocardial failure, though most were much older than Alison. Spare a thought for the only other young one, someone aged 34, whose cause of death was 'general paralysis of the insane'.

I went back to my friend Frank.

'No autopsy?' he asked.

'None.'

'Hmm. Without an autopsy,' he said, 'it's impossible to tell exactly what happened.'

'It seems like a lot of drugs,' I said.

'They weren't very accurate and yes, it was. It's hard to know but basically it looks like they overdosed her and that put her into cardiac arrest and she died.'

'They killed her?'

'Basically. Given her age. That's a convulsant they gave her. It seems the most likely explanation.' He continued: 'She would have been restrained for those last few days.'

'That's what confined to bed meant?' I asked.

'Yup. In a mental hospital. Leather straps.'

There was only a small death notice for Alison in the papers and no obituary. This may not be surprising, given the nature of the death. Perhaps in another age there may have been a deeper investigation into the death of a 29-year-old, but she was just one of two or three deaths that week at Sunnyside.

Alison was buried beside her mother on 5 June 1942, a year and three days after Julia. I don't know who attended but since Canon Redgrave took the service, I assume it was held at St Barnabas. The death was registered on 12 June, the day, according to Beryl's letters, that Tracy had originally picked for his wedding. He had the grace to delay it five days and remarried on the 17th, 12 days after burying his daughter.

28

The various contemporary court processes grinding away in the background had also inspired my brother to undertake his own investigation into family history. He'd been curious about some of my findings and decided to do his own digging. He lived overseas but could research from a distance and one day he called with a breakthrough.

'You remember how Beryl was the one who filed the first case in 1955?' he opened. 'And you couldn't find the court records?'

'Yes,' I agreed, 'It sounded like they'd been lost.'

'Well, I've found them. I went direct to the whole justice archives, not just the High Court. Turns out the court had no record because Beryl applied for relief under the Family Protection Act. The Family Court didn't exist then but when it was set up, in the early 1980s, all these sorts of family actions were retrospectively filed in the Family Court archives. An archivist thought of this, checked and found it. I'll send you a copy. Have a look.'

Fifty-two pages had survived. The bulk of them were procedural or pro-forma material, including simple submissions and a court minute around the appointment of counsel for the unborn or otherwise unrepresented. There was in fact only one substantive document in the file: Beryl's original affidavit. It was just three pages long, a total of 19 paragraphs, but it was the only formal comment I'd seen from her. Beryl's subject was her father's death and estate but, as I'd been finding, accurate context was important.

She opened as required: 'I, Beryl Daisy Gough, of Christchurch, Spinster, make oath and say as follows.' Then followed a basic summary of events that I already knew. The only surprise was that she said she didn't know, but had been 'informed' of, the value at which her father's estate was sworn. It seemed to confirm what was implied by the other records, that the children had no formal role following their father's death – Margaret and Frank Wilding might have sought probate without reference. Having thought so much about the deaths of Julia and Alison, I wondered now how Beryl and Owen would have heard about their father's death. Would they have been told on the day? Possibly not.

Beryl only started to talk about herself halfway through the short document:

> I was educated at St Margaret's College in Christchurch until I was eighteen years of age and after school I continued to study music.
>
> My father did not want my sister or me to go to work and at his wish we remained at home and assisted with household duties. During my schooldays we lived at Sumner but later moved to Mona Vale at Fendalton.
>
> Mona Vale is a large house with about 16 acres of grounds, and there was plenty of work for my sister and me in connection with the house and garden. I also continued my musical studies.

Tracy's views didn't surprise me. He was a beneficiary of twentieth-century capitalism but he'd also been born and brought up a late Victorian. Wearing formal dress for parties, travelling the right way, buying the right pictures. I could quite imagine him imposing his view of taste and decorum on his children and those around him. I might have been known to do it a little myself.

Beryl moved onto Julia: 'For about six months before her death, my mother was confined to bed and I looked after her with the assistance of a trained nurse. About this time, my sister Alison also became ill, and she died a year after my mother.' This was new information – a much longer period of illness for Julia. I hadn't considered this possibility but it made sense once you thought about it: not a short, sharp decline, but a longer, slower one in which visits to the garden were noteworthy and it was fine to go to Wellington for an operation, or agree to perform in a concert.

I was, however, no closer to knowing what might have happened to Julia medically, and still wondered whether it might be drug misuse, even by misadventure. This is akin to what happened to Judy Garland, for whom a long-term use of barbiturates led to accidental, gradual overdose. For Julia this seemed less likely, with a nurse present. The presence of a nurse also indicated that at least she was getting good care, and Beryl and Alison weren't having to carry the burden on their own.

Beryl continued:

After my mother's death I kept house for my father until he remarried the following year. Shortly after his marriage I went to St George's Hospital in Christchurch to work as a VAD. I then decided to train as a nurse and in 1944 I commenced my general training at the Oamaru Hospital, several hours south of Christchurch. After a short time at Oamaru I suffered a breakdown in health and returned to Mona Vale.

My health did not improve and in March 1945 I went to Hornby Lodge as a voluntary boarder. I was discharged on the 9th day of June 1948 after making a full recovery from the nervous condition from which I had been suffering, and I have remained in perfect health since that time.

After leaving Hornby Lodge I spent some time with my grandmother, and then with my brother, in Christchurch. I am now living with a friend in her house and sharing household expenses with her. It is my intention if possible to purchase a home of my own.

So Beryl, too, had left, had a breakdown. That made four of them, four women from the same family dead or driven out: Vida, Julia, Alison and now Beryl. And Owen was gone already, as of March 1942. By 1944 – assuming Beryl did not live at the hospital during her VAD work – all the original residents of Mona Vale bar Tracy had gone.

Poor Beryl. The last survivor of the women from the big house, and then packed off to this lodge. Its reputation didn't precede it the way Sunnyside's did. It was possibly innocuous, but really, what were the chances? The term voluntary boarder gave it away. You don't specify voluntary unless there's another kind. And the only places that have other kinds of boarders are not the sort of places you want to go, especially not if you've had a breakdown in the early 1940s.

I searched the newspaper records to learn a little more about Hornby Lodge but found nothing. I tried lists of historical mental health facilities but also found nothing. Okay, I thought, maybe it wasn't that bad. Maybe, just maybe, Hornby was some recuperative paradise for wealthy girls with a case of the nerves?

With this in mind I also tried the historical building register of the Christchurch City Council. If it was a garden-encircled old home it might be recorded somewhere. It turned out to be a lucky guess. There was a listing for a building called 'Stoneycroft/Hornby Lodge' at 79 Carmen Road. An accompanying photo showed a large masonry house with the thick structural forms and deep balconies of the Lutyens-inspired 1920s and 1930s. In the photo the house was bathed in sunshine behind a high brick wall. It had been originally built as a home for local businessman and landowner Richard Morten, but the listing went on to say, as I'd suspected, that 'The former dwelling Stoneycroft/Hornby Lodge' has 'high historical and social significance … for its long connection with progressive mental health treatment in New Zealand'.

If I hadn't already discovered what I had I might have stayed optimistic. But I had an inkling of what progressive mental health meant in those days. The house, originally a family home, was sold to the government in 1919 and converted 'to become a mental hospital'. Initially, I discovered, 'the house was intended to serve as a sanatorium where fee-paying patients could enjoy some of the domestic comforts to which they were accustomed before they became mentally ill'. Hornby Lodge was, it seemed, 'the first state facility of this type to be developed in New Zealand'. Aha, this might be okay, I thought; maybe I'd misjudged after all. Maybe it was more like a sanatorium for the well-off, paying fees for their time away from the cares of the world. I conjured an image of Swiss mountain retreats, villas on Lake Como, prim nurses in sparkling white uniforms gliding about in soft focus, quiet voices. Hornby Lodge was rectilinear, stripped Georgian with high ceilings and a deep loggia. It was simple and, for its time, progressive. I read on.

In the late 1920s the use of Hornby Lodge changed. By then the old idea of a mental disorder 'had evolved in line with the latest thought in mental health treatment. As the social revolution of the 1920s progressed, the idea gained currency that mental disorder was not necessarily a life sentence and that those who were diagnosed as recoverable should be treated in a humane domestic environment with the aim of returning them to the community.' Hornby Lodge became one of four 'curative neuropathic hospitals' in New Zealand. It would also take people transferred from Sunnyside.

I was still nodding. Humane sounded good. It was set on 27 acres (10.9ha) and the council file noted the lodge's unusually modern design. A good setting for the supposedly modern treatment being delivered. It might well have been just what Beryl needed after the trauma and grief she had endured. She may have been well cared for. But still, Beryl was there for three years.

Beryl's admission date of March 1945 rang a bell too. By now I was swimming in old papers, letters and photographs from which I'd created my papier-mâché theories and any date's echo could as likely be false, but there was something … It wasn't in any letters, it wasn't in medical files, it

Beryl at Sumner, c. 1935.

wasn't in Owen's military record – which meant I'd likely encountered it in the affidavits. And there it was: Margaret took over as managing director of Tracy's company on 27 March 1945.

I wrote once again, asking to see yet another childless aunt's records and received seven pages in a familiar buff folder. Beryl's file told me that she admitted herself to Hornby on 21 March 1945. She was examined on arrival: 'She lies quietly in bed, is fully oriented and realises her obligations as a Voluntary Boarder.' This was interesting: obligations, not options.

> She co-operates willingly on examination and gives a fair account of herself. She states that for the past year she has had a very strong feeling that she should go into the Mental Hospital and cure the patients. 'It feels like a divine power. Then I begin to get worried about this because after all that is really blasphemous to think one can perform miracles like God. I don't really know what to do about it. It has been getting me more upset all the time.' She is hallucinated and deluded but shows partial insight for her condition and is anxious to have treatment. She is suffering from schizophrenia.

Beryl was described as displaying:

Fair physical condition
No sign of recent injury
Teeth natural
Tongue clean
Height 5' 2½"
Weight 7st 8ozs

All her measurements and tests were healthy and normal; under 'Family History' there were no notes, no mention of Vida or Alison. 'Probable Cause' was likewise blank. There was no attempt to explain what might have happened to Beryl or why she might be suffering from schizophrenia. No link seemed to be made, for instance, between Beryl's desire to heal people in a mental hospital and the death of her sister in such a place a few years earlier. It may be that staff just wrote down whatever voluntary boarders told them and didn't question further, but they still had obligations under the Mental Defectives Act and this seems to have been a thin overview of Beryl's case.

I turned the page. Next was a yellow sheet, shorn from a legal pad and darkened at the edges with age. It was the start of Beryl's notes from her stay. The first entry was 26 March, five days after arriving. The entry beside this date was very short, in fact just three letters: 'E.C.T.' – electro convulsive therapy.

• • •

As for many people, my view of ECT was an unconscious derivative of such works as *One Flew Over the Cuckoo's Nest* and *An Angel at My Table*, but what I read about ECT's early days, around the time Beryl would have been subjected to it, did little to change my mind. I'm ignorant of the science but am amazed it's still in use. It seems so brutal: tying someone down and shocking them repeatedly and telling them it's helping.

Partly the development of ECT grew out of an observation that people with epilepsy didn't suffer from schizophrenia. This negative link was later disproved but it led to the idea of mental health treatment via seizure. Shaking people out of it was a cure and the thinking gradually hit on ECT as the safest way: you could adjust and control the charge even as you were delivering the treatment, and hence minimise excessive impacts.

ECT had been started in 1938 by two Italian doctors who picked up on the thesis that seizures were, in effect, good for mental health. Up until the 1950s a form now known as 'unmodified' ECT was practised. This involved no anaesthesia and no muscle relaxant. It also involved less tailoring to the individual patient. Every skull has a high but differing electrical resistance, meaning that there can be a large difference in the size of electrical dose needed for a patient. 'Seizure threshold increases, and seizure duration decreases, with age.' Contemporary ECT allows for adjustments to reflect this. Unmodified ECT did not. There was a fixed high dose – but they could turn it off.

I can't say the evidence from Beryl's file is compelling but ECT has endured despite ongoing controversy and uncertainty about how precisely it works. These days they provide patients with breathing masks to keep the mouth open and protected, but not in Beryl's day. This is what Beryl would have had: strapped down, buckles over the arms and legs and likely a belt around the head; wide awake and given repeated large shocks to the head.

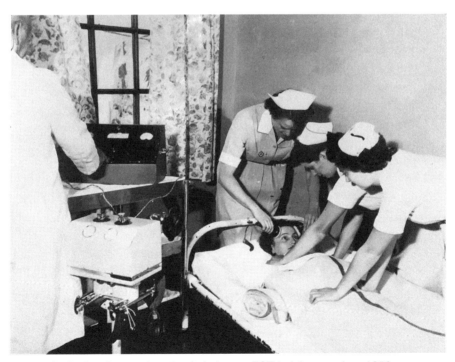

Nurses (including the mock patient) during an ECT training session, 1950s.
PORIRUA HOSPITAL MUSEUM

Either that or she would have been held down by several nurses at once, as an image from a training session in 1956 shows.

There have been claims recently that ECT was used as part of gay conversion therapy. One of the victims described her treatment in the 1970s, when the technology and precision were more advanced: 'They would give me muscle relaxant to paralyse me. It felt like razor blades going through my body. You were fully awake, and could see the silver machine and the assistants holding the electrodes and placing them around my head before I became unconscious.' She endured burns to her scalp from the electrodes and the treatment would make her vomit.

ECT was initially heralded as a harm-free, almost magic solution. But the side effects were obvious to those who had to endure it. Some of the obvious negatives included the extreme pain of the delivery of the electrical shock, damage to the mouth (and jaw), muscle aches and trauma and sometimes collateral injuries such as limb fractures as patients flailed around just shy of death itself.

There was also confusion, and complaints about damage to memory. In *The Emigrants*, W.G. Sebald's elegy for a broken and lost Europe, he describes an Uncle Ambrose being subjected to this unbelievable process: 'I see him lying before me … the electrodes on his temples, the rubber bit between his teeth, buckled into the canvas wraps that were rivetted to the treatment table like a man shrouded for burial at sea.'

And this was in the 1950s, when sedatives were starting to be used to reduce physical trauma injuries that could be caused by sudden, violent writhing.

That most careless but therefore most impartial of all social barometers, Hollywood, gave ECT its first appearance on screen in *The Snake Pit*, which was released in November 1948, just five months after Beryl was herself. The film starred Olivia de Havilland as the schizophrenic Virginia Cunningham. Her concerned husband sends Virginia to Juniper Hill State Hospital, where she's given ECT. As she goes in for treatment fully awake, she asks: 'Why are you electrocuting me?'

But although the film shows the bureaucracy of the hospital system and the malevolence of some staff, overall it's positive about the treatment. Virginia is cured. The husband is not the baddie. As such, *The Snake Pit* – the name came from the padded ward for the most recalcitrant patients – stands in contrast to the films from the 1960s and later, by which time forced shock treatment was presented as damaging and barbaric. *Shock Corridor*, made in

1963, shows a patient strapped to a table with leather bands on his arms and legs and a rolled-up bandage in his mouth. The treatment ultimately leaves him in a vegetative state.

Apparently De Havilland considered this role one of her toughest. She was a similar height, age and weight to Beryl at the time. She was born in July 1916, Beryl in August the same year. As part of her preparation, De Havilland visited Camarillo State Mental Hospital where she 'met a young woman who was very much like Virginia, about the same age and physical description, as well as being a schizophrenic with guilt problems … What struck me most of all was the fact that she was rather likable and appealing. It hadn't occurred to me before that a mental patient could be appealing, and it was that that gave me the key to the performance.'

It could have been Beryl. Beryl, so small and so smiling and so soft, went to Hornby to be electrocuted. According to her file, she had three sessions in her first 10 days, then a note: 'There is a slight improvement.' Five more sessions followed over the next two weeks, resulting in 'Condition improving', then an unintelligible series of words and then, 'gaining weight'. Then another five bouts over the following fortnight and 'she has been much better'. That's a total of 12 sessions.

Beryl had two months off before they started again on 12 July 1945. The notes for the session that day said that Beryl 'has been quite unsettled lately. Very deluded, introspective, pre-occupied with religious ideas. Believes mysterious things are happening to her.' It wasn't that mysterious. They were plugging electrical nodes to her skull and turning them on.

Another seven sessions followed at two- to three-day intervals, ending on 6 August 1945. The accompanying notes didn't register much improvement: 'Condition has been very unsettled for some time. She is very deluded, fantastic, see's [sic] God's interference in some everyday happenings.' Beryl displayed some modern views that alarmed the staff enough to record them: 'she refuses to eat well saying it was killed by human hand'. A few months later, again noted as a potential sign of mental illness, Beryl was 'very worried about the cruelty inflicted upon animals and so is refusing to eat meat. Also beginning to refuse eggs as hens are locked up.'

There was no visitor record with the file; I hope that, like Alison's must have been, it was lost.

Two more months passed before there was another observation. That next note was October 1945, with the war over and spring arrived. Beryl was described as 'rather more settled lately. Still very delusional and a little erratic in her behaviour but on the whole conducts herself well and makes herself useful in the lodge.' Beryl had trained as a nurse; it sounds as though she might have used her experience to help out, and the work could have been therapeutic. By early December the positivity of October had slipped: 'Has been very erratic in behaviour lately and her bizarre delusions are very prominent.' They decided to put her back on ECT – 12 sessions stretching from 17 December to 24 January 1946. Beryl was electrocuted on both Christmas Eve and New Year's Eve. The doctors seemed to observe the statutory holidays, so she was able to skip the horror on Christmas Day and Boxing Day; after New Year's Eve she had a gap until 3 January.

Nothing was recorded until after the seventh session, when there was an entry of only one line: 'There has been little change in her mental condition.' Then they strapped her down and started again, finishing the series. Ten days later the notes recorded: 'Little change in mental condition.'

There were more notes on Beryl's concerns about red meat and the killing of animals followed by nothing for seven months, and then only: 'No change apparent. Still very delusional. Most of her delusions centring around the animal kingdom. Has recently been feeding the cats a vegetarian diet of porridge, pudding, soup etc.' This just sounded like the Beryl I knew. Which could mean either that she was fine at Hornby Lodge, or was truly unwell all her life. Given that society seems to have caught up with her views, I am inclined to the former.

It was an entire year before anyone made any more notes, and for all that time the entry was just: 'No change at all.' But it seems that Beryl didn't stay at Hornby the whole time – she was allowed out. This might have been one of the privileges accorded a voluntary boarder. The only evidence I have, though, is another brief comment in her notes: 'When she visits her parents at home, she sometimes indulges in an outburst of screaming and will not be pacified.'

And it wasn't her real mother, was it? Another six months passed: 'Calmer of late but occasionally becomes excited and agitated.' Then it was June 1948, three years and three months since Beryl arrived, and the file said, 'Discharged relieved.' Relieved was not the same as recovered. Beryl went to stay with her grandmother, Elizabeth, in Sumner. Like Owen, she never went back to Mona Vale.

29

Both my brother and I had by now learnt that almost every aspect of family history merited further review: any gap, any event, any date, any person. Any stick dropped in the current had to be watched all the way to the next bridge. I found him often running ahead of me to do this, spurred by his earlier success, looking at things his own way.

He would come home about once a year and stay at Owen and Avenal's for a night or two. Maybe, like me, he needed to be among the ruins to have a feel for the story and what might be at stake. Maybe he just didn't trust my research. Either way, he'd do his own trawl through shelves and drawers, looking for mementoes, looking for explanations.

One visit came not long after I'd discovered what had happened to both Alison and Beryl. He stayed in Christchurch for a few days, then made his way north to visit me. He stayed a couple of nights, noticing that a lot of decoration plundered from Christchurch had migrated: 'I'm just keeping it safe till the house gets fixed,' I said. 'It'll go back.' He probably believed me. He'd brought a folder with him, which he now laid between us and took the chance to outline his latest theories.

'You know the date of Tracy's will, don't you?' he asked.

'Yes, 15 November 1946.'

'And the first codicil, the first change – just minor proofing issues – that was dated the same day.'

'It was probably faster than typing up a whole new will.'

'Yes, probably. Then nothing else changes until mid-1946. Then the next two codicils are rushed through side by side. The second one is late May, the third and final one was five or six weeks later, the 16th of July 1948.'

'So?' I said.

'Beryl was locked up in Hornby Lodge. She only got out on the 9th of June 1948, between these two events.'

'I'm not sure I follow you?'

'The second codicil was the one that reduced the power of Tracy's future trustees and gave Margaret, his new wife, the controlling interest in the business. It appointed her managing director for life. It just seems surprising that Beryl is locked away for three years, then a week before she's released there's this major change.'

'She was a voluntary boarder,' I reminded him. 'Supposedly she could come and go. She might have got out any time. It might be happenstance, it might just be coincidence.'

'I know, but apparently you had to have someone vouch for you still – to get let out. One of the uncles told me this once. Beryl had told him.'

'What's your point?'

'I just don't know how truly voluntary any of this was – I mean we're talking 1940s psych wards. Anyway, look at this.'

He pulled out a copy of the will and codicils from his folder and placed it on the coffee table between us. 'You tell me you've read this?' he asked.

I nodded.

'Well, tell me who witnessed the second codicil?'

'I can't remember that sort of stuff.' I said, reaching for it. His hand got there first and he picked it up.

'One was a nurse,' he said.

'Nineteen forty-eight, wasn't it?' I said, 'So Blair …' I was thinking of the birth of Owen's half-brother. 'He would have been two? It could've been a nurse for him?'

'Maybe. Anyway, I've looked her up. She was 18. And the second witness – you know who it was?'

'No.'

'Now, remember, this is the second codicil, the one that included Margaret in the receipt of real capital.'

'Yes. Got it. Still no idea.'

He folded back the pages and pointed. I read 'M.A. Fife, Domestic'.

'Fife? As in her surname? A relative?'

'Yes, yes and yes.'

'Not a coincidence?'

'No.'

'Who was she?' I asked.

'It was Margaret's sister. Margaret employed her as a maid at Mona Vale.'

'What? Is that allowed?'

'The employment or the signing? One's a little socially unacceptable.'

'The signing,' I said.

'I doubt it. You're not supposed to be related. But it was never challenged in the courts and so there it is. Maybe they were fine with it? I mean, they already knew the surname well enough.'

'You're sure of who it is?'

'Yes. I called up her will at Archives – her name was Mary, by the way, she was younger. Mary and Margaret. It looks like they emigrated together from Scotland. Margaret seems to have had the brains. Mary died in the 1970s. She was described as a spinster and a retired domestic. She had very little, but she left it all to one person, who was also her executor, and I think it proves the connection.'

'Who?'

'To Blair, her sister's child. He must have been the light of her life – she'd known him since he was a newborn.'

'I've never heard of Mary before.'

'Well, we didn't even know Margaret's name till recently, so it's no surprise. But do you want to know the most interesting part?'

'Go on.'

'The codicil itself is on one page, it's very brief. The signatures – including Tracy's – are on a separate page. No codicil on the signing page, no signatures on the codicil page.'

I took a look. 'But it does record that he's signing a codicil, beside Tracy's name, so I mean …'

'I know. But it's interesting, if not odd, right? Now look at these other dates too. Do you know when Tracy got sick?'

'If I'd realised this was going to be a quiz,' I said, 'I probably wouldn't have let you come and stay.'

'Come on.'

'He was travelling somewhere, wasn't he, Tracy?'

'Exactly.' He had a copy of Margaret's affidavit. 'Look at section eleven.'

I read it: 'During August 1948, I accompanied my said husband on a business trip overseas. During this trip his health deteriorated and in February 1949 he became totally incapacitated.'

'Do you see?' my brother asked.

'Yes, I read that affidavit too. Also I looked up Tracy's immigration records to see if he'd been in the country when Julia died. I found this trip in 1948 when I was doing that.' I went off to shuffle around for a small brown cardboard-backed notebook that I'd haphazardly filled with notes, dug it out and brought it back. 'Tracy left on 24 August 1948 on the *Aorangi*. Just him and Margaret, no son. They were heading for Vancouver.'

'Anything else?' my brother asked.

'The next time he appears in the immigration records is boarding the same ship in Vancouver, bound for home. He embarked on 8 February 1949. I guess it's his return trip. It fits with what's said.'

'It does. That's good. What does it prove?'

'Well, I think it explains the nurse. They'd have her in to get familiar with their son because they were going to be going away for a few months.'

'Good point. It does. Anything else?'

'Not really.' I answered.

'What about Beryl?'

'What about her?'

'She's been inside a mental health facility for three years, gets out in June and her father goes abroad in August?'

'It's over two months later, though?' I said. 'I don't buy it. It fits, but so do a hundred other possibilities. Tracy might equally have been waiting for Beryl to be released before he wanted to leave the country again. Once she's out he waits a couple of months to make sure she's fine, then he goes?'

'I suppose,' he agreed. 'But those liners to the West Coast of America wouldn't have departed that frequently, given how long it took to get there and back. There might only be a monthly run, so in effect he might have got on the next available ship.'

'He could just as likely have been waiting for her as avoiding her. And Beryl seems to have always been the warmest towards him.'

'Exactly. It's not about him. Your only surviving daughter – locked up for three years and within a month or so of her getting out, you're off abroad? I mean, who would do that?'

'I don't know,' I answered. 'But also – taking a ship wasn't risk free. It was probably common to sort your will before you went away for maybe six months.'

'Who would've booked the travel?' he asked. 'She's just had the July codicil done, getting two thirds of the business.'

'Doesn't prove anything, though,' I said.

He sat back. 'I know. But it sort of fits, doesn't it? Now, one more thing,' he continued. 'Have you ever seen TT's death certificate?'

'I'm sure I have. At some point Why? Do you want it? I could dig it out.'

Tracy and family on
one of his yachts,
Banks Peninsula.

'No, I have a copy here.' And he pulled something more from his file.

'Is this another test?' I asked.

He ignored me. 'You know where he's buried?'

'At Bromley, but not with Julia?'

'Yes,' he pointed to the death certificate, 'Ruru Lawn, it's sort of a separate section. I found this as well,' and another document emerged. 'It's from the cemetery guide. They've included biographies of some of the civic worthies buried there – Ruru Lawn has a few, including Tracy. I made you a copy – you need to read it.'

I was looking at it. 'I've just realised,' I said, 'that Tracy died the exact same day as Alison, twelve years later.'

I scanned the document he'd handed me. It started with Tracy's birth in Sydney, his family's move to Christchurch and so on. It mentioned his primary school, a private tutor, Gilby's (a technical college) too, and also St Aloysius. It felt like his parents tried to give him everything they could afford. There was an outline of Tracy's early career and then his business activities, including reference to his firm's expansion during World War II. It was familiar territory by now. The obituary then described some of the results of Tracy's success – the sequence of houses, gardens and even of Tracy's various yachts. It was amusing to see Mona Vale described as a 'modern' brick building. I'm not sure Tracy would have liked that.

But then the paragraph my brother had been waiting for me to get to: 'New Zealand's first shock-therapy machine was made by Gough, Gough & Hamer. Though the use of such machines is now banned,' it read, 'they were, at the time of Tracy's death, an "accepted part of the treatment of certain types of mental diseases".'

Beryl (left) and Alison in Sumner, probably around 1921.

It's funny how you can be used to certain conditions and yet still be surprised by them. Like a barefoot summer on the beach where the sharp pebbles still pierce. I was used to making family discoveries that stretched credulity, but I thought that I was finished. After all, I now knew as much as I could about how they all ended up: Beryl, Alison, Owen, Avenal, Julia, Vida. And yet here, seemingly, was more dreadfulness.

Surely some mistake. Tracy's firm wasn't remotely medical. It sold bulldozers. My hope was that whoever had written the note had picked up on some piece of bombast and blended it with ink and paper to make fact. Maybe something of the story of the Gough women had seeped via gossip into reportage? Or perhaps because ECT was then new and fashionable and Hollywood-endorsed, Tracy wasn't too bothered about dissociating himself from a fiction.

This was my hope, and I went to test it against what I could find about the domestic development of ECT. I searched through Ministry of Health papers and historical overviews and the like, but there was nothing that credited, or implicated, Tracy. As I expected, he wasn't mentioned – he'd never claimed to be an inventor as far as I could see. That was a relief, a close call.

I would have left it there but for the thought that Tracy was the sort of person who liked to show what he'd done: 'Look on my works, ye mighty.' If there was any involvement, mention of it would most likely be from Tracy himself. This meant in the newspapers – maybe some illustrated pages with him and his engineers and the machine?

I went to Papers Past, searching under different combinations of words. I found nothing under 'ECT' and 'Tracy'. Then some other, more obscure combinations. Nothing was revealed and I was pleased. He would be exonerated. Then I realised they had referred to 'electro' and 'shock' for the treatment. The ECT acronym might have just been for professional use. I tried again and discovered two articles, several days apart. The first was an interview given by Tracy and published in the *Press* on 7 June 1944, the day after D-Day. The heading told me everything I didn't want to know: 'ELECTRIC SHOCK TREATMENT – Introduction to N.Z. Mental Hospitals – MR TRACY GOUGH'S ACCOUNT.'

As Tracy explained to the reporter, he

> had not claimed any credit for having the first apparatus made in New Zealand, without the co-operation of the Mental Hospitals Department, but, now that the department was using the adoption of the treatment to suggest that it was progressive, he thought the Director-General (Dr. T.G. Gray) should make the real facts known. If that were done the public would know that the department was not justified in claiming all the credit. 'Is the Mental Hospitals Department just as backward as it has ever been, although it looks as if it is progressive?' asked Mr Gough.

His interest had begun in 1941, 'when he learned of the undesirable features associated with the cardiazol treatment for depression cases, and heard that two Italians had experimented with electric shock treatment'. That date meant Alison. It seemed that Tracy had seen the effects of cardiazol – used to induce shocks on his daughter – and decided to act.

As the article explained, 'The chief disadvantage of shock treatments with the use of drugs was that the estimation of the quantity of drug for any particular patient was made by a hit or miss method, which sometimes had distressing results. With the electric shock treatment the resistance of any patient could be accurately determined.' Although Tracy 'tried to get the apparatus from overseas … treatment was still in the experimental stage, so he decided to get one made in New Zealand'. After studying 'all available references to the electric shock treatment in medical journals', Tracy turned to 'an expert electrical engineer on his staff, Mr L.S. Johns. All they had to go on in the way of constructional details was a rough sketch of the circuit used, but from this, by experiment, Mr Johns was able to build up the apparatus.' The stakes were higher than designing a sports car or fixing a lamp but the auto-didacticism and tenacity – sourcing information from an enemy nation in wartime – reminded me of Owen. To work something out and then get it done by hand. Beryl had mentioned Leonard Johns in a letter: Tracy had been fighting to keep him out of the war draft. Was it so he could complete this machine? I also wondered what they meant by experiment. The machine was finally assembled in 1943, a year after Alison died.

Tracy was clearly not shy about being associated with such a machine or a treatment, which at the time was a major patient-centric technology (if you didn't ask the patients). It was the new frontier of medicine, a new cure. He was doing a public service. But there was no reference to his own daughter's death, just plenty of huffiness about not getting the credit and asking Dr Gray to 'put the facts before the public'.

'Then came the question of its use in New Zealand,' continued Tracy. 'Although the treatment by then was well established overseas, the Mental Hospitals Department delayed its being tried. Finally, permission was given for tests at Sunnyside. Since then highly successful results had been achieved … He had had no payment of any sort for the use of the machine, which was not made with any commercial interest.'

The newspaper gave Dr Gray right of reply on 14 June and he began by saying he welcomed Tracy's invitation to set out the facts, but believed that Tracy had not been wronged. 'In May, 1943, an assistant medical officer at Sunnyside informed the Medical Superintendent … that he had privately acquired the necessary machine and had made a selection of patients whom he wished to treat.' Permission was given and the treatment started. They did not find out until August that Tracy and Johns had made the machine and were 'unaware and, indeed, unconcerned as to how the assistant medical officer had become possessed of the machine,' which seems remarkable given they were talking about a potentially lethal piece of kit.

Beryl on a West Coast beach, c. 1970s.

It was a peculiar argument to be having, let alone having in public. Dr Gray comes across as a sensitive soul who, when he arrived in New Zealand from Scotland in 1911, commented: 'I was struck by the singularly isolated position which the mental hospitals occupied in the public life of the country … their existence was merely tolerated as a necessary evil and their drab and dreary structure and routine symbolised the hopelessly pessimistic attitude of the public towards the prognosis of those who had to be admitted.'

So, yes, Tracy did have a role in the development of ECT. From the dates it seems likely that his interest was a response to Alison's condition but not, maybe importantly, developed 'for' Beryl, which gives some comfort. But it was still used on her. Was his motivation grief or something more akin to remorse or even guilt? He might have been saddened by what happened to Alison and thought the treatment methods barbaric.

ECT was developed to replace the convulsant cardiazol that was delivered to Alison. Insulin, of all things, had also been used for drug shock therapy for the mentally ill. Another odd coincidence. Insulin shock therapy had also been treated as a miracle cure when first introduced, appearing as the saviour in a 1940 film called *Dr Kildare's Strange Case*. But it sounds even worse than cardiazol: patients were repeatedly injected with large doses in order deliberately to produce daily comas and sometimes convulsions over a period of weeks, months or sometimes up to two years in order to cure their manias. The massive seizures sometimes turned patients blue.

Beryl survived ECT, Alison didn't survive drug shock. So you could also say Tracy had two sick daughters, but that his intervention in mental health technology saved one of them and that, of the various approaches, ECT was seen as the most humane. Though when I went through all I'd discovered with an uncle he wasn't surprised. He said Beryl would be threatened with ECT if she was naughty or out of line – where I don't know, but I presume and hope this was at Hornby – and she always went white when recalling it. Apparently the machine still exists and he saw it a decade ago or more. It has a plaque on it, noting Tracy's work. I guess he won the battle for acknowledgement then.

30

The Tracy whose life I admired, whose style I envied, had taken on darker textures. I hadn't found just a crumpled old man behind the face of Oz, but something more sinister. I couldn't understand how he could have remained the family hero, the name above the door, the portrait in the boardroom.

As I searched through the wreckage of those sad lives, charting a family's destruction and shattering an image, around me great swathes of Christchurch were demolished and cleared, to be taken over by rabbits and carparks. I felt like the friend of Richard and Madeline Usher, narrating their downfall to myself in a house that was also disintegrating.

Wasn't I too young to be mourning the loss of the world I knew? That's what seemed to be happening. And I began to see portents. I'd become accustomed to looking twice, to constantly finding tragic significance in small events, and I started to unconsciously apply this lens to everything around me.

My brother took a collection of Tracy's old books to have scanned for posterity. While they were there the photographic studio burned down. The removal and liquidation of Tracy's trusts continued to grind its way through the legal system – the abolition of his remaining influence. Christ's College abolished the rounded Edwardian shirt collars that had always made its uniforms so distinctive; these were the collars that both Owen and I had worn. The cathedral was broken, mired in dispute, a pile of expensive rubble rotting in full view. Even Robin Hood Oak came under attack, apparently too tall now for the suburb that had grown up around him. Calls came for him to be cut down. After seven years of frustration on my part, met with apathy from the insurers, we were finally able to start repairing the house. Yet no sooner had this begun than it was burgled, as happened often on Christchurch building sites. Strangely, the only items of value to be taken were a chandelier and the old, very heavy garden urn that came from Mona Vale's grounds and had long stood under a silver birch at Owen and Avenal's.

Like a modern haruspex I stood over these entrails and decided there was a message here: the story was fighting back. That world has gone and you can't follow. It has ended. Thus far and no further.

I just didn't feel as though I could comply. In J.L. Carr's *A Month in the Country*, ex-soldier Tom Birkin is hired to uncover and restore a mural of Christ. As he progresses he reveals the figure to be severe and vengeful, and the more he uncovers, the more curious he becomes about its creator. I felt the same. I'd found not a life of elderflower and fancy but something altogether more fierce and, if anything, it made me want to understand more. But I'd exhausted every avenue of inquiry – every document, every shipping record, birth certificate, company file, graveyard map and will. What I had left was speculation, maybe informed but still, speculation. Where would it take me?

• • •

About the time the family moved to Mona Vale, Julia began to worry about Tracy and Margaret. She might have had suspicions before, but for some reason they became more acute now. These concerns and fears caused her to wither, or she let herself wither. Julia might have been misguided but the perception become her reality. I have a sense that Alison was closest to Julia. I can see an echo in my own family, the intense adoration of my elder daughter for her mother. I think Alison was the strongest, the most forthright, probably, in fact, the most like her father. She was bolder than Julia, maybe even more worldly, possibly more practical. Alison took Julia's plight the hardest and blamed Tracy and that bloody woman. She stood up for Julia, but then broke down. Alison lost herself, and was removed.

Owen already had a complex relationship with Tracy. My guess is that working at Tracy's company did not help. He would have been an eyewitness to his father's relationship – whatever form that took – with his secretary, at least when Owen wasn't sent away to projects in remote parts of the country. Was there anything there that might have torn at Owen's loyalties to father and mother? I actually don't think Tracy was culpable. Owen would also have had a direct working relationship with his future stepmother, which would have had its own complexities.

I know how Owen – passive, gentle, maybe even fatalistic – responded.

He didn't need Alison's death to make up his mind. He walked out a few months after that first miserable Christmas without his mother. Owen left Mona Vale for good. He left Tracy and Margaret to it. He didn't want any of it. You keep the house and your gold, I'm off.

But of course he said nothing of the sort. He wrote a dignified letter to his father's paramour (not to his father direct) and exited. Then he scratched her name from his vocabulary and his father's image from his life. You could see it as slinking away. I saw in it stoicism. He refused to be involved in what he saw as unpleasantness or wickedness, and his path of opposition was non-violent objection. With Avenal's help and support, he kept his temper, took whatever he felt and bundled it up deep inside, beneath a beautiful suit and overcoat.

Did Owen then disappear into himself? It made me reconsider the calm and quietude he presented the world. Was it capitulation? Or was it a form of triumph: to be able to survive at all and to live a life of gentleness, without rancour? When it came to Tracy's new marriage, Owen dug in. This was perhaps the schism, more so than the deaths.

Beryl, gentlest of all and caught between them. It would have been worse for her. She didn't have Owen's options. An unmarried young woman without qualifications, she had to remain, alone, watching the tragedy play out in her home. She must have missed Owen so much. I don't think he abandoned her, I just think he was too broken-hearted by his mother's death to be able to stay. Then came Alison, another death, and Beryl was truly on her own. Her letters to Owen, in hospital, echoed: come back to Mona Vale, Owen.

Beryl was no less sorry or upset than the others but her Christian philosophy compelled her to try to keep what remained of the family together, to keep the peace. She stayed by her beloved father's side; she urged Owen to forgive. But where was her home? After Tracy's new marriage Beryl didn't feel welcome, or was made not to feel welcome. I could imagine Beryl retreating to her bedroom and feeling as alone as if she'd been floating through the blackness of space. She was probably terrified, haunted, unbelievably sad. For her too, survival was triumph. I realised that her wedding breakfast in her old bedroom was almost a form of conquest over the trauma she must once have hidden from in there and a memory of a happy time before her mother died. But first she had to leave too, succumbing to the pressure of her family's total disintegration and entering Hornby Lodge.

Tracy? The tombstone said Alison died 3 June 1942. A fortnight later he had remarried. The best – the absolute best – I could tell myself was that Alison's death left Tracy so bereft that he needed the comfort of marriage.

Owen in Christ's College uniform and Beryl (right). The woman in the middle is most likely an aunt.

But with children myself now, Tracy's behaviour is bewildering. My elder daughter is only seven and apart from when she's infuriating, I can't imagine anything worse than her not being there. To follow a death like that with a wedding – I don't know how you could. On 17 June 1942, Beryl and Owen's world suffered its final collapse.

The survivors built and rebuilt their own lives. For those of us to come, Tracy became a name only, Margaret not even that.

I'm only certain about this last part.

• • •

We were all still going in and out of court, trying to decide precisely what Tracy's will meant. Seventy years after his death, this was Tracy's final requiem.

Godfrey, my lawyer friend, was helping my mother and I was helping him. I would run through slush piles of the more humdrum evidence to save him the bother and the time. There were vast volumes of papers, thousands of documents.

I planned to spend the summer after my mother left hospital doing just this. We were all off to the Sounds, to Owen and Avenal's old house there, on what is now called Arapaoa Island. My parents would go whenever they could and sometimes we'd go with them. You can sit there with blue before and above you and green all around. You can stare at the ever-changing sea for days on end, while splotches of white under power of sail or engine dart back and forth along the main channel. It's like a plane coming in to land over a city: there's a world out there but you're sitting back, unseen and almost uncontactable. Not everyone likes it – they're unimpressed by the cold water, stony beaches, summer storms and stingrays – but my mother loves it. That was why we were going: it was to be her first trip since the operation. There was no better place. This time we all travelled down together, my parents, my wife and I – and our new daughter, just a few weeks old.

I also took a bundle of evidence from the trustees (just the one bundle, mind) and while the baby girl slept and the house was silent in the noonday sun, I sat at the kitchen table and read through over 2500 pages: statements, affidavits, old deeds, legal correspondence, company minutes, constitutions, articles of association, offers, re-offers, indemnities and so on. Page after page after page of typewritten words and fading signatures. Another kitchen, another table, still scribbling notes about family history.

The truth was that everything that I'd found out about Julia and Alison and Beryl and Vida and Owen wasn't legally relevant. Julia and Alison's deaths might have caused alterations in Tracy's behaviour, but from a legal perspective the background was a distraction and possibly prurient to boot.

Julia died, and it was natural for a widower to remarry. Alison died, but before Tracy, and so of course didn't count. Beryl had entered a mental hospital and so was also excluded, which was, in any case, consistent with the more patriarchal values of the era. Their stories were tragic but immaterial. Their erasure was almost self-fulfilling. They held the foreground for me, but only for me. What counted was legal reasoning and legal rationale.

I stuck to my dry task for several days, Queen Charlotte Sound catching the warm, clear sunshine out there over my left shoulder, ultramarine ringed by emerald. It was painful to be inside out of the summer. Thankfully there was a lot of repetition in the pile so it was faster than you might think. A letter would refer to another letter and they'd both be there. Then the next reply would have them both appended for reference, and so on. I learnt to scan at speed, flick quickly to the next page and only jot down really worthwhile references.

The blandness of the material made me eager for distraction and every couple of hours I'd stretch, walk around the house, yawn. The place is just as I've always known it. Everything that Owen and Avenal lived with has remained. In the main room there's the organ. It's now unemployed but, like most of the stuff, would need a barge to move. There's a television that looks like a microwave, beside piles of videos – and a video player, still. There are two record players and many of their old records, a woodburner, more sofas than I can count from memory.

In a dark corner with a small window facing the hills behind the house there's a desk that used to be Avenal's sewing station. Beside it is a bookshelf filled half with detective novels, half with books on fish, birds, Captain Cook and other Marlborough seaside subjects.

There are fishing rods cluttered into one another and a tall pile of board games. Near the top is Masterpiece, in which players buy and sell Old Masters, never knowing which is a forgery and which is valuable. It's a game of bluff, deception and chance and was the family favourite. My brother would always pay anything for Goya's *Duke of Wellington*. I rather liked one of the Gainsboroughs. There are playing cards, chess sets and, next to all of this, a rolltop desk where Owen used to avoid doing paperwork and children would play at slamming fingers, sometimes succeeding.

My regular but arbitrary breaks kept bringing me back to this corner. I'd browse the books, telling myself I desperately wanted to learn the different types of gulls. Or reread *The Mysterious Affair at Styles*. What was whaling life like? What's the difference between a skate and a stingray? Who's keen for a game of snap? Anything to avoid the homework I'd set myself. In the lead-up to university finals, I once read a history of the White Rajahs of Sarawak in one sitting when I was meant to be studying Victorian welfare systems. The result was predictable.

I was trying to resist the same temptations now and return to my piles of pages. These kept the story of Tracy and Mona Vale top of mind, even as I loitered. Gradually, I started to think more carefully about what was right in front of me. This desk, for instance. It had been a part of Owen's life for decades and was just the sort of place in which things might hide. It had in fact been transported from Christchurch with its contents intact. I could imagine Owen touching nothing, locking it with a key and then saying to Avenal it was ready.

It was a long shot, but I'd known luck before: in safes, briefcases and boxes. Maybe something within would draw me back to the human story and away from the drier legal one? I rolled back the desk's lid. Its movement was smooth but noisy. Inside, and in line with experience, was a diverse range of clutter that probably hadn't been touched for years. There were the blueprints for a boat, photos of other boats, plans for the house, piles of old business cards, unused pencils, blank curling notepads. It was reminiscent of my own desk, if I'm honest. The drawers were the same. The sewing table behind it held hardware, nails, a hammer and string.

The only thing of interest was a packet of photographs, colour, but

The view of Queen Charlotte Sound from Owen and Avenal's holiday house.

faded, showing Owen and Avenal and Beryl on holiday in Europe. All three looked close in age to how I remembered them and so I guessed it was the late 1970s or the early 1980s. There's Greece, the Corinth Canal, Mykonos. Owen in a white trilby, Avenal in a white summer dress. Aegean churches. I showed my father and he said that was when they went to the Passion Play at Oberammergau, the hours-long recreation of the death of Christ that's been performed once a decade for almost 400 years. These three made a retirement pilgrimage to attend.

It was while looking at the desk that I realised a gunmetal-grey filing cabinet stood beside it, obscured by the fishing clobber in front and games on top. I cleared things out of the way and started going through the cabinet's drawers. They were full but in good order. No paper flopping out to get crushed. There were named files for the company, for legal affairs and so on and I took each out in turn and flicked through it. There was nothing new. This didn't surprise me. As I was finding, the formal record was well documented.

When I'd finished, I went to put the final folder back in the cabinet, thick fingers trying to attach those flimsy metal arms onto the drawer's runners. I'd worked from front to back, maybe an error, so I had the drawer pulled all the way out and was trying to reach to the back to stuff this file in. I was holding the drawer against my knees so that the cabinet wouldn't tip over, bringing the games down with it. I could barely see and my hand was getting stuck. It was embarrassing, wrestling with a filing cabinet and being bettered. I was getting a little hot and bothered and sweary.

I finally managed to force the file back into place but, in doing so, felt something give at the back of the drawer. Overcoming laziness with a sigh, I took a bunch of files back out of the drawer so that I could get a proper look. The back was a metal plate, itself hanging like a file to create a false back. I fiddled with it and it came out easily. It hid only a few centimetres but in here was another of the brown-paper sandwich bags that Owen had apparently used to store anything significant or private. This one was large but folded over on itself and contained only a brown leather writing case.

Seated at Owen's desk, I unzipped the case. Inside was a replay of so many other discoveries: lawyers' bills and formal letters. Nothing new, but they were older than I'd found for a while, all from the 1930s, 1940s and 1950s. The newest item was a receipt from the 1970s. It made sense. That was just before they built this home. The filing cabinet must have been Owen's principal archive, moved up here with its contents like the desk. But then there was a bundle of small handwritten pages, as if from a notepad, folded over and stuck into a pocket. They weren't in an envelope and I could see they'd been written in fountain pen and, after flicking through a few pages, in aging pencil.

As soon as I'd digested a few words, I realised this was the best discovery I'd made in my circuitous and coincidental journey through family detritus. They were not always complete and not always legible, but the bundle turned out to be four distinct documents, discernible by headings and writing style. Though mostly undated, in what I determined as chronological order, they were 'Beryl's Story'; a further note from Beryl, untitled but in her hand; an incomplete memo by Owen; and a long memo, also by Owen, forming the complete and likely final version of the above and largely, it seemed, written by Avenal.

I was excited but nervous. I also wanted to be careful, so tried to move methodically. I washed and dried my hands, then came back and took the four documents through to the dining table where I'd been working. I laid them out page by page, being careful to keep them out of the Sounds breeze. My nerves extended to not wanting to see a page flutter off into the blue eternity. I laid them in rows and took a photograph. If anything happened, at least I'd have this.

Only then did I sit and read them, the water still sparkling outside but these documents saving me from drudgery.

• • •

I started with 'Beryl's Story'. It wasn't dated, but for reasons I'll come to I think it's the earliest. The handwriting was Avenal's, though I imagine she transcribed from Beryl's narration. It starts:

> As a schoolgirl, my first memory of Margaret Fife was of a bright young Scotch girl, employed by my father. We all liked her, and she appeared more than anxious to become an intimate friend of the family. Expensive gifts were given to us children which embarrassed our mother. We enjoyed her company and she was always a welcome visitor to our home.
>
> We had looked upon her as a friend of our mother's until one day my sister Alison and I found our mother shaking with a letter in her hand. She handed us the letter, which she had found in Daddy's coat, which stated that she [Margaret] loved my father, but that she knew it was 'like crying for the moon'. She had worked a cross-stitch picture, and stated that 'every stitch was a stitch of love'.

This seems a minor thing to be upset about. It sounds almost childish; more suited to a mystery Valentine in a school bag than evidence of a serious betrayal. Julia is so upset I sense she suspected more. This discovery was confirmation, for Julia at least, and a floodgate.

> We were all absolutely staggered at this stab in the back [that] Miss Fife had given our mother after appearing to be such a friend to her. Needless to say, my mother, who had been so completely oblivious of Miss Fife's true designs, was very deeply pained at this revelation of deceit. Of course she approached my father on it afterwards, & he assured her that there was absolutely nothing in it and that Miss Fife was just going thro' a silly schoolgirl phase.
>
> Unfortunately for my mother Miss Fife, in her capacity as private secretary to my father, handled all his affairs.

Beryl then outlined various ways in which this caused difficulty, such as how bills were paid and household finances handled. It was all ugly. Then she turned to Alison, still the most mysterious of them all.

All the way through, it was my elder sister Alison who seemed to see most clearly what was happening. We were a very united family and of course my sister spoke up for what she thought was right. Alison and Miss Fife had many open duels, Alison always supporting my mother if she felt she had endured a slight.

Some time after leaving school Alison took a commercial course and when this was completed she wished to take a clerical position in the company. Miss Fife would not allow Alison this position, yet she permitted her own sister to take just such a position as Alison would have wished.

My sister was deeply worried about the family situation which seemed to be ever present and becoming more complicated. In addition, she had the frustration of not being allowed to make use of any of her talents to take a job either making use of her shorthand & typing or at anything else.

Over all these years Miss Fife seemed to be continually disparaging us children, and questioning our normality. An aunt of ours on our mother's side had had a goitre operation from which she never fully recovered her faculties, and time and again we were reminded of this.

At the end of this paragraph there was a sketch of a smiling woman's face.

My father and I were always very firm friends and we used to have long chats in the evenings, and often when he came home tired he would ask me to sing to him. He was always very interested in our music and gave us every encouragement. No doubt he had no idea of the agony of mind which Alison and I suffered in worrying over Miss Fife's suggestions as to whether or not we were able to do things other girls could do.

My sister suffered a nervous breakdown [this must be the event of 1939] and I will always remember that in her saddest moments she kept referring to Miss Fife and the havoc she was working in our mother's life. Even when Alison had recovered from her breakdown, she had lost a great deal of her brightness and she still worried unceasingly about Miss Fife and her designs on Daddy. Of course this breakdown of Alison's gave Miss Fife another excuse to point a questioning finger at our normality.

Continued pinpricking worried us all, my mother especially, and in the late nineteen thirties we learned that she had contracted diabetes.

So Julia did almost certainly have Type 2 diabetes. This in turn meant that her coma was more likely caused by her blood sugars being too high.

> Returned To Kirkwood Avenue
> ... July 1944? and Stayed
> with my Brother's family
> for several months (5 months
> I think). Spent Xmas at
> "mona Vale" & also at Kirkwood
> Avenue. Stayed at monavale
> from before Xmas until
> mid February and then
> Voluntary Went To Hornby
> To Receive Shock Treatment
> incidentally my father had
> been the instigator of this
> machine. Having seen his
> eldest daughter drugged while
> ill my father searched for
> a better method of
> Relief. I Remained at
> Hornby for three years,
> hoping all the time
> that I would be able
> To resume my general
> nursery Training. Mrs Gough

Front page of memo by Beryl, found at the house in Queen Charlotte Sound.

After we moved from Sumner to Mona Vale things seemed to go from bad to worse … Things reached a climax one night when my sister and mother were utterly beside themselves, & I realized that their worrying had taken possession of them, and that there was nothing that could be said to comfort them. My mother was ill for about two weeks and during that time she was continually under the delusion that Miss Fife was poisoning her food and that of everyone else in Mona Vale. She was always so concerned for the nurses and continually warning them that Miss Fife had poisoned their food.

What a scene. I could imagine a doctor seeing this and easily diagnosing Julia with acute mania; maybe even full-blown persecution anxiety. But I could also imagine Julia's frustration and how this could morph into a breakdown as she saw that the more she protested, the more she was doomed.

Julia considered Margaret a rival but this realisation, and the consequent breakdown, brought the latter's success in this rivalry closer. There was something very Greek about this inescapability of fate.

Even if Tracy's concern and affection for Julia remained genuine, in the face of her spiralling concerns he perhaps developed his own frustration and his own despair. He might have felt he could do nothing to help Julia or convince her of his bona fides. He might have felt Julia goading him into infidelity with her accusations.

T.H. White talks about precisely this dynamism of concern begetting its own reality, in book three of *The Once and Future King*: 'For her … as for all women, the dreads were in advance of the male horizon. Men often accuse women of driving them to unfaithfulness by senseless jealousy, before there has been any thought of unfaithfulness on their own part … Seeing so much further into the future than he did, she pressed towards it with passionate tread, wrecking the present because the future was bound to be a wreck.'

By the time Julia's death came it would have been easy to see it as a tragic release for a troubled woman. Tracy might have mourned. He might have shaken his head over her grave as a friend patted his shoulder and told him he did all he could. But he might also have felt liberated. Emerging from the cold bath of death with new vigour.

The one thing Beryl's note did confirm, though, was that no matter what the medical or even the social cause, Julia died unhappy. She believed her accusations to be correct: that she had been abandoned by Tracy.

Julia was ill for almost a fortnight – acute mania – before finally slipping into a coma just as Alison was taken away to be assessed for Sunnyside. Julia's death wasn't coincident with other sadness, it was part of it. And Alison herself? Beryl's words: 'A year later Alison died terribly distressed, a few days before the proposed wedding of my father and Miss Fife.' This sentence told me that Beryl saw the stark significance in the timings, despite her best efforts to make things right.

And so it came to pass. Everything Julia and Alison allegedly claimed would happen, did happen, and therein lay the key problem for interpreting Tracy's role.

'After Daddy had married again,' Beryl continued, 'I'm afraid there seemed to be continual arguments going on, which made me sick at heart. Often Daddy and I would be talking together when in would come Margaret & accuse us in heated terms of talking about her. Actually neither my father nor I ever mentioned her to one another.'

This is where Beryl ended her first note. The second was dated 1951 and took up the story after a gap of a few years. It was also by Beryl, but now in her own handwriting. It was almost like part of a larger document, a chapter in a longer book. She opened by writing that she 'returned' to stay with Owen and his family on 25 July 1944. She didn't say where she had come from, but I think it must be Ōamaru, where she'd gone to train as a nurse after Tracy remarried.

> I stayed at Mona Vale from before Xmas until mid February [1945] and then voluntarily went to Hornby to receive Shock Treatment. Incidentally my father had been the instigator of this machine. Having seen his eldest daughter drugged while ill my father searched for a better method of Relief. I remained at Hornby for three years, hoping all the time that I would be able to resume my general nursing training.

• • •

Given the legal entanglements the family found themselves in after Tracy's death, and the taste for complexity exhibited by his own last will and testament, it's almost surprising that he didn't take some form of action against Sunnyside. But, then again, many people stung by tragedy don't think it's worth extending the pain once there's no chance of bringing someone back. Such humanity is implied by Beryl's tone, and by Tracy's own actions, even if those three letter, ECT, keep obscuring it for me. There was just such a dichotomy: Could he really have cared for Alison and sent her to this? Was he just doing his best, under pressure, his wife dying, false accusations flying?

Back and forth, back and forth, back and forth I went. A moral metronome still. Sunnyside was the best care on offer; seeking it out took courage too. But did Alison need help because she was inherently unstable, or was that illness brought on by events? If by events, was Tracy culpable, or was it merely a sequence of unfortunate coincidences that summed to tragedy?

By now I had the outline of what happened next, and this timeline more than anything else condemned. Would you watch your wife die, send your daughter away, watch her die and then remarry, knowing that it causes your next daughter and your son to flee?

But Tracy's world collapsed too. His wife died; his eldest daughter blamed him and then herself had a breakdown. What was he supposed to do? How would anyone be equipped to respond? He buried Julia, he sent Alison away to what was theoretically the best care available. He remarried quickly, to a woman he knew well.

That was all reasonable – if you didn't look too closely. Then you saw that his secretary was his girlfriend within three months of Julia's death; the frequent coincidences of dates; Alison's admission to Sunnyside with bruising; the few short days between her death and Tracy's marriage to Margaret, even with his knowledge that the family was worried about her.

Back and forth between blame and sympathy; between anger and despair. Between Tracy as villain and Tracy as victim. Between relative probabilities. And then I would wear myself out. I'd run out of permutations and think, does it even matter? It's done. These people have died and this family was destroyed. The cause is academic, the results are the same.

Beryl seemed less confused. Her note bore her father no ill-will. I'm inclined to think that was because Beryl herself was as close to a saint as I'd ever met – though she did not extend the same compassion to Tracy's second wife.

'Mrs Gough,' Beryl's next paragraph began, and how strange a way it must have been for referring to her stepmother, her father's new wife, 'had stated that I would never come out of Hornby.' But Beryl was 'determined to prove that with rest I was as normal & sound as any girl'.

While at Hornby I asked to take on the duties of a Junior nurse, working a full nurse's hours and did so for the last six months of my stay out at Hornby as well as attending some of the Lectures.

On learning that my father & Mrs Gough were planning to take a business trip abroad I asked if I could not take some employment and take my place in the world. Mrs Gough was strong on the point that I should remain at Hornby until they returned from their trip.

My brother approached the doctor on my behalf on the subject of my leaving Hornby and was told I was well enough to leave but that they could not do anything without my father's consent. I approached my father again on the subject of leaving Hornby, as I felt well able to make myself useful in Life. Previously I had stated that I would never go back to 'Mona Vale' to live, and [so] have it thrown up at my father by Mrs Gough that she had to look after his abnormal daughter.

I asked if I could not look after my Grandmother, to which, at last, my father consented much against Mrs Gough's wishes. It seemed as if Mrs Gough had steeped my father in thoughts that I was not capable of taking my place alongside other folk in Life. These are thoughts that I wanted to sweep away from my father's mind, most of all, for what is sadder to any father than to be continually told that his children are inferior.

I came out of Hornby and stayed with my brother & family, but had no financial support. I did possess a post office savings account of £40. My brother asked for an allowance to be given me while my people were over seas and I was given forty pounds. This allowed me one pound a week. I spent a fortnight with my grandmother and then returned to my brother's Home again, eventually taking a position in the Record Dept at Beggs [music shop] for 2 years nine months. My father had always impressed upon us as young girls that there was no need for us to earn our living but I now realized that I was placed in a position where it was necessary for me to earn my own living.

So much for being a voluntary boarder. It just meant you served at your guardian's discretion, not the state's. In this case Beryl was subject to her father and his new wife, who happened to receive all his correspondence and manage his affairs. What a coup.

Beryl was not long out before Tracy and Margaret travelled abroad. It was an intriguingly busy few weeks in the middle of 1948. Beryl got herself released with Owen's help on 9 June. Tracy's will was changed on 19 July and on 24 August he and Margaret departed on the *Aorangi* for Vancouver. The *Aorangi* was a leading luxury liner complete with music room and Jacobean-inspired smoking room, and this happened to be its first voyage following a major refurbishment after war service. It was on this trip that Tracy had a stroke.

'My Father Returned' – Beryl had a way with redundant capitalisation – 'from his business Trip abroad a very ill man.' According to passenger records this was early February 1949. From then on Tracy was incapacitated.

On July 5th 1949 I sat my teacher's singing examination and went over To 'Mona Vale' to tell my father all about it. Daddy was sitting up in the chair and Mrs Gough was massaging my father's bruised leg, which only seemed to irritate my father. She told my father that he was not going to get away with everything. I told her that Daddy was tired and to leave him alone. The Next minute I was pushed off the stool on which I was sitting, with Mrs Gough rushing at me Like a mad thing.

Mrs Gough had been drinking and all at once I realized she did not seem to know what she was doing. I told her to pull herself together and think of

Daddy sick in the chair. She grabbed me around the neck, but I managed to free myself of her. She told me that I was mad and had always been so, and that we as a family had done nothing for our father but that she and her family had done everything for Daddy and that I should never be allowed to see and visit my father again.

I Told her That I would not Leave my Father's side until she was in control of herself. Before I knew where I was, I was flung onto the bed, face upwards, with Mrs Gough punching the breath out of my lungs. I Felt everything going black, but knew that I must not let my poor Father see Mrs Gough overpowering me. Fortunately the bed that I had been pushed onto was a high one, and the fact that Mrs Gough had been drinking making her less accurate in her aims at me, was to my advantage. I do not know to this day how I managed to wrench myself free from Mrs Gough. Poor Daddy had tried to come to my rescue, but had fallen back in his chair helpless.

In my father's condition I knew that such a scene as he had witnessed was enough to give him another stroke. Daddy called out to me 'You Have Done The Right Thing Beryl.'

I turned to Mrs Gough and told her that she must assist me [to] put my Father to bed. He was looking very ill and distressed. We put him to bed. The nurse came into the room. Mrs Gough Bent over my father & kissed him. I felt sick with the misery and insincerity of it all. Picking up the button that had been wrenched off my coat I left the room.

If the words attributed to Margaret were at all accurate – and there was no reason to think otherwise – they revealed an obsession that seemed close to psychosis: the allegations of drinking, the violence. It also shows the humbug at the heart of the mental health treatment. Similar scenes are what got Alison sent away. But Alison wasn't mistress of the house. Poor Beryl, and maybe Tracy too. He might be more sinned against than sinning.

Beryl finished her note by saying that she was now living with a friend, teaching music and singing. It sounded like an attempt to show that she had prevailed and was living a normal life. As such, it was effective. It sounded ordinary. It gave me the sense that Beryl was a reliable witness to her own condition. She was honest about herself.

31

Finally there were two documents, a partial draft and a final version of the same memo from Owen's point of view. The draft, as I think of it, is briefer, angrier, less professional. For that reason alone it is worth quoting, especially a telling first paragraph excised from the fuller version:

> To return now to the order of events leading up to the death of my mother & sister. Round about 1936, Miss Fife, who by this time had asserted her influence to such an extent took control of the household accounts. By a series of clever accusations and inferences, Miss Fife led my father to believe that my mother was extravagant and incapable of managing the ordinary family accounts. In consequence my mother was required to suffer the indignity of passing all accounts to Miss Fife for approval and payment. Such an opportunity was never missed by Miss Fife to criticise every item of expenditure. The most appalling part of the whole business was the fact that each week Miss Fife paid on behalf of Mr Gough the sum of £8 to Mrs Gough to cover the current small needs of the family.

The full version filled 36 small lined pages of writing paper. When I laid them out to be photographed they covered the whole kitchen table. It was Owen's writing at the start but it changed part way through to Avenal's, then went back and forth between the two. That was the way they worked, finishing each other's thoughts, helping with each other's work, keeping each other together. Saying that, even when the script was Owen's, I could tell some of the tone was Avenal's.

> This is a brief account of the manner in which Margaret Blair Gough (née Fife) entered the Gough family and has, in the opinion of the writer done everything in her power to dissolve a perfectly natural and happy family consisting of

husband, wife, two daughters and a son. Up to 1929 this family was living as happily at Sumner as any other New Zealand family. Mr Gough enjoyed a modest income as the proprietor of a Christchurch City shoe store. Mrs Gough attended to the running of the home while all the children were at school.

About this time a Miss M.B. Fife entered the employ of C.D. Gough and Sons as confidential secretary to the principal of the firm – Mr T.T. Gough … About 1932 Miss M.B. Fife was appointed private secretary to the Governing Director of Gough Gough & Hamer Ltd, Mr T.T. Gough, who had a controlling stake in the firm.

It was during this early period Mr T.T. Gough received an embroidered picture of a boat [the boat amused me – she guessed the way to his heart was via fancy toys] from Miss Fife together with a letter indicating that every stitch was a stitch of love, as such indicating her feelings towards Mr Gough. Naturally Mrs T.T. Gough was much perturbed at this show of affection for her husband but had the assurance of Mr Gough that there was nothing in it the matter.

I'm inclined to agree with Tracy, at least as far as this single event goes. Even if there was nothing in it from his point of view, what could he do? The problem is that once a scenario like this has arisen, at least one person won't escape unscathed. Perhaps Tracy, confident of his abilities in managing people, thought he could handle a young admirer? But if he didn't solicit the letter and it meant nothing, then the sensible course of action was to move Margaret into another job, another office or another firm. After a confession like Margaret's, it wouldn't be professional to keep his relationship with her on the same footing. Even leaving aside professionalism, the same rules of human affection apply now as then. Tracy was the only one who could solve things. You couldn't expect Margaret to just resign.

I could think of several reasons why Tracy might not have acted, other than the existence of an actual liaison: Margaret was probably good at her job, administratively efficient and knew the business; for personal or professional reasons Tracy may have been loyal to her; these were still Depression years and he may not have wanted to force her onto the job market (though I imagine he could have manipulated some other position for her across town); perhaps he even thought that Margaret should not suffer as a result of Julia's misplaced anxiety.

But then again, sometimes people don't mind a little flattery – especially when they're successful and they think they can keep everything in check. He might not have been pursuing her but maybe he enjoyed the admiration. If

Owen in London, 1962.

he was either innocent of the charges or just being sensible, he should have moved her; but the fact that he didn't doesn't prove guilt.

Owen continued:

> On looking back this appears to be the first indication of Miss Fife's intrusion into the personal lives of the family. The first visible sign of antagonism against the children came in 1935 when Mr & Mrs Gough were on a trip to the U.S.A. They were just arriving in Australia when Mr Gough was presented with a cable from Miss Fife indicating her intention to resign if Alison continued to interfere in the boot business. This impression was quite without foundation as at no time had Alison attempted to take any active interest in the affairs of either business. Any accusation that she was interfering was quite without foundation and was purely a product of the imagination of Miss Fife.

This ire towards Margaret was the most emotional thing I'd ever read or heard from Owen, Beryl or Avenal. It felt as though he was drawing on years of anger and upset.

Margaret might have run a campaign against the family but she also might simply have seen them as effete and useless, getting in the way. Maybe Margaret was brusque, efficient, a little vulgar, less refined, but she got things done and she knew how to run a business, even if she couldn't sing an aria. I could imagine, too, Margaret Fife, the Glasgow migrant, being defensive and protective of her patch. No professional wants the owner's children swanning in from their luxurious home. I'm sure Margaret found the parables of the prodigal son, and of the workers in the vineyard, as hard to swallow as I do.

It read as though Owen didn't understand this natural human reaction. But given the rawness of his loss and the replacement of his mother by her tormentor, it was hard not to take his side.

> When Mr & Mrs Gough were preparing to move to Mona Vale in 1939–1940 a further act of antagonism became very much apparent. Mr Gough was out of town at the time the house was being renovated prior to being occupied and Mrs Gough on requesting the keys from Miss Fife with a view to inspecting her future home was given a flat refusal to hand them over. Had she, Miss Fife, been given instructions from Mr Gough to this effect, her actions would have been explainable, but to take it upon herself to prohibit a woman from looking through her own home is I think without precedent.

I feel I need to intervene again here. I can imagine the premise. Technically the house was owned by the company, as the chairman's residence. No doubt then, as now, this related to tax structuring. However, from a legal perspective, Miss Fife may have been able to say that it was a company asset and Julia was not a company employee and hence without Tracy had no right to access the building. Certainly not until Julia was resident. At least, that's the way I would have played it in Miss Fife's position. But it was an action designed by Margaret to irritate, in fact designed with an almost pathological precision: Margaret as a young girl would essentially babysit and keep house for Julia; now Margaret was in charge. It would be a very odd husband indeed who didn't act to rectify this situation.

From this time onwards a definite campaign was launched to antagonise the children & Mrs Gough. The object of this was not at first apparent but on looking back over the past it was obvious that the whole scheme was designed to keep as many of the family out of the business as possible in order that one day Miss Fife would assume control of both the business and property of Mr Gough. Some of the incidents I am about to relate will show without doubt the intentions and objectives of this woman.

One of the earliest attacks was upon the mentality of the whole family. I can recall one instance of having heard from a third party that Miss Fife had made numerous references to Miss V. Philpott (sister of Mrs T.T. Gough) inferring that she was mentally incapacitated and that her disability was of a hereditary nature + generally inferred that other members of the Philpott family were of a similar condition. These statements were quite unfounded as Miss Fife well knew – in point of fact Miss Fife was aware that the Medical Records of Miss Philpott proved conclusively that she was suffering the after-effects of a Thyroid operation.

If Margaret knew, then so did Tracy. These notes were almost contemporaneous. There may have been medical confusion between mental issues and hypothyroidism but if Owen knew of the link, then Vida's case must have been clearer than others. Tracy has little excuse, and I presume Owen wasn't aware that Tracy had cited Vida when sectioning Alison.

Owen then, in his own words, diverted from the chronological order of events to 'give a brief description of the manner in which my sister Beryl was victimised'.

Beryl on leaving secondary school was keen to take up a position somewhere but her father insisted that there was no necessity for her to work, he stressed that his financial and his social position were such that there was absolutely no call for his daughters to have to work. Instead she was persuaded to assist with the running of the house, devoting her spare time to the study of music. Beryl's total income during this period was 25 shillings per week paid by her father. When her Mother died in 1941 Beryl remained in charge of the house and continued to do so until shortly after Miss Fife's marriage to Mr T.T. Gough one year later.

It was soon apparent when Miss Fife moved into 'Mona Vale' as Mrs Gough that Beryl was not wanted, numerous insinuations were cast at Beryl's inability to keep house & manage the household affairs apart from the veiled accusation as to the girl's laziness and general inefficiency.

From Margaret's point of view it could be a fairy tale. The lazy, inefficient, entitled wife dies. The righteous, hard-working, overlooked orphan gets the chance to marry her Prince Charming. The collateral damage wasn't her concern. It should have been Tracy's. He might have told himself events had been taken out of his hands, but he'd handed victory to Margaret as surely as if he planned it.

'In sheer desperation,' Owen went on, 'Beryl took a position at St George's Hospital as a Nursing Aide. After twelve months living in at the Hospital & spending her off duty hours at her home Beryl decided to take up nursing as a career and proceeded to Oamaru Hospital where she entered the hospital training school.'

Beryl's affidavit had mentioned going to work at St George's shortly after Owen and Avenal's wedding. That was November 1942. And it appears the job was residential. This means it took a total of 18 months to clear Mona Vale of Julia and her three children. The first Christmas with Margaret had sounded awful. There wasn't a second. By then Alison was dead too and Owen and Beryl were gone. Margaret was there on her own, with Tracy.

> The strain of nursing upon a girl who had been used to a comfortable quiet home, associated with thoughts of her Mother's death followed a year later by her sister's death, resulted in Beryl having a nervous breakdown. She was brought to Christchurch by car and upon advice from the Medical Superintendent of the Hospital was examined by Dr Baxter in Christchurch who certified her as being perfectly well mentally but requiring rest treatment.

This must have been the Dr Quentin-Baxter we met earlier (and who Tracy called Baxter).

> Miss Fife made it quite obvious that Beryl was not wanted at 'Mona Vale' so for the next five months she stayed at the writer's house in Riccarton. Miss Fife did not come to see her during this period nor did she receive any allowance or support from her family. Such treatment seems almost unbelievable as prior to her mother's death Beryl was considerably favoured by her father and one can only conclude that his mind had been poisoned by Miss Fife's repeated and consistent attacks on his children.

It was Disney's stepmother again. I felt sorry for Beryl and Owen, but was it really plausible that a successful businessman, already married once,

Four generations: Owen (rear) and his four children, with Tracy and Tracy's mother Elizabeth (Tiny Granny), c. 1950. The author's mother is on Owen's knee. All photos of Elizabeth show her dressed in black.

with two daughters whom he supposedly loved, should turn against them? Today we'd talk of agency – the agency lay with Tracy. He was the business owner after all. Tracy was weakened by stroke and ultimately incapacitated. Before that, though, he was hardly meek and impressionable. But it's also not without historical precedent for a strong older man to defer to a stronger, younger woman at a cost to his former allies. Is there culpability in this, a willingness to go along?

To understand if Tracy was under some sort of spell meant casting judgment on whether his later actions were consistent with his character as I'd come to understand it. It was tenuous, but it was all I had.

Tracy seemed to believe in hierarchy, in tradition, in the patrilineal line. He was taken into his father's firm and rose upwards. He in turn took Owen into his own firm from school. In this context then no, it didn't seem natural to overlook Owen with just a few months of his military service to go. By all means appoint someone like Johns, who Tracy had fought to keep out of the war effort, but to appoint his second wife and send Owen to the outer darkness felt inconsistent. And if we talk about ability, then it is clear that Margaret was skilled, but Owen took over from her in time and the company appeared to flourish.

Tracy seems to have been committed to family, and to his family. He gave his children a charmed life and fine educations. He encouraged Beryl in her singing and stepped ashore at Pago Pago to wire her about her success. Yet he effectively left her out of his will, and this affected Owen as well. And he married so soon after Alison's death.

The question is ultimately in two parts: Did he change? I think he did. Can he avoid responsibility? I don't think he can.

• • •

From the way the memo moves into the present and then stops, it appears it was written soon after Tracy's return following his first stroke. I think in this situation, with his father too ill to attend to business affairs, it might have been hard to blame Tracy, no matter what.

> Beryl was well enough to visit Mona Vale which she used to do and after a while her father insisted that she stay there again. The writer is of the opinion that Miss Fife conveyed to Beryl's Father the impression that she had no desire to live [with] or see her father. This was not so. Beryl certainly had no desire to live

under the same roof as Miss Fife after the treatment she had received after Miss Fife's marriage, but she always had an earnest desire to see her father.

Beryl did go back to Mona Vale. From all accounts there were some fairly terrific scenes between Miss Fife and Beryl. Mr Arbour, a friend of the family witnessed one of these and would be able to give support to this evidence. Later a Dr McKillop [Alexander McKillop, the superintendent of Sunnyside] was called in to medically examine Beryl and, on his recommendation, Beryl was sent to Hornby when [sic] she was visited only by Mr Gough and Miss Fife. The writer and friends of Beryl's were not permitted to see her and no monetary allowance was made to her during the early weeks of her stay there.

This confirmed my worries for Beryl at Hornby. Those long blank periods on her file of three, four or even six months – at one stage a whole year. No visits from friends, and if anyone came it was her father and his new wife. I can't imagine Margaret would have encouraged Tracy to visit often. And when they were there, what must it have been like? It also seems that although Beryl was technically a voluntary boarder, there was, at the very least, encouragement for her to send herself away. Imagine if Dr McKillop's opinion had been for Sunnyside? Beryl was lucky.

Miss Fife claimed that she was supplying all the necessaries to Beryl and her Father believed this to be so. I am sure that at times Beryl was short of such small articles as writing paper soap & stamps. The writer was permitted to visit Beryl occasionally while he was in the air force stationed at Wigram. It was not until about 1946 that we were permitted to see her at fairly regular intervals, but Miss Fife still maintaining the intense desire to keep Beryl at Hornby opposed any suggestion of her coming home.

Any days' absence that were granted were spent at the writer's home, however Beryl used to visit her Father on these occasions by going round to 'Mona Vale' for a few hours accompanied by the writer. During the last few months, before Mr Gough & Miss Fife were due to go to America, attempts were made during our visits to get her father's permission to come out of Hornby. On each occasion Miss Fife either remained in the room or gave us very definite instructions that we were not to discuss Beryl's release. The excuse given each time was that Beryl's Father was not well enough to discuss such things. On one of these visits Beryl & the writer found Mr T.T. Gough on his own and after a short discussion on the subject he agreed to Beryl coming out.

These facts have been written at length as the writer feels that the indignities suffered by his sister could & would have been avoided had not the full facts of Beryl's case been concealed from her Father by Miss Fife. During the whole of her stay at Hornby he was under the impression that Beryl was being more than adequately provided for financially and that she was not fit to return home. Both of these impressions were contrary to fact especially the money side as Beryl's Post Office Savings Bank Pass Book (containing a credit of about £60 saved while at Oamaru) was in the Safe custody of Miss Fife.

I suppose Margaret controlled the domestic affairs and finances and was a gatekeeper for Tracy's official correspondence, but this absolution of his father by Owen is tendentious. It ascribes to Tracy the role of ingenue, at odds with his commercial success and apparent hardness in other areas. Margaret might have kept information back from Tracy, saving him the bother of petty details. But was he helpless? Not before his stroke. Blameless? It's hard to accept. And the one person who never accepted that was Alison: 'Blames her father for the death of her mother.'

• • •

Justified or not, the family worried about Margaret and then grew to dislike her, which might have clouded their assessment. But this was where it got complicated. Margaret might have been unpleasant, or just unpleasant to Owen, Beryl and Avenal, and they to her, but that didn't prove she ran a conspiracy.

'Shortly after Beryl's return from Hornby she went to her grandmother's home as an assistant & a companion. This was not satisfactory and she returned home to the writer a fortnight later. Eventually with the assistance of Miss Fife a position was obtained for Beryl at Begg's Music Shop where she has remained ever since.' I was sorry to read that things did not go well at Tiny Granny's, and it was considerate of Margaret to help Beryl with a job. So long as it wasn't near her own.

Owen jumped backwards at this point and, just as Beryl did, recorded matters to do with household allowances, his sisters getting upset and Julia prophesying her own death.

About a year before my Mother's death I had just returned by air from Auckland arriving at Mona Vale about 12.30pm and found my Mother, Beryl & Alison generally discussing Miss Fife & her associations etc. I remember my mother saying that Miss Fife was interested solely in the family & the business from the point of view of monetary gain and at the end of the discussion (which by the way was around the dinner table) she made the following statements. They were that although she would never ask Miss Fife to Mona Vale in her lifetime, Miss Fife would be at her funeral – would be staying in our house not later than a month after her death and would be married to my father within twelve months of her death. This information worried me quite a lot although I did not actually let any of the family know this.

From then on I used to see & hear a lot about Miss Fife at the office and it was from this time onwards that I realised how much Miss Fife was interfering with our lives. My Father began to think that I was not much of a success in the firm. Things seemed to go from bad to worse and there was always heated discussions going on about Miss Fife at home.

My Mother died less than twelve months later – May 30th 1941 and Miss Fife married my Father on June 12th [actually 17th] 1942. I mention this not as any criticism of my Father but to show that Miss Fife's intrusions in to our family eventually caused the complete breaking up of our family. During my Mother's illness she would not take any food as she felt she was being poisoned by Miss Fife. My eldest sister Alison died on June 3 1942.

I remember seeing Alison just before I went to Wellington a few months before she died. She had just learned of Miss Fife's engagement and she said she felt there was not much left in life to live for.

• • •

Owen's refusal to comment on his father's behaviour kept pushing me in the opposite direction. Marriage is the quintessential duet. If Owen and Beryl were upset about Tracy remarrying, Tracy himself could not be blameless.

'I remember seeing Alison just before I went to Wellington a few months before she died' answered another question: there was no telegram, no rushed overnight passage on the *Rangatira* to Lyttelton. Owen saw Alison about the time he wrote that mournful farewell letter to Margaret, but never again.

I should like to say here, that over about five years before she died, my sister Alison had periods of being acutely worried. At those times she would let out a lot of her secret anxieties, and I am afraid that Miss Fife and her activities always appeared to Alison as a threat to the unity of our family. It was in fact that threat which worried Alison more than anything else … Both my Mother and Alison then, died pre-occupied with the thought of Miss Fife, and desperately concerned about her ultimate intentions.

The remainder of Owen's note was devoted to other grievances against Margaret: how she complained about the family's overspending, which led Owen to leave school early (another mystery solved); how she complained to colleagues about the quality of his work; how he wasn't allowed a name on his door and was banned from handling cheques in his job. It was tragic but also petty. It was petty to complain about; it was pettier to do.

When I was transferred to Wigram I contacted my Father who was more than pleased to see me back in Christchurch. My sister Beryl who at this time was at St George's Hospital as a V.A.D. + spending most of her 'off duty' time at 'Mona Vale' recalls the frightful rows that took place because I was allowed to re-enter the home. Miss Fife declared that my father could choose between myself & herself & if he received me in to the home then she would leave. My Father did welcome me whenever I came to see him on my leave times, but [handwriting changes to Avenal's] Miss Fife did not carry out her threat.

Owen was being outmanoeuvred by a pro: after all, she'd managed to secure the biggest prize of all by marrying the owner. His grievances sounded not unlike the sort you hear over an after-work glass of wine on any given Friday evening. Maybe he deserved it? Maybe he was ineffective? Owen was perhaps 31 when he wrote this, but he would have been fresh from school when he first encountered this treatment, and as shocked as any teenager by his first view of adults behaving like children. He was sensitive; he'd come from a life where he'd likely known only kindness. And maybe, again, you might say he should be grateful for that. But I felt sorry for him, bewildered as he was by Margaret's behaviour. I could understand how this experience might have swirled though him over a decade to finally fall in blue lines onto these pages.

Also, if I believed Beryl and Owen – not their opinions but their narratives – Margaret could be unpleasant. There might have been some justification, a hard background, a chip on her shoulder. She may have found the three siblings spoiled where I thought of them as well-mannered and kind. But her actions were still her actions.

Owen concluded:

I got to feel I was a failure, and as the months went by this was more and more impressed upon me. Miss Fife did not confront me with instances of inefficiency, but always appeared to pass it on to other people. I used to wonder why it was that I was not able to make a success of anything … I became very depressed and felt that life in general had very little to offer. After my Mother's death I spent a period as a clerk in the sales division of the company. While in this position I made application to enter the R.N.Z.A.F. The day after my Father became engaged to Miss Fife I left home for Wellington to try and enter the Air Force.

• • •

Tracy's engagement made Owen's bewilderment complete, and it cast a long shadow. Decades later I was spending my summer holiday reading through the documents it generated. But for now it was time for lunch at this isolated seaside retreat that Owen and Avenal had made for themselves. I cleared everything off the table and set it for pie and salad. I packed the dozens of small pages into plastic files for safe-keeping. Later that day I began to type them out word for word, including the errors, the typos, the crossings out. As I did so, I realised that they were all written several years before Tracy died and before the legal fighting started. These were memoirs for Owen and Beryl, or maybe for someone like me to find and ponder.

32

One of the first things I see when I wake up is a black and white etching. It shows a man in what I'd call cavalier dress leaning on a desk, his back to an open window. Avenal found it in London in the early 1960s. The whole family were there on holiday, all the way from Christchurch, the opposite ends of the earth.

I in turn found it in a drawer after Avenal died. On the back were two opposing claims, scrawled in pencil. First, that it was by Rembrandt. Second, that it cost £5. I believed the former and chuckled – what luck! – at the latter. This response was the reverse, demonstrably, of Avenal's. She must have regretted this tourist purchase and so hid it under a pile of dress patterns for 40 years. It's not a very good picture, but I got it framed and now I live with it and enjoy being reminded of its story.

Not far from the etching, on my bedside table, is Avenal's old Bible. She kept it beside her bed and read it every night with Owen already asleep beside her. I keep it beside my bed out of a more secular reverence. 'This belonged to your great-grandmother', my mother wrote inside its cover when she gave it to my second daughter for her christening. But that page is bent back from the book's regular service as a missile. Seeing it splayed on the floor so often made me feel uncomfortable. I decided the good book deserved better and I would keep it on trust for a few years.

Outside my bedroom door – heading towards the girls' room whence I rescued the Bible – is a sketch of the corner of a stone building. It's a small drawing, just a few centimetres, showing an arched door and lancet windows. On the first floor is the study I had in my last year at school. Beneath it was the laundry and below that, incongruously, the college armoury. The study may not sound salubrious but I had my own oak staircase, and the small room was a luxury after years of dormitories and cubicles. Owen and Avenal knew how much I liked it, and before the new theatre was built they could see it as they drove past into town. They arranged for someone to draw it and gave me the picture the week I finished school. That was when I left Christchurch the first time. Just below this hangs that old watercolour of Leeham, from Beryl's house.

Avenal herself used to paint in watercolours. There's the picture of the old provincial council building that she took off the wall of her home and gave me shortly before she died. Then there's one of fairies dancing in a glade. When he's older my son may be surprised to hear that this hung in his nursery in his infancy.

In my daughters' room I've hung the photograph of Alison in ballgown and long gloves. The girls saw her picture often and hers was one of the first names they learnt to say. It was funny watching them, in nappies, standing and pointing. They recognise her, which I never did.

Beryl, too, lives with us in a way. I took her portrait with us from Christchurch when we moved. The same went for her sideboard, a large ungainly thing but stuffed full of her life. The earthquakes released it from its purgatory in Owen and Avenal's garage. Once living with it face to face, I finally cleared the drawers, throwing away rubber bands and paperclips and notepads and half pencils and cassettes of liturgical singing. At the back of one I found a handbell the size of a sherry glass. The handle was wood and the brass tarnished to the colour of coffee. It was an oddity among oddities and it took me a moment to place it: it was an old servants' bell from Mona Vale. That's where this piece of furniture had originally come from too. I still don't know if I'm pleased by that or not.

Near Beryl is a grandfather clock. It's not an antique and it's not the one from Owen and Avenal's. I followed local auctions and whenever one came up for sale I would go and check, but viewings are silent affairs and I didn't feel I could open anything up, wind it and set it going just to satisfy my curiosity about its chime. This clock, though, had a lever visible to the side of the dial. It showed the ability to select Cambridge Quarters. That was all I wanted. When my mother-in-law found me trying to sneak it into the house it confirmed everything for her, but now our home rings with a familiar sound and the girls shout, 'Big Ben!'

I have a portrait of Tracy, too. It's unframed, the paint is crackled and the board it's painted on is damaged. I've had it for years and it's in need of restoration but I can't quite bring myself to extend this courtesy, even to a dead man, even to my great-grandfather. Instead he faces the wall in a bedroom upstairs, covered by a cloth.

There are aspects of Tracy that make me smile. There are large parts I recognise as achievements, and at times this respect might even stretch to envy. I like the idea of the grand seigneur, the connoisseur, the collector. I like the house full of treasures, the cars, the yachts, the travel by ocean liner, the lily pond, the winter garden. If I'm honest, I admire these material results more than I do the achievement that furnished them. I like the look of it all: leather helmet and goggles in a Tiger Moth. The man in a blazer, watching the cricket, smoking a pipe.

I know I already have a habit of draping stories, let alone myself, in history or drama that may not always be deserved.

I like the idea of furniture that tells tales. I can imagine collecting paintings as if they were seashells. I prefer old-fashioned houses. I've been known to dress formally at the least provocation. I enjoy the picturesque. I like traditional gardens (though hydrangeas, not azaleas). I have a feeling that if we'd been thrown together at about the same age, Tracy and I might have got along. He might have found me flouncy, I might have found him brash, but I know we'd have had tastes and interests in common. Recognising this shared sensibility gives me pause: to condemn him would be to condemn a part of myself.

Owen and Beryl almost save me the bother. Their extant writings imply a campaign engineered start to finish by Margaret. It's impossible to either fully refute or, given the inherent bias of the sources, accept. They're near silent on Tracy's role. By implication he was manipulated, taken advantage of.

It just doesn't ring true. Tracy was someone who'd built airports, done deals with governments, sold a lot of machinery to loggers, roaders, builders, miners. He'd designed and built tanks, military defences. He'd been brought up in inner-city Sydney and travelled around the world. He knew how to take advice, he knew how to get things done. He knew, by all accounts, how to cut out the nonsense.

The photographs, the letters, the publicity. Tracy was confident, prominent. Until his stroke in 1949, he was in control. He was the person most able, and likely, to intervene in events and change how they proceeded. There was nothing to suggest Tracy was Superman at work and Clark Kent at home. How, or why, did Beryl and Owen skirt around his role in the sequence of tragedies?

The most obvious answer is that their dislike of Margaret absorbed them. If she had remained a secretary with a crush, they would still perhaps have felt betrayed – but not devastated. As it was, Margaret became a natural source of enmity.

A stepmother's role is a hard one, no matter what. Here the conditions, the events before and after the marriage, were awful. I doubt she'd have ingratiated or assimilated; I doubt she'd have cared. Owen and Beryl claimed they saw conspiracy. I've no reason to disbelieve their privately recorded claims, never meant for prying eyes, of finding a billet-doux in Tracy's overcoat pocket. Maybe Margaret was conniving. She was certainly successful. She was also, it seemed from Beryl's testimony, violent and erratic and protective of her own position. But this approach risked becoming circular and unsatisfactory: Owen and Beryl didn't blame Tracy because they disliked Margaret; but they could only dislike her with such intensity if they thought Tracy blameless. There must be other explanations for their view.

I came up with five, all linked.

First, their memories of Tracy would have been of him helpless in his bed while Margaret wielded complete control both at Mona Vale and in the company. This would have made a powerful impression. Those first memos I'd found were written when Tracy had been sick for two years. By the time he died in June 1954 he'd been lying mute, helpless and immobile for some time. He would generate pity from Owen and Beryl. To make him persona non grata in their own lives would be to reinforce Margaret's position.

Second, more speculatively and more conceptually, I think Owen and Beryl judged Tracy through the prism of their own characters. They were gentlefolk. They had a kind mother and a comfortable upbringing. They were products of Christchurch's private Anglican schools. Tracy had been born an immigrant's son. He had advantages but his life was far from what he gifted his children. It's almost a cliché: the father's rough and tumble career; the pretty and artistic wife; the calm, cultivated, beautiful offspring who wouldn't even recognise Tracy's childhood. Everyone has some ambition, some ruthlessness. I just think Tracy's personal cocktail had fewer parts compassion and empathy than did Beryl and Owen's. Tracy had luxury but Owen and Beryl had more. Tracy was a tough businessman who took his place in the world. He had privileges but he also worked. In Beryl and Owen's world, everyone had been good and kind – at least until they moved to Mona Vale.

Third, maybe for Beryl especially there was the filial link: Tracy was the father whose wedding she must attend even over her brother's. I think she would have found it hard to think ill of him.

Fourth, both Beryl and Owen possessed a strong strain of Christian-tinctured forgiveness. Even if they'd seen Tracy as a transgressor, they'd have absolved him. He was family after all. It doesn't seem such forgiveness was extended to Margaret, however.

Fifth, last and maybe simplest, I'm afraid I think that both Beryl and Owen just didn't like Margaret. The scene of hitting Beryl is maniacal. The intrusion into Julia's home is contemptible. Beryl and Owen's reports of Margaret's treatment of them are pathetic; in the true sense, they may also be base, they may also be unfair. Whether fair or not, they just didn't like her and in comparison their father shone. This is a clear change from Owen's earlier view: the standoff over the wedding, the tension at Christmas that Avenal tries to heal. I think what happened is that over time Owen's animosity to Margaret hardened, while that towards his father softened.

Maybe it was a combination of all of these, but Tracy escaped the judgement of his surviving children – leaving it to those who came after, like me, to answer whether he'd been victim or culprit. I feel I have to weigh both options. I worry about people's lost voices but Tracy, too, lived for years without one and he can't defend himself now. Maybe he planned a different ending. Perhaps if he hadn't been so affected by the stroke there would have been a happy, internal resolution for the family, despite Julia. I'd like to think it was possible.

In the first narrative Tracy is beset by circumstance, as indeed, and in time, is Margaret. Tracy delivers a life of plenty. The family accepts it and appears to treat it as natural. They don't live in the real world the way Tracy does, and then, gated, cossetted, unused to hard work, they start to go barmy. Tracy's wife comes up with crazed theories about his secretary. Julia just doesn't understand how many hours Tracy must spend at work. He tries to help her but to no avail. Try as he might, he can't talk her round.

Amid this, Julia's health worsens. No medical connection to her state of mind is established but she dies, suddenly. Tracy is heartbroken, but maybe he's relieved. He's upset that Julia died thinking the wrong thing about him and Margaret, but there's nothing to be done about that now.

Then one of his daughters starts blaming him for Julia's death. Poor Tracy. He's given the family so much already, he deserves their loyalty. He bought them a palace. He bought them gentility and leisure. He took his wife travelling. He gave his family a life of material perfection. And now they turn on him? He's not Lear on the heath but he is Tracy on the lawn at Mona Vale, trying to get some peace amid his own grief while his daughters wail inside. In the end there's nothing for it and, with great sadness, he decides that Alison has to return to Sunnyside. It means more heartbreak, but it's the only thing for her. She doesn't forgive.

Tracy is left bereft. And if his family has turned on him, where is he to get support? He'd be within his rights to remarry anyway, but now, abandoned by all – son left, surviving daughter run away – what is there to do? Lucky he has Margaret to look after him. A man should have a wife, and the woman who had helped look after the children (and keep house) when young, and who now looked after his own affairs, would be perfect.

At the other end of the spectrum: Tracy in charge but doing nothing to make things better. After all, men can be peculiar with women, and never more so than when they're rich and the women are young. In this narrative he gives up on Julia, and she gives up on him and slides towards a miserable death. Maybe the relationship with Margaret hadn't predated Julia's death, but her death released it. They can be together at last and, indeed, it only takes a few weeks.

Alison raves and threatens and she's better off alone, imprisoned. So be it. Then there's Beryl too, come to think of it. Margaret's never got on with her either and something must be done. Owen, well, he's walked out and won't be any trouble. Alison's death is sad, but not sad enough to postpone a wedding. Tracy's given his word to Margaret and a gentleman wouldn't break that.

Neither narrative answers all the questions. Scattered across the story are all sorts of shards and slivers, sometimes darkening, sometimes brightening. How much depends on interpretation?

• • •

In the Sounds, again, a recent summer. No documents now to read but the same stories still swarm in my head. There are, oddly, several dead birds around. A cormorant on the beach; a tiny green bird the size of a sparrow which, according to the bird book, is either close to extinction or very common; a blackbird … It's more than I've seen before. I think more possums. But a friend, visiting, looks back from the jetty up at the hills and remarks that now the pines have been killed the bush is regenerating wonderfully. More trees, more ferns, more birds, more bird deaths.

The same holiday and a hat is washed up on the beach. 'CAPTAIN FIN' it reads across the front. I show it to my wife, 'Amusing,' I say, thinking anthropomorphic shark.

'How sad,' she responds; she's more European than me. 'The end of the captain.'

Or imagine an old photo, of a face perhaps: torn, crumpled. 'He never took care of it,' someone says. 'He carried it in his wallet till the day he died,' says the other.

So much of interpretation depends your angle of vision. I had spent so long in the company of Owen and Beryl, Avenal and Alison that I was bound to take their side against Tracy, even as they themselves did not condemn him. I needed to turn over each of these shards and look again to make sure I'd not been mistaken. I might have come to a conclusion but I felt I owed him, in his enforced silence, a final re-evaluation.

Julia's death: medical misadventure, persecution or persecution complex? I could imagine Julia sobbing into a handkerchief or into her daughter's shoulder. I could imagine Tracy shuffling and huffing through papers, trying to ignore the racket and muttering about slander.

Alison could be sent to the only place that might cure her.

Margaret had already waited a year and it wasn't fair to keep her waiting longer.

Owen could have all the chances he wanted, once he'd re-learned the ropes and seen enough of the company.

Beryl would get the best help money could buy – and she could stay there.

• • •

The children again: Owen, Beryl; Tracy telling himself he could manage it. Maybe he did, initially, or thought he did. I know many successful people who are used to waving a hand at problems and considering them resolved so long as the problems no longer reach their ears. Then he had the stroke. He at least deserves sympathy for that.

Owen's boat trip to the Sounds – that was kind of Tracy. He also helped Owen to buy a house. It wasn't a large amount considering what he had, but then anything was a help and Owen had decided to get married and so should be able to pay his own way. Besides, Tracy wouldn't want to spoil him. And he wanted his son to come up through the ranks; Tracy wasn't going to be soft on him. Owen should have learnt to be less sensitive, to stand on his own two feet.

Alison did some form of secretarial or administrative training, so Tracy must have allowed something. He put Beryl in charge of the 'exchequer' – admittedly only after Julia and Alison were out of the way – but it shows support for her.

And, yes, Tracy left Beryl out of the will, but he gave her an annuity. Still, she was uniquely treated relative to her brother and, more tellingly, Tracy's second wife.

I even rechecked the reference to that story of Absalom. I wanted to make sure received lore wasn't condemning by accident. What were the chances the story got twisted and it wasn't some biblical retelling but a famous novel of the day? William Faulkner's *Absalom, Absalom* was published in 1936 to wide acclaim. Tracy could have picked up a copy on a trip abroad. He might just have been trying, like Avenal, to get Owen to read, to broaden his horizons. Until you look at the plot: still the story of a wayward son rebelling against his father's empire. There's a conflict between half-brothers and a ruined plantation. If my suspicion was right, it was the most prescient thing Tracy could have given his son.

To each point a counterpoint. I was no further ahead than before I found those memos. And so always, I end up back with this: remove the opinions, give someone the list of dates, tell them what happened. Would they say it was all just a series of accidents? Julia's breakdown, Alison's bruises, Julia's death, Alison's death, Owen's flight, Tracy's remarriage, Beryl's flight, Beryl's struggle to be free.

With the best will in the world, I find it hard to explain that Tracy is merely a victim of an unlikely combination of unrelated circumstances that have all gone against him.

I'd wondered at times whether my family's idealisation of Tracy showed us to be unaware of what occurred. I thought I'd been uncovering horrors for the first time. But of course this wasn't right. Owen and Beryl lived through it. They survived. They had every right to blame Tracy – more right than I have – and yet they didn't. When Owen's first son was born the war had just ended and Owen wasn't welcome at Mona Vale. But he named that first-born son Tracy and recorded his father as next of kin on his enlistment documentation. Avenal was listed as fiancée, then wife, to be advised in case of casualty. It also records that Owen has a will with a solicitor in Wellington, and the executor is Tracy.

I may think it seems implausible to absolve Tracy but I can't support that view unless I ignore Owen and Beryl's. I can't accept Beryl and Owen's views unless I ignore some of Alison's last recorded words.

Beryl and Owen's accounts may be biased by affection or sympathy, but in that bias, too, lurks something. I'd never known Beryl and Owen to be cruel or rude about anyone. Their views on Margaret are such an epic departure from their usual quietude that it sways me towards Tracy, a little. Margaret may have captured him, but he had a chance to stop it and he didn't.

Hisham Matar in his book *A Month in Siena* writes about the impulse to take the place of one's adversary – a dark, secret jealousy. If there's truth in this, then it's logical that condemning that enemy must mean condemning one's own inclinations, impulses, desires.

I've ended up with the same disposition of children as Tracy: two girls followed by a boy, over a marginally shorter timespan than that from Alison to Owen. Looking at how mine interact I feel I'm seeing Owen's younger years and getting to know him over again. I watch the two older girls with the younger boy – the fussy mothering, the leading by the hand, the attempts at discipline, the embraces. I like to think it tells me something about how these three got along, especially about how Owen turned out the way he was: gentle, sensitive and friendly. I can see my son and second daughter grow close, as Beryl and Owen did. You'd think, in theory, it would bring me closer to Tracy. It doesn't. It makes me judge him more harshly.

If anything, Tracy's best defence is my own pride. How much of myself do I see in him? The look, the extravagance, the carelessness. The objects he acquired. As I say, there's much I like, much I admire. Too much? Is there too much of him in me? The thought that I'm not my own man is shocking enough but worse, if we're alike, am I too capable of such actions?

This selfish concern for my own future brings me to sympathy. How might I react to finding my family hysterical? To having to watch my wife die? To having no other option for my daughter than state care? To searching the world to try and find a better cure? I can understand how Tracy's heart might have been broken by what happened. But the truth is I can't hold this sympathy for long.

I can't see Tracy's swift second relationship – mere weeks after Julia's death – as validation of his love for the family he lost. I can't forgive him the marriage ceremony days after burying Alison. I can't help but blame him for what happened to her and Beryl. Tracy was trying to find a new cure, you might say. And the medical and social standards of the time were different. Sure. But even with incomplete evidence it is impossible to tell myself that Alison and Beryl would have got sick if Julia stayed alive. And I cannot detach Julia's death from her concerns about Tracy. Whether those concerns were justified or not – at the time – is important but I'll never know. I do know that Margaret turned out not to be a figment of Alison's paranoia.

Alison complained, became psychotic over Margaret. She was forced back to Sunnyside where she died, possibly with only her poor aunt beside her. Or maybe Beryl too. Perhaps that's how Beryl and Vida forged such a friendship.

This is perhaps the one indisputable fact that tells against Tracy, and this is where I decide I have to end my coiling and recoiling around him: he knowingly married the person who had caused his wife and his three children incredible anxiety. That is something I can't understand and never will. It's more than eccentric. It feels calculated, narcissistic. Wilfully, cruelly blind to what had happened over the previous few months. And it caused worse in the months and years to come.

This is my final view. I know it's unfair to judge on patchwork, seen from a distance. Tracy might have died regretting it all, or some of it. He might have repented during those years he lay in bed. I won't know. But I do know that his family was destroyed, and that he could have done more to stop it.

How ungrateful, you might say. I've benefited since birth from what Tracy created. I know that, and I like to think I know how much I've gained from it and I am thankful. But gratitude doesn't insist on ignorance.

• • •

I may not hang Tracy's picture on the wall but I've been back to Mona Vale. After the earthquake it took almost six years to repair. They removed almost all the bricks, numbered them, stored them, and then put them back together around a new steel and wooden frame. Inside, the refurbished era is High Edwardian. It's not Tracy's natural period but it's what he aspired to. There are pressed tin ceilings and yards of polished oak and mahogany. When the house reopened at the start of summer, several relatives went along and were photographed leaning over the upstairs bannister. There was a bold green and gold Morris-style wallpaper behind them that I'm sure Tracy would not have had.

Most of the ground floor is given over to a café and we went along for lunch a few weeks after it opened. We were a family of four by then, a second girl having arrived to join the first. We were meeting some friends and their children. We parked Owen's car by the rear entrance near the rose garden. I chose a spot under the shade of a rhododendron to protect the woodwork. We walked via the lily pond to the front of the house. It looked good, almost the same, though the stucco was creamier. More authentic? I took a photo of my two daughters with the house behind them and couldn't help thinking of the two sisters who had walked here in the 1930s.

We chose a table on the patio, looking down the bank to the Avon. Across the river were wide expanses of lawn where houses had once stood: soft land by the water's edge meant they'd succumbed to the February 2011 shaking. Cafés in splendid locations often leave you a lot of time to look at the view. We sat for a while, looking around and then taking turns walking the children among the trees and gardens. As we idled there a cousin turned up – the naughty young one from the steps at Beryl's wedding. He was with his fiancée and their dog and had come to see the revived place too.

'When was the last time you were here?' I asked him.

'Years ago. Probably my twenty-first.'

'You had that here?'

'You were invited,' he protested.

I did some maths. 'I was in China, I think.'

We ambled a little way along the riverbank, with a terrier and a noisy child respectively. We were walking in the direction of that postcard gatehouse and Fendalton Road.

'I'll show you something,' he said and motioned for me to follow him a little further. We came up behind a green wooden bench and then walked around to face it. A brass plaque was attached to one of the back slats, telling the world that this seat had been given in honour of my cousin's birthday. 'Great-grandson of Tracy Thomas Gough,' it read.

I was amused by it. 'Rather grand. I never knew about it.'

He shrugged. 'I know. My mother arranged it.'

The bank was less steep here. The river ran just a metre or so below us and the remaining houses on the other side were hidden by willows and ferns and shrubbery. The river is shallow and the reeds sit just below the surface, the clear water almost trembling over the top of them.

We turned to make our way back to the house. Just behind the bench was a rimu. It looked young but they can be slow growing. Its trunk did little to spoil the view. I noticed now that it also had a plaque, shining and silvery, set on a low concrete plinth.

'That's how we chose the spot for the bench,' my cousin said.

The plaque reads:

This rimu tree was given as a tribute to my father
MR TRACY T. GOUGH
from the men logging in New Zealand bush.
My father said that these men were some of the finest gentlemen he had met.

The rimu tree weeps, but in maturity lifts its leaves to the light
which is our heavenly Father.
Given by his daughter, Beryl

Good, generous Beryl. And so again, I find I have more to learn. About myself now, about forgiveness.

Owen's response was different from Beryl's. He chose to create a new life. There's tenacity in sticking with things, but there can be strength in abandonment. Owen was able to turn his back on Mona Vale and start again. Many people going through such trauma turn to anger and bitterness. Instead he built a life with Avenal in which warmth and kindness prevailed.

• • •

Running almost parallel with the discovery of the story of this family at Mona Vale were the efforts to repair Owen and Avenal's home. In the end we succeeded, thanks largely to a patient builder and a good friend. It took eight years but we were finally able to move into a repaired home. It was updated in places but with the same feeling: the glazed front door, the long hallways, the mirror, the chandeliers. The pictures are back on the walls, the books back on the shelves. Owen and Avenal are back above the stairs, the clock chimes in the hall and Mephistopheles provides the heat in his low growl. It's nice to be back. It's a memorial, not just to my mother's childhood or my own: I can now see it as a memorial to Owen and Avenal and to the way they overcame those horrible years.

In contrast, just as I was coming to the end of this story, Tracy's estate was finally dissolved and, mere months later, his company veered towards collapse and was sold. Its disappearance was quick and brutal and, despite it all, I was sorry. The age of success was long behind it, but it was destruction of a sort, the toppling of an old monument. It was 90 years old, and those who have lived long lives, whether moral or not, leave big gaps.

With the company's liquidation the last concrete vestige of Tracy disappeared. Jan Morris once argued that the best solution to a decaying Venice was to let the city sink. Morris was perhaps being playful, but you can see in the idea a certain symmetry, the completion of a story. That's how it seemed now. It was at an end. It was history, all 130 years of it, from Birmingham to Fendalton. Tracy's world now dissolved; Owen and Avenal's enduring.

Beryl's rimu tree at Mona Vale.

One of the books that emerged from a box as we unpacked in the repaired house was Avenal's copy of *Paradise Lost* in two small hardback volumes with olive-green cloth bindings. Milton's epic presents the expulsion from Eden not as a loss but as mankind's quintessential experience. Forced out into the world by the tree of knowledge but with a chance of redemption through our own actions, we are given the chance to flourish.

Owen, Beryl and Avenal were never going to be able to bring Julia and Alison back. They could never go back to Mona Vale. They could have lived in bitterness and regret but instead they created lives of happiness. Somewhere deep that sorrow remained, hidden to prevent infecting others. Owen wept when I drove him to Mona Vale before he died. I didn't know why at the time but I assume now it was for his sister, his mother, the whole godforsaken tragedy that he carried inside himself. The pain had never abated, it had just been cauterised by silence.

Such silence can protect. Haruki Murakami recounts his father telling him a rare, awful story about his time as a Japanese soldier in World War II. He must have felt a need to relate it, Murakami says, but in so doing 'it would remain an open wound for the both of us'. I think Owen understood something like this. Silence kept the family safe from carrying his scars and resentments in perpetuity.

Which raises the question: were these memories to be resurrected? Does the importance of knowledge override all things, even good taste?

After thinking about this for the best part of a decade, I've decided that there's value in discovery for its own sake, in moving ever closer to a truth even if you can't say it's the truth. But though I told myself this, I worried that a part of me wanted the stories for myself, not for others. That I didn't care what I found, I just wanted to be the one to find it.

I've resolved this by telling myself that my motivations don't matter. It feels correct to give events a voice. These people couldn't speak for themselves. This was a way of restoring their stories.

That brought me back to Owen, Beryl and Avenal. I don't think they wanted to forget; I think it was just too painful for them to remember. Instead, Julia and Alison's names were wrapped in tissue and placed in a drawer, out of view, like ancient parchments or delicate watercolours that can survive only out of the light.

But with that comes the risk of loss. Out of view for long enough can become out of mind. Alison and Julia didn't get to live in the world as long as they deserved, and they lived barely longer in the telling. I can't believe this was what was intended by their survivors. Matar goes on to say that the dead's last argument is their silence. There's no way I can alter that. It might have been too hard for Owen, Beryl and Avenal to tell their stories, but it's not too hard for me.

Their stories should endure: that's all they have left. But stories can last longer than fine houses, pictures, cars and yachts. They can last longer than family names and companies and vainglory. They can endure because people find them interesting, not because a complicated testament obliges obeisance.

And there is a value in their telling. If nothing else I'd like to think it would be a comfort to Julia and Alison to know that some unknown descendant, 80 years later, might take the time to say, 'Look at what happened.' I know it would be a comfort to me.

Epilogue

I started looking into the history of my mother's family in detail around the time she first became seriously ill, in 2013. This was a coincidence only. The court processes for the wind-up of her grandfather's estate were already under way; it was the illness that was unplanned.

My mother survived but became sick again a few years later. My parents were living abroad at the time but she needed to be home for care, so she came and stayed with us. We moved my old bed from their house and set her up in it. By then I had much of the story together in my head. She had seen parts of it, and had appreciated the telling.

As I've noted, the family history proved to be of limited legal relevance, but this didn't make it any less interesting, or horrifying, for me. I felt the lives of this handful of young people from many decades ago deserved more than just a few paragraphs of legalese for affidavits. I therefore joined some night classes, one in memoir and one – because this is what it felt like – in detective fiction. I wanted to learn how to tell the story properly but, like anyone trying to write in any form, I struggled with structuring and shaping: guilt over elisions, frustration with loose ends and despair over sequence. I must have started and restarted at least a dozen times. I'd go out around a hundred pages before giving up and returning to line one and once upon a time.

I told myself that I just wanted to get the story down, tidily and to the best of my ability. I don't want to pretend this was a saintly exercise in ancestor veneration. I did feel an obligation to the subjects, an obligation that grew as I discovered more. But if I'm honest, my motive was primarily selfish. I wanted to satisfy a preference for completion.

Once I had it all done I thought I would print it and be happy. It might not be great but it would be a record and it would no longer nag me. A few friends helped me along the way, friends who knew the joys and troubles of writing. Their time and kindness and advice were always accurate and constructive, but always left me with more work to do. I knew they were right when they said tweak this and excise that, and I couldn't receive good advice and pretend I hadn't.

After about seven years I felt I'd done all I could. I'd tried every permutation and what remained was no worse than any of the others. I might not have been happy, but I'd worn myself into benign resignation. As importantly, I felt I had the whole story now and understood what had occurred. I was less shy by then, too, or had used so much energy on the telling that I had none left for proprieties. I approached some people about the story. There wasn't much interest, which was fine. This left me with what I had told myself I wanted and had happily pursued: a private manuscript, tidily spiral bound by my local copy shop, sitting in a box under my desk.

I can't thoroughly explain what happened next. First, after 90 years Tracy's company was sold. It felt symbolic. If there was any time for a post mortem it was now. Not that my story – their story – had any commercial sensitivities but I suppose I'd have been more reticent about invoking a name and a brand that was still operating in a marketplace. The new owners proved this to have been misguided by changing the company's name as soon as they could.

The sale was in 2019. In 2020 the world started imploding. We watched it on screens until everywhere was consumed, ourselves included. We spent seven weeks at home and then, like many others, went travelling over the winter. It was during this time, first in Arrowtown and then in a log hut between the south bank of the Rakaia and the base of Mt Hutt, that I decided to try and distil 120,000 words into 4000. Maybe being back in the South Island had something to do with it. Maybe seeing that life was uncertain: if I wanted to do something, I should do it now, even if my ambitions were only mild and sedentary. In late July 2020 I submitted the result of these efforts to *Landfall* for the annual essay competition. They invited entries: I wouldn't be forcing anything on anyone. I wouldn't say I sat back and waited but I did feel that here, then, was an end. I had done something formally and was satisfied with that.

In early September my mother had some more tests. These were quarterly and for years they'd been fine. For some reason, complacency or distraction, I didn't ask how these ones had gone. In fact it was an uncle who asked me. We'd had a small Father's Day gathering, hosted by my mother, and he'd thought she wasn't as chipper as usual. He asked whether the results had been bad. That's when I realised I hadn't received the usual cheery all clear from her. That's when we found out her news wasn't good.

My father's birthday was a few days later, on the 10th, followed by mine on the 14th. We planned to celebrate with dinner out together on Sunday 13 September. Two days before, a message arrived from Otago University Press. I'd managed to win a prize and the essay would be published in November. I was delighted, of course, and surprised.

I was also pleased to have some nice news for my mother. We were heading to the restaurant where we'd dined the night before her first operation, when we'd proffered the hopefully consoling news that we were expecting our first child. This news wasn't quite in the same league, but the essay did star my mother's beloved Auntie Beryl and I thought she'd be amused and maybe proud. At dinner I told her and handed her a printed copy of the essay. She folded it into her bag. I think she was distracted. But she later told me she loved it.

The news about the prize was embargoed for about a month. Once Mum was allowed, she told a few friends, including one of their oldest and dearest, bumped into outside a deli in Karori, whose wife had won the same prize a few years before. He danced a jig, he said, and his joy spread to Mum. She needed it as she was enduring daily radiotherapy, her only option by this stage. It was better than the drain of chemotherapy and each session lasted only a few minutes, but she still disliked it. 'It sounds like sharpening knives,' she said. The treatment made her tired where she'd previously been full of energy. We also saw her become less able, less dextrous.

The *Landfall* prize essay represented the total of my formal literary output. Despite, or because, of this, I was emboldened to mention to Otago University Press that I had a full manuscript on the same topic that might be of interest. I do feel sorry for publishers. It's hard enough to read a book that a friend gushes over, let alone a rough patchwork by a complete unknown. Otago replied generously and said maybe they'd have a look, in the equivocal way that I knew was the best I could hope for. Thus I laboured through one further edit of this long version of the story and sent it off at the start of December.

On 12 December we held a birthday party at home for our elder daughter. My parents came. Around this time, maybe the week following, I also told my parents that there was a full manuscript floating around. They didn't know. My work on it hadn't so much been a secret, I simply didn't think it merited broadcast. I was just a fossicking amateur. Mum was interested for a moment, then switched to another topic.

By then it seemed something else was wrong. We had ascribed it to the side-effects of the treatment but it was more than that. We worried that further tests would drain and depress her – she disliked hospitals – and worry her too much. But in the end they proved necessary. They found shadowing in the brain. An MRI was ordered and the next day we were to see the oncologist about the results. That day was Christmas Eve. What they found was completely unrelated to what she was being treated for and nothing could be done. My sister was already home; my brother immediately applied for a compassionate spot in MIQ.

Meanwhile, Otago University Press had replied to say they would send the work out for a second opinion and I'd hear in February. That was again as much as I could hope for, but there was a lot else going on.

The summer was a sad and disjointed one. Mum lost more mobility and needed more sleep. The illness drained her at an astonishing speed. But she was able to be at home, in her own bedroom. The weather was beautiful too: hot days, warm evenings, birdsong unruffled by wind – even in Karori. Mum would sit on the upstairs balcony in the evening and listen and watch the light in the beeches and sycamores and be peaceful. The rooms filled with flowers.

A month almost to the day after her diagnosis I got a message about Robin Hood Oak. We hadn't visited Christchurch together – my parents and our family – since late 2019. Now it was clear Mum never would again and it seemed this quiet, noble tree would suffer alongside her. Once a prince, now a beast with the people gathering to seek his limbs. Too tall, too old, too grand, too beautiful for a city, we were told. Too much, perhaps, a part of some old Christchurch that I still mythologise. A part of Alison and Beryl and Owen's Christchurch of gardens and gentleness and beauty for its own sake. The Christchurch from which my mother unfolded. But what did violence against nature matter now? Unsheathe your scythes.

A month later I heard once more from Otago. The news was good. They wished to publish. That was late February. Four days later the chopping on Robin Hood occurred. Less than two weeks after that my wife and I, our three children and my sister went round to my parents' house for dinner. It was another beautiful evening. We ate in an upstairs room that faces north and fills with light. We have a lovely photo of our second daughter leaning on the edge of the sofa, yabbering away to my mother, who looks at her and smiles.

We put Mum to bed, as we did each night, and left the room. It was a little after 7pm. She complained of a headache, the first time she'd complained of any pain. But she was asleep by the time her head hit the pillow. I never saw her conscious again. She died the next evening, 12 March. We were all there. And now I realised why she'd cared so much about her parents' old home, about those lives captured in rooms and objects. I thought I understood before, but now I *felt* it. I felt that impulse for preservation at all costs, never more sharply than when returning to her bedroom the next day.

I didn't tell my mother before she died that the family story would become a book. It was never the right time. By then unusual or unexpected news could confuse, and this would be unusual. It also felt unseemly to spout good news amid the unwinding tragedy, though she wouldn't have judged it such.

I regret her not knowing, but I blame the illness and tell myself I don't regret my silence. I thought about it a lot at the time, every time I saw her in fact in the 17 days I had from the news to her death. I knew time was precious but it never felt right. And I thought it wouldn't matter, because I was so certain Mum would be happy with the result. I don't mean happy with the quality of the writing or the storytelling, but that she would love to read and hear about her lost Auntie Alison, whose dressing table she used her whole life, and about her Auntie Beryl, and about her parents.

My brother pointed out that Mum was the first in her family to die in almost 20 years, the first since her father Owen in fact. Our grief was out of practice. We used the same rite we'd used for Owen as we buried her. I helped to carry her to her rest. The spot was a churchyard, consecrated ground, in a little village out the back of Wellington on the way to a rocky cove that she used to love. The sun shone and the cicadas sang and we covered her in flowers and a giant bumble bee tried to join her. Her last season was a flowery one and that was perfect. She lived in summer, died in autumn and now I wished it were winter: a winter to let you move in darkness and turn your collar up against the world. Not that that's what she would have done: as I said at the service of thanksgiving, she was always moving towards life.

Reading helps, stories help. The book I had with me when Mum died was *Chroma*, by the artist Derek Jarman. It's his paean to colour, written in the last year of his life as he went blind and died painfully. I thought its subject and melancholy context appropriate. Mum loved colour. She loved reading about art, about nature too. Not the nature of science but the nature of woods and fields, hedgerows and footpaths, shepherds and foresters, bees and flowers. Among such writers she loved Roger Deakin and Robert Macfarlane the most.

In faint echo I have picked up Naipaul's *The Enigma of Arrival*, where the narrator finds himself planted in a cottage on the edge of the Salisbury

Plain, surrounded by lanes and farms and tumuli. He writes: 'Already I lived with the idea of death, the idea, impossible for a young person to possess, to hold in his heart, that one's time on earth, one's life, was a short thing. These ideas, of a world in decay, a world subject to constant change, and of the shortness of human life, made many things bearable.' I can think she is with her parents and friends, and we will all one day join her. But that doesn't yet make it easier for me.

Since that day at the churchyard at least three people have given trees for her, and an uncle has nurtured a sapling of Robin Hood Oak to transplant to Mum's side. And I have spent time making lists in my head of things I will plant in her memory: blackwood, walnut, magnolia, chestnut. I spoke about some of these with her. We often planned trees. My siblings have planted a tōtara for her already.

I received the edited version of the manuscript about a fortnight after Mum's death. Then we all went down to the Sounds to her parents' old place – my family, Dad and my two siblings. We'd never gone there in this combination before: the whole family but not Mum. But I think we all travelled with her in some way, or she with us. On the island I sat at the same spot at the same table and looked at the same view as I had done years before, sorting through Beryl and Owen's memos. Now I edited, and I wrote this.

I was discussing my story one evening with a few of those friends who helped me. Someone asked, 'What's it really about?' Before I could stutter a response – did I even know? – another friend, a proper writer herself, said, 'It's about losing your mother.' I had never thought of it like that, but maybe it was always meant to be an elegy.

I have created my own collection of mementoes now, notes and letters. It's not in a brown leather satchel with straps, just a cardboard box, but I store it near my desk as Owen maybe once did his. It all helps to keep her world alive. This book might too. I hope it helps, I hope it works, for I miss her very much.

Alexander McKinnon
Queen Charlotte Sound
Easter 2021

The author's mother, by Stuart Pearson Wright.

The following sources are referred to in this work

Blofeld, John, *City of Lingering Splendour* (Boston: Shambala, 1989)

Frame, Janet, *An Autobiography* (Auckland: Century Hutchinson, 1989), quoted in Michael King, *Wrestling with the Angel* (Auckland: Penguin Viking, 2000)

Hisham Matar, *A Month in Siena* (London: Penguin, 2020)

Jackson, Shirley, *We Have Always Lived in the Castle* (Australia: Penguin, 2010)

Lewis, Cecil, *So Long Ago, So Far Away* (London: Luzac Oriental, 1997)

McKinnon, Malcolm, *The Broken Decade: Prosperity, depression and recovery in New Zealand, 1928–39* (Dunedin: Otago University Press, 2016).

Murakami, Haruki, *New Yorker*, October 2019: www.newyorker.com/magazine/2019/10/07/abandoning-a-cat

Naipaul, V.S. *The Enigma of Arrival* (London: Picador, 2011)

Rice, Geoffrey, *Christchurch Changing* (Christchurch: Canterbury University Press, 2008)

Sebald, W.G., *The Emigrants* (London: Vintage, 2002)

Twain, Mark, *Following the Equator: A journey around the world*: https://archive.org/details/followingequator00twaiuoft/page/n7/mode/2up?view=theater

White, T.H., *The Once and Future King* (New York: Ace, 1987)

Woodward, Christopher, *In Ruins* (London: Vintage, 2002)

Acknowledgements

I'd like to start, not end, by thanking family, the closest first: R, M, B and P. They put up with the time spent on this more than most, more than anyone. Other family have always been supportive, even when they didn't realise: my siblings, uncles and aunts and of course my parents, without whom nothing.

Several people helped a great deal with the writing and drafting over the years, both in final form and in earlier snippets. I'd especially like to thank Diane Comer and Anna Jaquiery, and those friends toiling in neighbouring fields: Mike, Hilary, Kate, Des, Edmund; Guy, Jenny, Lauren and Bruce. Godfrey and Frank too – you know who are.

Anna Rogers took charge of the editing and was a revelation. I thought I'd got things quite tidy. Her acumen and attention to detail is exactly what someone sloppy and lackadaisical needs. It was a privilege for me. It's obviously an honour to be published by Otago University Press too. Thank you to Emma Neale for my initial luck with *Landfall*, Rachel Scott for taking a chance, Sue Wootton for following through and for all the help from Laura Hewson, Imogen Coxhead and Fiona Moffat.

The serendipity and happenstance of moving from idea to draft to essay to book has reminded me that we go through life subject to the benevolence of others. If there is any credit in this book, then it should accrue to the teachers. I'm lucky to have had a great lot, right from Mrs Keller (the first I can properly remember) to those at the Day School, to Christ's College. This last had an incredibly strong English department when I was there (RAD, JB, JEB, NHL). I'm grateful to all of them as well as others, notably CJPW, GJW and MJR.

At university I similarly benefitted from the patience of people who had much better things to do. Thank you especially to Dr Hughes, the late Dr Linehan and to Maggie Hartley. Also to Dr Szreter for – I doubt he remembers but I always will – his kindness in letting me switch to history. It's taken me a while to do anything with it, but I suppose you never know where education might lead, and that's part of the fun.

Alexander McKinnon was educated in Christchurch and overseas, and lives in Wellington. His essay 'Canterbury Gothic', a summary version of this story, won the 2020 Landfall Essay Competition. This is his first book.

Published by Otago University Press
Te Whare Tā o Te Wānanga o Ōtākou
533 Castle Street
Dunedin, New Zealand
university.press@otago.ac.nz
www.otago.ac.nz/press

First published 2021, reprinted with amendments 2022
Copyright © Alexander McKinnon
The moral rights of the author have been asserted.

ISBN 978-1-99-004806-7

Editor: Anna Rogers
Design/layout: Christine Buess

All photos are from the family collection unless otherwise stated.

Printed in Hong Kong through Asia Pacific Offset

MIX
Paper from
responsible sources
FSC
www.fsc.org
FSC® C136333